Mass and Parish in late Medieval England: The Use of York

Mass and Parish in late Medieval England: The Use of York

Edited by:

P. S. Barnwell, Claire Cross and Ann Rycraft

Spire Books Ltd
PO Box 2336, Reading RG4 5WJ
www.spirebooks.com

Spire Books Ltd
PO Box 2336
Reading RG4 5WJ
www.spirebooks.com

Publication of this book was assisted by generous grants from the
Marc Fitch Fund and the Yorkshire Architectural and York
Archaeological Society.

CIP data:
A catalogue record for this book is available
from the British Library
ISBN 1-904965-02-4

Designed and produced by John Elliott
Text set in Adobe Bembo

Printed by Alden Group Ltd
Osney Mead
Oxford OX2 0EF

*Cover illustrations: Stained glass from All Saints', North Street, York.
Front cover: A miraculous Mass - part of the stained glass window that
stands over the altar of St James (© Dean and Chapter of York: by kind
permission. Photographer: Dr Tom French).*

*Back cover: Part of the east window of the chancel showing the donors. This
was probably a memorial to Nicholas Blackburn senior who died in 1432
(© Allan B. Barton).*

*Opposite: The Absolution of the Dead. Book of Hours, Fifteenth century,
French. York Minster Archive MS XVI.N.9 f. 89r. (© Dean and Chapter
of York: by kind permission).*

Contents

Preface

This book has its origins in a day of talks given by members of the Centre for Medieval Studies at the University of York before a reconstruction of a Requiem Mass held, according to the Use of York, in honour of Nicholas Blackburn junior (†1448), in the parish church of All Saints, North Street, York. Interest in both the reconstruction and the talks was so great that the latter were repeated at a later date. Continued expressions of interest encouraged the authors to create this book, which, although largely based upon their talks, provides a broader context and seeks to convey as much of the experience and performance of a late-medieval Requiem Mass as can be achieved on the printed page. The contribution of John Hawes to both the reconstruction and the inspiration for this volume is greater than his authorship of chapter 8 suggests: he has been a significant inspiration at every stage of the process.

During the course of assembling the volume, the authors have worked closely together so that, while the individual essays stand alone, they are properly complementary and take account of material drawn from outside individual authors' areas of academic specialisation. The venture has depended upon the goodwill and assistance of many people beyond the immediate authors, who wish to express their gratitude to Allan T. Adams for preparing Fig. 4.8b, and to Amanda Daw for preparing the other drawn illustrations and for much other assistance; to Paul Gameson for typesetting the musical examples in Chapter 3; to Peter Rycraft and Paul Simpson for assistance with the Latin text of the Requiem Mass; to Brian and Moira Gittos and Sally Badham for advice concerning the grave slabs in All Saints', North Street; and to the staff of the Borthwick Institute of Historical Research for assistance rendered to the various authors in the course of their research.

The editors owe particular thanks to Gordon Forster and Philip Lankester for their thoughtful support and encouragement at various stages, and to Spire Books Ltd for readily agreeing to publish a volume which is thematic rather than working within a single academic discipline.

Various organisations and individuals have kindly given permission to reproduce illustrations: The Borthwick Institute of Historical Research, University of York (Figs 3.1–3, 5.7 and 5.8); The Centre for Medieval Studies, University of York (Figs 5.5 and 5.6); Christopher Daniell (Figs 7.2, 7.5, 7.6 and 7.17–20); The Dean and Chapter of York Minster (front cover and frontispiece); English Heritage (Fig. 4.8b); R. Skingle (Fig. 4.8a). Finally, but by no means least, publication would not have been possible without the generosity of the Marc Fitch Fund and of the Yorkshire Architectural and York Archaeological Society, which is gratefully acknowledged.

Editorial Note. Throughout the spelling of all English quotations has been modernised.

The Mass and church life in late-medieval York

1

The Mass in its urban setting

Claire Cross and P. S. Barnwell

The Mass in the Late Middle Ages

The Mass exercised a defining influence upon the life of the late middle ages, affecting clergy and laity alike. All members of the laity were expected to attend High Mass every Sunday in their parish church, as well as the other obligatory Sunday services of matins and evensong.[1] Although High Mass was the most solemn and powerful of the regular services, on most occasions the congregation hardly participated in it directly, since communion by the laity was restricted to one or two occasions in the liturgical year, and the service, conducted in Latin, was largely incomprehensible to most of those present (see chapter 7). The emphasis was therefore on witnessing the Mass, rather than on direct participation by the congregation. This, which is a particular feature of the Mass in the later middle ages, was the result of changes in belief which had occurred between the middle of the eleventh century and 1200. Central to the late-medieval Mass was belief in transubstantiation, which meant that the bread and wine were transformed into the actual body and blood of Christ. One of the consequences of the spread of this belief, which was a requirement following its official adoption as a Doctrine of the Church at the Fourth Lateran Council in 1215, was that the bread and wine were treated with increasing reverence. The laity was not deemed worthy to touch the bread and wine, and therefore to share communion, other

13

than on very rare occasions, such as Easter or Pentecost. On those occasions when the congregation did communicate, great care was taken to avoid crumbs from the bread, parts of Christ's body, falling to the floor and being lost, and the risk of spilling drops of wine was deemed so great that the laity were never given the chalice. As a result, increasing emphasis came to be placed on the ability of the congregation to see the Host at the moment of consecration. This led to increased elaboration of the east end of the church, around the altar (see chapter 2), in order to provide a suitable backdrop against which to view the Elevation of the Host, the moment, immediately after consecration, at which the priest raised the Host above his head for all to see. So strong was the belief in transubstantiation that some late-medieval depictions of the Elevation show the priest holding the Christ child rather than bread. The potency of the Host was such that it was popularly believed that no-one would fall ill or die on the day that he saw it: this encouraged people to try to attend a Mass every day.

Another defining late-medieval belief, and one which also encouraged a proliferation of Masses, was in Purgatory, which became an official Doctrine in 1274.[2] Like belief in transubstantiation, the understanding of the fate of the soul after death had been subject to a complex and protracted evolution. According to the late-medieval understanding, souls which were not damned but which were yet not sufficiently pure to enter heaven, were held in Purgatory for a time sufficient to be purified from their particular sins. Although purgation took the form of fire and torment, souls were comforted by the fact that they knew they had been saved from Hell, and their time in Purgatory could be reduced by the intercessions of the living. Of particular importance for late-medieval Catholic religious practice was a belief that the most potent form of intercession was the saying of a Mass dedicated to a specific soul or souls: the more Masses were celebrated for an individual, the shorter that individual's suffering became. For this reason many people left money for Masses to be said on their behalf after their death, the richest endowing perpetual chantries, or permanent foundations for the purpose of saying dedicated Masses, and those of lesser means establishing similar foundations for a specified number of years. Such private, or soul, Masses were less elaborate than High Mass celebrated on Sundays and feast days, but contained the same benefits for both the priest and such congregation as was present (see chapter 4). Most churches contained several perpetual or temporary chantries, providing many opportunities, often several a day, for parishioners to engage in public worship and to witness the Elevation of the Host.

In addition to the normal daily and weekly services there were many other occasions, often marking the most significant staging points in life, when people gathered at their church for purposes of thanksgiving, worship or prayer. Since mortality was high and baptism guaranteed absolution from the original sin with which they were born, babies were christened no more than a week after birth, even though the haste with which the ceremony was arranged meant that very often only parents and godparents could attend.[3] Marriages and funerals (see chapter 4) also took place in the parish church, as did various commemorations of the anniversary of the deaths of individual parishioners, including obits, the repetition, without the corpse, of the funeral Mass (chapters 5 and 6). In the course of a generation, even a medium-sized parish would accumulate enough deceased parishioners for such celebrations to form at least a weekly event in parish life. In addition there were special ceremonies at the major festivals of the liturgical year, particularly in the week before Easter, when, following very elaborate ceremonial and processions on Palm Sunday, the church was in almost continuous use from Maundy Thursday to Easter Sunday. The Purification of the Blessed Virgin Mary, on 2 February, was marked by processions in the church and churchyard, which all parishioners were expected to attend. The feast of Corpus Christi (Body of Christ), the Thursday after Trinity Sunday, was the occasion for a major religious festival and holiday on which whole neighbourhoods processed together behind the consecrated Host. At Rogationtide, the three days before the feast of the Ascension, further compulsory processions made their way through and around each parish, bearing crosses, church banners and a standard of a dragon to drive away evil spirits. The patronal festival of the parish church took pride of place among the numerous saints' days celebrated each year, while in the parish at large priests performed all kinds of religious ceremonies including the blessing of houses, boats, and bridal chambers, the visitation of the sick and administration of extreme unction to the dying.[4]

During the day time, churches were almost continuously used by the parish priest, by the stipendiary ministers who served its chantries, and by the laity; most had several Masses daily, and incidental services on many days. In addition, the nave of the church could be the setting for much social activity, including funeral wakes and anniversary feasts, and feasts and 'church ales' to raise money for the church.[5] In these very different ways, parish religion with its very particular festivals and other observances both conferred a unique sense of identity upon each parish and at the same time helped to integrate it into the wider community of the locality and of Christian Europe.

The Church in York

The daily celebration of the liturgy affected and in its turn was affected by the architectural and social context in which the clergy served. Second only to London in importance in the high middle ages, York possessed the largest Gothic cathedral in northern Europe, three monasteries and a nunnery, a huge hospital, four friaries (Fig. 1.1) and no fewer than 40 parish churches. In the later medieval period the city entered into a long period of economic stagnation, when its population, which had peaked at perhaps 20,000 before the Black Death, contracted to about 15,000 in 1400 and to around 10,000 a century later. Yet, notwithstanding this fall in the number of inhabitants and the much harsher economic climate, its ecclesiastical provision remained virtually unchanged.[6]

Then as now the Minster towered over the urban scene. In an almost constant state of rebuilding from the thirteenth century onwards, it was not finally completed in its present form until 1472 (Fig. 1.2). Despite its position as the metropolitical church of the northern province, the cathedral normally saw little of its titular head, and in the case of Thomas Wolsey, its most notorious early Tudor incumbent, nothing at all. Even when he did reside in his diocese, the archbishop no longer lived in his mansion within the Close but some miles outside the city in one of his palaces at Cawood or Bishopthorpe.[7]

Responsibility for the administration of the Minster, like that of the other English secular cathedrals, lay with the dean and chapter. In addition to the dean, its presiding officer, the chapter consisted of the three other chief dignitaries, the precentor, chancellor and treasurer,

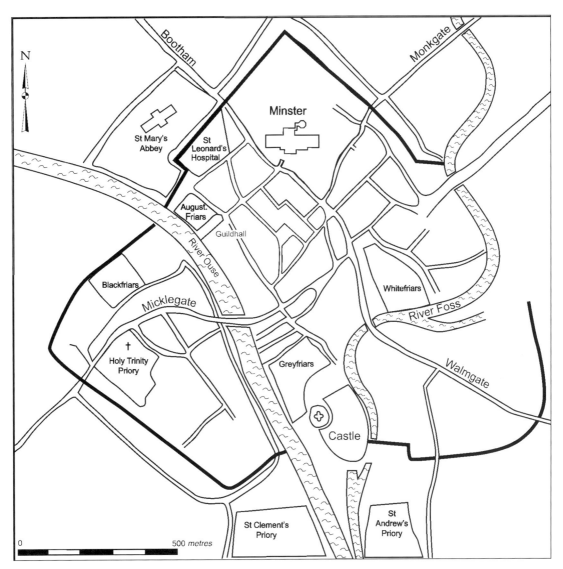

and 32 canons, all since at least the end of the thirteenth century supported by individual estates or prebends, which ranged from Masham worth a princely £120 a year in the mid fifteenth century to Thockrington valued at under £3. Since a deputy might perform the duties of a prebendary, prebends had rapidly come to be regarded as rewards for meritorious service in church or state, with the result that the majority of canons never had any direct connection with the city. In practice the day-to-day running of the cathedral rested with a small inner group of wealthy residentiary canons, usually no more than

Fig 1.1 Principal religious institutions of late-medieval York. Based on a map by the York Archaeological Trust. (© Amanda Daw.)

17

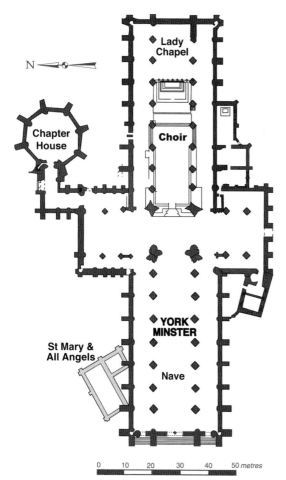

Plan of York Minster showing Lady Chapel, Chapter House, Choir, St Mary & All Angels, York Minster, and Nave with a scale of 0 to 50 metres and a north arrow.

Fig 1.2 Plan of York Minster. (© Amanda Daw.)

three or four at any particular time. In addition to his prebendal income, on protesting residence a canon became entitled to a share of the cathedral's common fund, which could amount to a further £100 a year.

In the absence of most of the prebendaries, the chapter largely relied upon the vicars choral to conduct the worship in the Minster. Every canon was required by the statutes to maintain a deputy in priest's orders, and in the thirteenth century these vicars formed themselves into a corporate body with a chapel, hall and individual chambers in a part of the Close called the Bedern. Largely dependent on rentals of urban property, the college found it could no longer afford its full complement of 36 vicars in the later middle ages and the number fell to 30 at the end of the fifteenth century and to rarely more than 20 a generation later.

With salaries of only about £6 a year the vicars choral could double their income by serving a Minster chantry, and by the Tudor period almost every vicar choral was supplementing his living in this way. Quite apart from the chapel of St Mary and All Angels, a very early collegiate foundation of a sacrist and twelve canons offering perpetual prayers for the dead, some 60 individual chantries had been established in the Minster by the end of the middle ages. The chantry priests tended to be local men who lived in the city largely outside the control of the dean and chapter until the creation of St William's College to house them in 1461.

The dean and chapter ran a song school as well as a much larger grammar school open to boys from the city and its hinterland. Admission to the song school could lead to a permanent career in the Minster with some of the choristers moving on to the grammar school and subsequently serving as thurifers, incense-bearers, and deacons in the cathedral worship. At the age of 23 they became

Fig 1.3 St Leonard's Hospital, York. (© Allan B. Barton.)

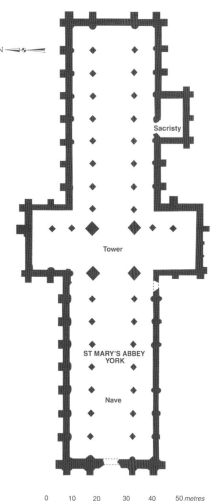

N

Sacristy

Tower

ST MARY'S ABBEY
YORK

Nave

0   10   20   30   40   50 *metres*

Fig 1.4 Plan of St
Mary's Abbey
church, York.
(© Amanda Daw.)

eligible for ordination to the priesthood which enabled them to become vicars choral, posts many then retained for the rest of their lives.

Constantly challenged by two rival institutions of almost comparable influence and size, St Leonard's Hospital and St Mary's Abbey, the Minster never enjoyed an undisputed pre-eminence in medieval York. The largest hospital in the whole of England with 200 beds and revenues of over £1,200 in 1287, St Leonard's occupied the area adjacent to the Close from High Petergate to the city walls (Fig. 1.3). It fulfilled a dual purpose throughout the middle ages, functioning partly as a religious house with thirteen Augustinian canons celebrating the divine office in the priory church, and partly as a hospice with a staff of eight sisters, four secular chaplains and innumerable lay servants to care for the foundlings, the poor and the sick. St Leonard's like the Minster supported both a song school and a grammar school. Though forced by a combination of financial mismanagement and the general economic depression to curtail its charitable activities and concentrate increasingly on out-relief in the late fourteenth and fifteenth centuries, it still played an important part in the life of the city until the Reformation.[8]

St Mary's Abbey, with an income in the region of £2,000 a year the wealthiest Benedictine monastery in the north of England, adjoined St Leonard's Hospital immediately outside Bootham Bar. Governed by a mitred abbot with a seat in the House of Lords, it housed between 50 and 60 monks and some 200 servants throughout the middle ages. In conscious competition with the Minster the community entirely rebuilt its magnificent church in the fourteenth century (Fig. 1.4). The Abbey also made a significant contribution to education, dispatching its quota of monks to the university of Oxford in the later middle ages in addition to keeping a boarding house for lay boys enrolled at the Minster school. Apart from education, however, it seems to have stood rather aloof from the concerns of the city, far more often recruiting its novices from the local gentry and yeomanry than from within York itself.[9]

Perhaps because the nave of its monastic church operated as a parish church, Holy Trinity Priory in Micklegate, a very much smaller Benedictine community of ten to a dozen monks, had much closer ties with its surrounding area and on occasions certainly opened its doors to local talent (Fig. 1.5). The last prior, Richard Speght, son of Henry and Margaret Speght of Micklegate, ordained priest from the priory in 1510, appears to have been born in the parish.[10]

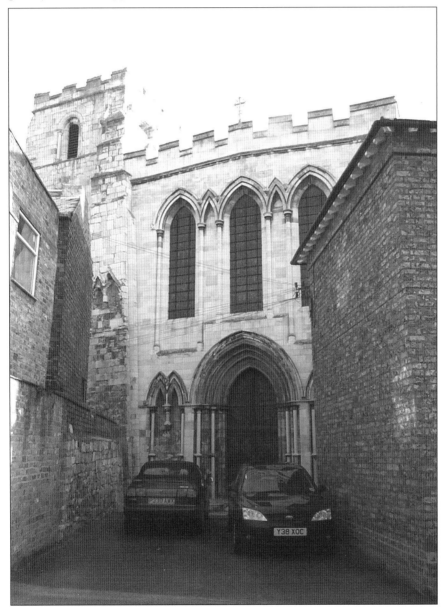

Fig 1.5 Holy Trinity Priory, Micklegate, York. (© Allan B. Barton.)

The Gilbertines also preserved a presence in the city throughout the middle ages. Unlike the order's much larger house at Watton in the East Riding, St Andrew's Priory, situated just outside the walls in Fishergate, never included any nuns. With an annual income of just under £50, the priory contracted to little more than a monastic cell after the Black Death and contained only a prior and three canons in 1538.[11]

In around 1130 Archbishop Thurston established the city's one nunnery across the river in the suburb of Clementhorpe, where over time the nunnery church also came to serve as a parish church. With assets of about £55 a year the community probably never exceeded the thirteen nuns thought appropriate for smaller female houses, and consisted of only eight nuns in addition to the prioress at the dissolution. Nunneries tended to be more socially exclusive than monasteries and Clementhorpe appears to have attracted its novices from local gentry families.[12]

Charged with a special mission to the laity, from the beginning the friars had more impact upon the city than the monastic orders. All the four chief orders of friars had established convents in York well before the end of the thirteenth century, with the Franciscans, or Grey Friars, settling near the Castle, the Dominicans, or Black Friars, on Toft Green, the Carmelites, or White Friars, near the Foss in Hungate and the Austins, Augustinians, between the Guildhall and Lendal Tower (see Fig. 1.1). While each priory may once have held as many as 40 or even 50 friars, the numbers had decreased by a half to three quarters by the early sixteenth century.

The friars always retained their reputation for learning, with many studying for a time at one of their houses at Oxford or Cambridge, and the more able proceeding to a higher degree. The York Austin priory possessed more than 600 theological and philosophical works in the late middle ages and the three other orders probably owned comparable libraries. At his death in 1544 the last warden of the York Franciscans, Dr William Vavasour, left an extensive collection of books which may well have come from the friary at its dissolution. The civic authorities turned to the friars for sermons on special occasions, and literary historians have detected the influence of the Austin friars behind the York Cycle of Mystery Plays. Some inhabitants preferred to make their confession to a friar rather than to their parish priest, while others bequeathed money, rosary beads and household goods to the statue of the Virgin in the Carmelite church around which a cult had developed by the early sixteenth century. At their deaths virtually all the more prosperous York testators paid for the four orders of friars to celebrate Masses for the welfare of their soul.[13]

At Corpus Christi, under the directing hand of the corporation, the Minster clergy, the monks and the friars joined with the city clergy and laity in a demonstration of civic unity, when for an entire day from dawn until after nightfall the craft guilds toured the streets, stopping their pageant carts at various stages on the route to enact scene after scene from the story of salvation. The celebrations culminated the next day in a solemn procession from Holy Trinity Priory via the Minster to St Leonard's Hospital, led by the master and keepers of the Corpus Christi Guild together with a multitude of priests in their habits, the best singers chanting as they went. Behind the priests came the Host in its bejewelled shrine, followed by the mayor and the citizens 'with a prodigious crowd of the populace attending'. The plays and the procession marked the climax of the civic year and attracted vast crowds to the city.[14]

Yet despite the dominance of the Minster, the monasteries and the friaries, the vast majority of the laity looked no further than their parish church. Apart from London, always a special case, Winchester and Norwich, York had more parishes in the middle ages than any other English town (Fig. 1.6). Even though the city lost five churches in the fourteenth century (St Benet, St Mary ad Valvas, St Mary, Walmgate, St Michael without Walmgate and St Stephen, Fishergate), it still had 40 parish churches in the early Tudor period.[15]

With one church for around every 200 of its inhabitants the Tudor corporation in the sixteenth century made a causal connection between the fall in the city's population and the decline in the quality of its parish clergy. Whereas tithes and the offerings had attracted learned incumbents in former more prosperous times, by that date only the most menial clerics would accept benefices which brought in a derisory 26s. 8d. a year. In an age when £5 was thought to be the absolute minimum upon which a priest could live, half of York's parishes produced well below that sum.[16]

Largely because of the laity's demand for prayers for the dead, a surprising number of priests, nevertheless, somehow managed to survive in the city. Driven by the same impulse which had impelled

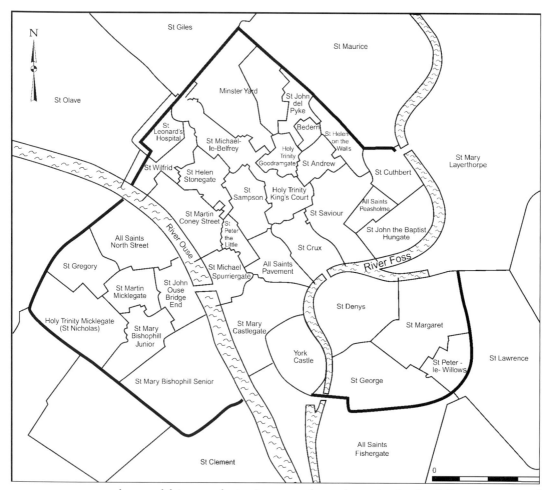

Labels on the map:

N

St Giles
St Maurice
St Olave
Minster Yard
St John del Pyke
St Leonard's Hospital
Bedern
St Helen on the Walls
St Michael-le-Belfrey
Holy Trinity Goodramgate
St Andrew
St Mary Layerthorpe
St Wilfrid
St Helen Stonegate
St Cuthbert
St Sampson
Holy Trinity King's Court
All Saints Peasholme
St Martin Coney Street
St Saviour
St John the Baptist Hungate
St Peter the Little
All Saints North Street
River Ouse
St Crux
St Gregory
All Saints Pavement
River Foss
St Michael Spurriergate
St Martin Micklegate
St John Ouse Bridge End
St Denys
Holy Trinity Micklegate (St Nicholas)
St Mary Bishophill Junior
St Mary Castlegate
St Margaret
York Castle
St Peter - le- Willows
St Lawrence
St George
St Mary Bishophill Senior
All Saints Fishergate
St Clement
0

Fig 1.6 The parishes of late medieval York. Based on a map by D. Palliser in *Yorkshire Archaeological Journal*, 44 (1974).
(© Amanda Daw.)

the wealthiest ecclesiastics to endow chantries in the Minster, some of York's richest merchants felt compelled to establish in their parish churches benefactions for the celebration of Masses in perpetuity for the salvation of their souls. At least 80 different chantries are known to have existed in the city at some time in the later middle ages. Only the most affluent could afford the expense of a permanent foundation, but those of more modest means could at least hire a priest to intercede for their souls for a term of years or months after their death. A whole array of stipendiary priests depended upon casual work of this kind.[17]

Such local clergy constituted the very lowest level of the ecclesiastical hierarchy. Born and bred in the city, when he died in 1528, William Simpson, the chantry priest at St Katherine's altar in All

24

Saints', Pavement, asked to be buried beside his father and mother in the church of St Lawrence outside Walmgate Bar. Like Thomas Worrall, the stipendiary priest of St Michael's, Spurriergate, William Coca, the priest of Nelson's chantry in Holy Trinity, Micklegate, interred next to his parents in the same church in 1537, may never have left the parish of his birth.[18]

Yet this localism did not necessarily exclude these priests from a wider ecclesiastical culture, even if they acquired their acquaintance with this culture only at second hand. York continued as a provincial capital with ties throughout England and indeed with many parts of the continent throughout the later middle ages. When the Minster and St Mary's Abbey embarked upon the rebuilding of their churches, both patronised the highest levels of contemporary craftsmanship, and some citizens seem to have wanted the same high standards in their parish churches. A generation after the Minster canons had erected their great east window at the beginning of the fifteenth century, the wealthy merchant Nicholas Blackburn gave two fine, though smaller, painted windows to All Saints', North Street. The churches of St Martin, Coney Street and Holy Trinity, Goodramgate owed their east windows to the generosity of their incumbents, Roger Semer, vicar of St Martin's from 1425 till 1443, and John Walker, rector of Holy Trinity from 1471 to 1481, while clerical and lay benefactors combined to donate the new glass in St Michael le Belfrey, rebuilt by the dean and chapter in the early Tudor period.[19]

Lay and clerical testators chose also to adorn the liturgy of the city churches. At St Michael's, Spurriergate, alone John Barton, alderman and spicer, donated the substantial sum of £26 in 1461 to buy a suit of damask vestments for a priest, deacon and subdeacon, while three years later the rector, William Langton, left the church three vestments, his Missal, Manual, and chalice. In the early sixteenth century another parishioner, Thomas Geffrey, bequeathed to the church his best candelabra, Alice Blakey presented her hanging candlestick to the statue of St Anne, and John Roger, fishmonger, gave enough cloth to make an alb for the morrow Mass priest in the adjoining St William's Chapel on Ouse Bridge.[20]

Perhaps most interestingly of all, by the end of the middle ages at least some of the parish churches were aspiring to compete musically with the Minster and the monastic churches. There were certainly song schools at different dates in the parishes of All Saints, North Street, St Mary, Castlegate, St Martin, Micklegate, St Michael, Spurriergate, Holy Trinity, King's Court, in the chapel on Ouse Bridge and perhaps elsewhere in the city. When arranging for the celebration of Requiem Masses for the souls of themselves and their families, a number of testators specified that they should be sung with 'pricksong' by 'an honest priest being a choirman'. The chance survival of St Michael's, Spurriergate, churchwardens' accounts reveals that the parishioners purchased not one but two sets of organs in the early Tudor period. Clearly the more influential citizens both wanted elaborate musical settings of the liturgy and were providing the means to perform it in their parish churches.[21]

The Minster, the monasteries, the friaries and the parish churches together needed a huge clerical work force. In addition to the host of servants employed by the different ecclesiastical institutions, the city may well have accommodated over 100 members of religious orders and approaching 400 secular clergy in the later middle ages. With the active encouragement of the laity these priests were continuously extending and beautifying their churches, acquiring gold and silver vessels and precious vestments, and sponsoring ever more elaborate music. The prime purpose of all this endeavour was to glorify Christ in the Mass, the universal and defining feature of late-medieval Christianity.[22]

2

The ornaments of the altar and the ministers in late-medieval England

Allan B. Barton

Despite the interest in late-medieval liturgy that has arisen as a result of influential publications such as Eamon Duffy's *The Stripping of the Altars*,[1] little has been written in recent years that provides basic information on the visual setting of the liturgy in late-medieval England. Against that background, and with the aim of creating a sense of the aesthetic experience of late-medieval English liturgy, this chapter sets out to provide a brief guide to both the form and adornment of the altar and its immediate environs, and the distinctive vestments worn by the ministers.

The form of the altar

Medieval English altars were usually made of stone, and consisted of a structure which supported a large monolith, or mensa. The mensa, the consecrated part of the structure, was the altar proper: on it, and only on it, could the elements of bread and wine be consecrated by the priest during Mass. English mensa slabs, which survive in their hundreds,[2] are usually chamfered at the sides and their tops invariably bear five incised crosses, one in the centre and one at each corner.

These crosses were the points on the slab that were anointed with oil by the bishop during the consecration of the altar and symbolically represent the wounds in Christ's hands, feet and side, highlighting the sacrificial purpose of the Mass as the re-enactment of Christ's passion.[3] The main structure of the altar, below the mensa, was often hollow, and sometimes contained relics sealed into it during consecration.[4] Sometimes the structure supporting the mensa was made of wood and took the form of a chest which might be used to store vestments, as were two bequeathed to St John's, Hungate, York in 1435.[5] Although the width and height of medieval English altars was quite uniform, the length varied widely, the size usually being dictated by the physical setting of the altar (see below).[6]

The physical and visual setting of the altar

Late-medieval English parish churches were divided into compartments, each with a specific purpose and each containing an altar or a series of altars. The chancel at the east, often known as the high choir in the middle ages, separated from the nave by the rood screen, was reserved for the daily parochial performance of the Mass. Its focus was the high or principal altar, consecrated to the patron saint or title, such as Holy Cross, of the church. This was where the incumbent priest celebrated. The nave, that is, the body of the church, with its side aisles, formed the largest part of the building and was both an area where the laity gathered to witness the liturgy at the high altar, and a space where they practised their own devotions. It often housed subsidiary altars dedicated to popular saints, and used for the celebration of votive Masses, or private or corporate obits or commemorations. Such altars might be placed in a variety of places, in subsidiary chapels at the east ends of the nave or chancel aisles, or in the body of the church, set against the rood screen or the pillars, or in screened-off areas.

In parish churches the high altar usually stood above the body of the building, and the chancel was sometimes raised above the level of the nave by one or two steps, with the immediate environs of the altar, the presbytery or sanctuary, up another step.[7] The altar itself was either constructed directly on the pavement of the presbytery, or on an additional step, the predella or footpace. To the south of the high altar, usually built into the wall, but occasionally free-standing, were the piscina and sedilia. The piscina, a basin for washing the sacred vessels, often incorporated a credence or shelf to hold the vessels prior to and after use during the Mass. The sedilia, often next to the piscina, was a set of two or three (occasionally more) seats used by the clergy during the Mass.[8] On the opposite side of the chancel, and also built into the wall might be an aumbry, a locker, in which the sacred vessels were stored, and an Easter sepulchre, for use during Holy Week (the week before Easter).[9]

Side altars placed at the east end of aisles could stand on the floor but were commonly raised on a footpace. Altars in the nave, usually of lesser importance, were often built directly onto the pavement. Like the high altar, side altars could be provided with piscinae and aumbries, which were built into the walls of the church. Principal side altars occasionally possessed their own sedilia.

In early Christian basilicas the high altar, usually at that period the only altar in the church, was placed at the eastern end of the chancel, in a semicircular apse, some distance from the wall, beneath a canopy of honour, or ciborium, supported on four columns. The ciborium shielded the altar from contamination, and fixed curtains on all four sides hid it from view. The whole structure enshrined and enclosed the altar giving it visual dominance within the church building.[10] By the later middle ages in England and the rest of western Europe, the ciborium had been adapted in response to new doctrine and local circumstances. The doctrinal issue related to the gradual refinement of the teaching concerning the sacrament, which culminated in the adoption of the Doctrine of Transubstantiation in 1215 (see chapter 7). This led to greater reverence for the sacrament, and to the introduction of the ceremony of the Elevation of the Host so that the laity could see it. As a result the front hangings of the ciborium, which obscured the view from the nave, were abandoned. In England there was also a local factor in evolution of the ciborium, for the dull climate meant that as much light as possible needed to be cast on to the altar so that the priest could read the missal and sing Mass. As a result, the shade-creating canopy of the ciborium was dispensed with, and the altar set against the east wall of the chancel below the large east window.

The sense of enclosure of the altar was retained through the use of other devices. Textile hangings, known as riddels, were placed to the north and south of the altar, suspended between posts, known as riddel posts, or hung on iron brackets.[11] They were drawn forward at the beginning of the Canon of the Mass (see chapter 7) to prevent the priest being distracted during the devotions.[12] The canopy of the ciborium could also be re-created in other ways. The most common was an elaboration of the timber ceiling directly above the altar, either by the use of carving or by concentrated painted decoration and gilding. Occasionally a physical canopy or tester, a ciborium without posts, was either hung from the rafters or attached directly to them above the altar, but set higher than the head of the east window so that the light was not reduced.[13]

With the altar set directly below the east window, the chancel wall, rather than the enclosure of the altar, became the principal visual focus in the building. The way the wall was treated varied greatly according to the size and date of the building.[14] A large altarpiece or reredos might be erected behind the altar, as was usual on the continent, but more commonly in England the east window glass served the same function. In churches of the fourteenth and fifteenth centuries the windows were usually of generous proportions and their glass often incorporated a crucifixion scene or figures of saints under canopies which imitated three-dimensional structures, with the length of the altar adapted to the width of the window.

Textile hangings or small-scale backdrops of more substantial material were frequently used to create visual unity between the altar and its setting. A hanging known as the dorsal or upper frontal, a curtain slightly narrower and longer than the altar, was often suspended between the riddel posts or from hooks in the east wall. A more costly alternative was a small-scale altarpiece or retable, perhaps consisting of a painting, or a panel of carved wood or stone, or, commonly, a set of alabaster panels set within a wooden housing. In larger church buildings where the images in the window or on the east wall were too far away from the altar, the images in such smaller altarpieces or panels provided a devotional focus for the priest during Mass. If the backdrop was particularly bright, a dark curtain was drawn across it at the time of the Elevation, so that the white host was thrown into contrast and made visible from the nave.[15]

Canon law required two three-dimensional images, one of the Virgin Mary, the other representing the patron saint or title of the church, to flank the high altar. In larger buildings such images might form part of the altarpiece, but in most parish churches they were placed on each side of the east window either on corbels, some of which still remain, or in canopied niches known as tabernacles.[16] Since these images were intended to serve as a devotional focus for the laity, they had to be large enough to be seen from the nave. They were almost all destroyed at the Reformation.

The location of side altars necessitated different approaches. Altars set against the east walls of aisles might be treated in much the same way as the high altar. If, however, there was a screen behind the altar, it was usually incorporated into the backdrop, as at Ranworth, in Norfolk, where the two altars placed against the rood screen were provided with integral altarpieces made of painted panels, inserted between the uprights of the screen. Whatever the structure, the imagery around the altar again reflected its dedication or devotional character.

Textiles and lights

The rubrics of the Missal and the injunctions of bishops required that the altar be covered with a series of textile hangings before Mass was said. The front of the altar was usually covered with the nether or lower frontal, over which was suspended a shorter cloth called, the frontlet or, less frequently, the super-frontal.[17] These hangings may have evolved from the front curtain of the ciborium, perpetuating the sense of enclosure created by the canopy.[18] In England, the frontal was usually subdivided into panels by orphreys, applied strips of fabric often decorated with embroidery. The high altar at Durham Cathedral had two sets of frontals, one, for daily use, 'of red velvet, wrought with great flowers of gold in embroidered work', the other, for principal feasts, 'of white damask all beset with pearl and precious stones'.[19] In addition to the embroidery, fringing, often multicoloured, might be applied to the bottom and sides of both the frontal and frontlet.[20] There is some evidence that fabric frontals were occasionally replaced with painted wooden ones, the fourteenth-century Thornham Parva retable in Suffolk, for example, having a matching nether frontal, now in the Musée de Cluny in Paris.[21]

The top of the altar, the mensa, was covered with between two and four white linen cloths.[22] The 1229 Constitutions of Westminster, which probably represent general practice throughout England, ordered three cloths to be placed on the mensa, the top one blessed by a bishop.[23] Often the lowest layer was a 'cere', or waxed cloth, to prevent the oil used at the consecration of the altar soaking into the upper cloths. As is apparent from manuscript illustrations of medieval altars, the topmost cloth, sometimes ornamented with embroidery or drawn-thread patterns, hung down the sides of the altar, so that no part of the structure was visible during Mass.[24]

A standing cross was not considered a vital altar ornament in medieval England, as it would often have unnecessarily duplicated the imagery of the retable, east wall or window. There is, however, evidence that occasionally, and very economically, the head of the processional cross was detachable so that it could be placed on a separate base on the altar.[25]

According to late-medieval episcopal legislation, the only light required during Mass was a single wax taper. It was not necessarily placed on the altar, but could be held by the clerk or assistant ministers.[26] However, the evidence of inventories suggests that it was usual in parish churches for two candles, but seldom more than two, to stand on the altar during all services.[27] In larger churches it was also normal for two standard candles to be placed on the pavement in front of the altar. At the wealthy Lincolnshire church of Louth, for example, the high altar had two 'great candlesticks of latten [brass]', which stood in the high choir.[28] In addition, lamps were often hung from the ceiling in front of the altar, either singly or grouped in threes or sevens, forming sacrament lamps, burning in front of the sacrament which was reserved above the high altar (see below).[29] Large twisted torches called 'serges', often portrayed in medieval manuscript illustrations of the Mass, were carried by the ministers or prominent members of the laity at the time of the Elevation; wealthy testators frequently bequeathed the lights which illuminated their funeral hearses for use round the altar as 'elevation torches' of this kind (see chapter 4).

In cathedrals and large churches, the candles, standards, lamps and serges were sometimes augmented with other occasional lights, which stood around the altar or in the choir. Their number and use varied according to the solemnity of the occasion. In Salisbury, for example, the Use of Sarum indicates that, on the most solemn feasts, the two altar candles and standards were augmented with eight additional lights placed about the altar, in front of the principal images to either side and, probably, on a beam above it.[30] The amount of additional illumination was determined by the status, size and wealth of individual churches.

Reserving the Sacrament

Although there are occasional references in medieval inventories to tabernacles, lockers or 'sacrament houses' placed upon the altar,[31] it seems that the most common way of reserving the Sacrament in medieval England was to suspend it over the high altar in a pyx, a vessel of precious metal or gilded base-metal, usually in the form of a small box with a hinged lid, suspended by a chain and raised and lowered on a counterweight or pulley system.[32] At Durham Cathedral, for example, the pyx was hung from two gilded iron brackets let into the stonework of the altarpiece.[33] The pyx was covered by a pyx-cloth, canopy or sindon made of the finest linen or another rich material. The only English example to survive, from Hesset in Suffolk, now in the British Museum, takes the form of a square of fringed drawn linen weighed down with wooden balls at the corners, and with a hole in the centre for the chain from which the pyx was suspended.[34] The pyx cloth at Durham Cathedral was more expensive, being of 'very fine lawn, all embroidered and wrought about with gold and red silk', with the balls or 'knopes' being gold.[35] Occasionally, the cloth was surmounted by a wooden canopy like that which still exists at Dennington in Suffolk, or by an umbrella-like tester, which appears in many manuscript illustrations of medieval altars; at Durham it was surmounted with a gilded pelican.[36]

The ornaments of the ministers

Most of the vestments worn by the ministers were derivatives of the everyday dress of ancient Rome, and like the altar, had gradually evolved over time to fulfil the particular demands of the liturgy. They might vary according to the availability of materials and other local circumstances.[37]

At High Mass all the ministers and their attendants wore the same basic under-attire: a cassock, amice and alb. The cassock, a long-sleeved, skirted gown of black material, buttoned at the shoulders and

waist, was the everyday garment of the clerk in holy orders, and was worn under all other vestments. Next, to protect the outer vestments from soiling, a rectangular piece of linen was put around the neck. Known as the amice, from the Latin *amicio*, to wrap around,[38] it was placed on the head and secured around the neck and torso with tapes or cords (Fig. 2.1). After the alb had

Above:
Fig. 2.1 Amice, put on over the cassock. (© Allan B. Barton.)

Right:
Fig 2.2 Alb and stole, secured by the girdle; amice still over the head. (© Allan B. Barton.)

been put on, the amice was thrown back from the head to rest around the neck. The alb, or albe, in Latin, *tunica*, was a simple sleeved tunic, brought in and secured at the waist with a rope or band of fabric called a girdle (Fig. 2.2). It was usually made of linen, but there is evidence that some of those used at principal feasts could be made of silk.[39] The name 'alb', arose from the fact that the material was usually white (Latin *albus*), though a rose-coloured silk example is known to have been used at York Minster between 1360 and 1378.[40] Both the alb and amice were decorated with coloured embroidered panels called apparels. On the alb they were suspended at the front and back hem of the skirt and on the cuffs of both sleeves (Fig. 2.3), while on the amice they were placed on the outside edge, so that, when thrown back from the head, it appeared like a collar.[41]

Sometimes a rochet, a short ungirdled white linen vestment with tight sleeves was worn over the cassock instead of the alb. It had the advantage of being able to be slipped on quickly, but, since it was worn without the amice, it was not suitable for use under the particular vestments that distinguished the senior ministers at Mass.

Over the alb and amice, the priest celebrating Mass wore three additional vestments, the stole, maniple and chasuble. The stole (Latin *orarium* or *stola*), had evolved from a napkin used by deacons in early Christian liturgy to cleanse the eucharistic vessels, and by the late middle ages had become a long narrow strip of fabric which was placed over the shoulders of the priest, crossed at the breast and secured by the girdle of the alb (see Fig. 2.2). After its transmutation, the stole was superseded by a napkin, placed on the wrist, which, in its turn, became conventional, and developed into the maniple (Latin *mappula*) or fanon, as it was better known in England, a strip of fabric worn on the left wrist.

The celebrant's main item of clothing was the chasuble (Latin *casula*),[42] or Mass vestment, described in most medieval English contexts simply as 'the vestment' (Fig. 2.4). Very much like a poncho, it was descended from the *paenula* or *phaeilonen*, a practical outer

Fig. 2.3 Alb, showing apparels; amice turned down.
(© Allan B. Barton.)

35

Fig. 2.4 Chasuble, showing Y-shaped orphreys on front (a) and back (b). (© Allan B. Barton.)

garment worn by all ranks of Roman society, and took the form of a very full circular cloak, with a hole in the middle for the wearer's head. Until the fifteenth century, in England the chasuble was conical and made from a semicircle of fabric sewn down the centre; it was an elegant vestment which retained much of the fullness of the *paenula*. The central seam was covered by an embroidered strip or orphrey.[43] Since the deep folds of fabric impeded the free use of the priest's arms, the introduction of the ceremony of the Elevation of the Host necessitated a change in the form of the chasuble. At first the seams were moved to the shoulders to lessen the weight of the folds, and the burden of the remaining fabric was reduced by folding the vestment back over the celebrant's shoulders immediately before the Elevation.[44] Over time, and certainly by the fifteenth and sixteenth centuries, the amount of material was greatly curtailed in order to leave the priest's arms entirely free, the vestment thereafter commonly being referred to as a 'square' chasuble. On the continent, the reductions in the amount of fabric continued until, by the Baroque period, the vestment had evolved into the so-called 'fiddleback' or 'Roman' chasuble and its various local manifestations.

At a High Mass, the priest was assisted at the altar by a deacon and subdeacon (see chapter 7), both of whom had their own distinctive liturgical dress. The deacon wore a sleeved tunic or dalmatic (Latin *dalmatica*) derived from a Roman garment made of wool from Dalmatia.[45] Sometimes referred to in

Fig. 2.5 Dalmatic, showing slit sides and straight orphreys.
(© Allan B. Barton.)

medieval texts as a 'deacon coat', it usually fell below the knees at the front and back but had slits at both sides from the waist (Fig. 2.5). The dalmatic might be plain, but was often adorned with two parallel vertical orphreys on the back and front, with two horizontal apparels between them at the breast and skirt. It was also common for both the outer edges of the skirt and the cuffs of the sleeves to be decorated with fringing.[46] In addition to the dalmatic, the deacon also wore a stole and maniple. The stole was in fact the official garment of the deacon, which the priest only wore by virtue of the fact that he remained a deacon when elevated to the priesthood; it was placed 'deacon-wise', that is, across the left shoulder and tied on the right hand side at the waist.

Despite a quite different origin, the tunicle (little tunic) worn by the subdeacon was by the late middle ages almost identical in form to the dalmatic. To reflect his inferior status, it was usually less elaborately decorated, with one rather than two horizontal apparels on

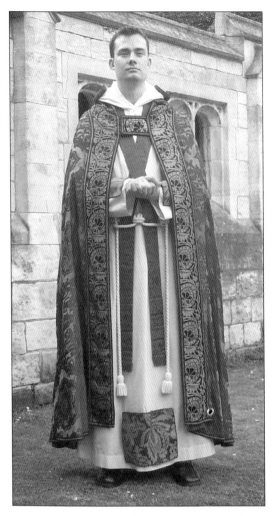

Fig. 2.6 Cope, showing the morse (a) and vestigial hood (b). (© Allan B. Barton.)

the orphreys. As the tunicle was not the exclusive preserve of the subdeacon, but was also part of the vesture of a clerk in acolyte's orders, who might act as a crucifer or thurifer, the subdeacon wore the maniple to define his particular status.

For processions, solemn choir offices and all other occasional services, the priest exchanged the chasuble for the cope (Latin *cappa*). Deriving from the Roman hooded cloak, it consisted of a semicircle of fabric held together at the breast by a clasp or morse (Fig. 2.6). During the middle ages the hood became vestigial, evolving into a symbolic flap suspended from the back of the vestment. If worn during a procession before Mass or at other extra-liturgical functions such as the Absolutions of the Dead, the cope was placed over the alb, amice and crossed stole. For choir offices it was worn over the cassock, a full white vestment or surplice, and a fur scarf known as tippet or almuce. A version of the cope made of black material, the *cappa nigra*, was worn out of doors, and also by the rulers of the choir.

By the thirteenth and fourteenth centuries it was increasingly common for dalmatics and tunicles to be made of the same material and carry similar decoration as chasubles, and they, together with the cope, formed matching sets or suits of vestments, sometimes described as a 'whole vestment' and its 'appurtenances'.[47]

Textile decoration and liturgical colours

In the thirteenth and fourteenth centuries England was famous for its embroidered textiles, *Opus Anglicanum* or English Work being much prized throughout Europe and particularly favoured by the papal court.[48] The main areas of decoration on the altar hangings and vestments were the orphreys, and the hood of the cope. The embroidery was couched in silk or metal thread on a backing of canvas, and then stitched to the main fabric of the hanging or vestment, which was usually of velvet or silk damask.

In general terms the type and level of decoration on a vestment reflected the prevalent architectural style so that, in the fourteenth century, for example, vestments were embroidered with tightly packed imagery set within naturalistic or architectural features. The backs of chasubles often had cross or Y-shaped orphreys containing a crucifixion scene, or subdivided into panels recording the life of a particular saint. In the fifteenth century the decoration tended to become more conventional. The orphreys of copes were adorned with two-dimensional tabernacles containing standing figures of saints, the twelve apostles with Christ in the morse being a common theme, while vestments were often 'powdered' with angels, fleur-de-lis, double-headed eagles and stylised plants or 'water flowers'. As with all elements of late-medieval art, liturgical vestments and altar hangings were a vehicle for self-display, with the patrons' armorial bearings and personal devices and images showing the kneeling donor becoming common by the end of the period.[49]

Although prescribed colour sequences for vestments and altar apparel for different kinds of service and seasons during the liturgical calendar are of great importance in the modern Church, they were virtually unknown in medieval England, and indeed on the continent before the standardisation introduced at the time of the Counter-Reformation.[50] Colour sequences did exist in some English cathedrals, but they varied widely and it is unclear how strictly they were followed.[51] In those churches which had less money for multiple sets of vestments and less ready access to costly materials, it appears that the usual procedure was to employ the best or newest vestments and altar hangings available, regardless of colour, for the most important feasts of the church and then to use worn or older vestments for the lesser ferial, or ordinary, days.[52] This is borne out by references in the fourteenth century fabric rolls of York Minster, which indicate that a variety of colours, including white, gold, red, and mixed red and green, were used for vestments at different altars on the major feasts. It seems that the only universal standard in the late middle ages was the use of unbleached linen hangings for Lent, the so-called Lenten array,[53] and darker colours, whether black or blue, for funerary rites. In the early sixteenth century York Minster possessed vestments of both the latter colours.[54]

In addition, it seems that no great effort was made to match vestments with altar hangings. Manuscript illustrations commonly depict black vestments against green or red frontals, red vestments against blue altar hangings, and many other combinations. Even a cathedral as rich as Durham only had two coloured frontals for the high altar, one of red for everyday use and one of white for feast days, and they must have been used in conjunction with vestments of widely varying colour.[55] Neither, it seems, did the alb and amice apparels have to match the vestments with which they were worn. Since the desire for maximum impact appears to have been more important than the need to signify the liturgical season, as with the decoration of woodwork, both contrasting and conflicting colours could be used in the later middle ages to lend a sense of mystery and wonder to the celebration of the Mass. The gift of rich vestments and hangings to embellish this, the most sacred of church services, was one of the most potent forms of offering to God which any medieval donor could make.

3

Choral music in York, 1400–1540

Lisa Colton

The nature of the evidence

This chapter describes what is known about choral music in York in the late-medieval period. Music before the Reformation fell into two general types. Plainchant, also known as Gregorian chant, was part of the services in Christian religious houses and churches across Europe, and consisted of Latin liturgical text sung to a single melodic line. By the thirteenth century, many institutions had also begun to perform polyphony, music in two or more parts. In the fifteenth century, the most prestigious churches owned manuscripts of polyphonic music, which might have contained choral settings of Mass items, antiphons or motets. In contrast to the one-to-a-part arrangements that characterised fourteenth-century choirs, the middle of the fifteenth century witnessed a rise in choral singing in which vocal parts were performed by two or more singers.[1]

Polyphonic music books differed from those containing plainchant in that they used a special type of notation, one that specified rhythmic duration, rests, and part distribution. Over time, different methods of notation were used for polyphony, and sources containing old-fashioned repertoire were disposed of, often as binding material for other books. It is likely that most churches kept only the most recent book or books of choral music to hand.

Furthermore, the Reformation of the sixteenth century caused those that remained to be destroyed. Choral music fared badly because it was specific to the Catholic rite and represented one of the most powerful aural elements of its liturgy. John Aubrey, a seventeenth-century natural history writer, reported that:

> In my grandfather's days the manuscripts flew about like butterflies. All music books, account books, copy books, etc., were covered with old manuscripts, as we cover them now with blue paper or marbled paper; and the glovers at Malmesbury made great havoc of them; and gloves were wrapped up no doubt in many good pieces of antiquity.[2]

For these reasons, only a tiny proportion of what was once performed has been preserved, and musicologists seeking to understand the sorts of music cultivated in a city such as York have to draw on a variety of forms of evidence, all incomplete. Questions such as how many singers lived and worked in a given location, or exactly what types of music were being composed there, are difficult to answer with any certainty.

The earliest evidence from York

Against this background it is, however, possible to understand something of York's musical life in the period before the Reformation.[3] The earliest choral music to have survived from the city dates from around 1400, and consists of a single parchment bifolium – that is, a rectangular piece of parchment folded down into the middle to make two leaves (Fig. 3.1).[4] The source originally consisted of a gathering of several leaves, within which this was nested, so that it contains parts of three incomplete pieces of music. The oldest piece is written in notation that is typical of the late fourteenth century. The remaining pieces seem to be later, perhaps by a decade or more. One is identifiable as a three-part setting of the antiphon *Nesciens mater,* and is also found in the Old Hall Manuscript where it is attributed to Bittering.[5] *Nesciens mater* was sung in devotional contexts associated with the Virgin Mary, and a few polyphonic settings have survived, in line with the increased importance of Marian feasts in the later middle ages.

The Old Hall Manuscript is England's first substantial source of choral music to have survived almost intact. Its contents, mainly

Opposite:
Fig. 3.1 The earliest choral manuscript to have survived from York. BIHR MS Mus. 2 f. 1v. (Reproduced from an original in the Borthwick Institute, University of York.)

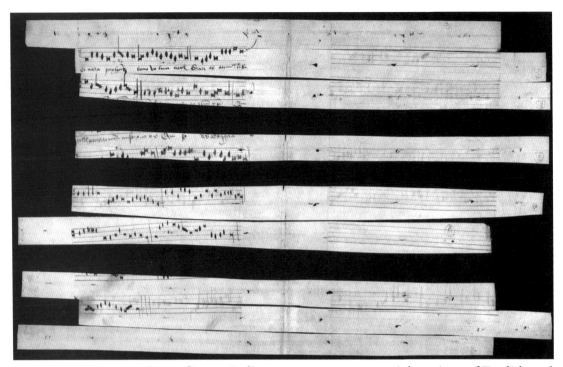

settings of Mass Ordinary texts, represent a rich variety of English and continental pieces, many of which are found with a composer's name attached to them, such as 'Roy Henry' (probably Henry V), Queldryk and Leonel Power. The second son of Henry IV, Thomas, Duke of Clarence, is thought to have owned this impressive collection. The main contents were completed by about 1420, shortly before the manuscript passed to the royal chapel following the death of its original owner. The York copy of Bittering's *Nesciens mater* gives a more convincing version than that preserved in the Old Hall Manuscript, and it was probably copied from a third source, since lost. The *Nesciens mater* by Bittering is an important link between a major source of English choral music and York's own musical heritage. That a York church owned a reliable copy of this music is particularly interesting, since it suggests that singers in the city were familiar with the latest repertoire. There is little reliable evidence linking the name Bittering to any specific institution, and it is possible that his music was composed in the York diocese and later copied into a southern source, rather than, as is usually assumed, that the best music was written in London, and only later copied and passed on to the north of the country.

In 2001, staff at the Borthwick Institute of Historical Research in York found further pieces of music in the binding of a sixteenth-century book.[6] The fragments of music, which had been torn horizontally from a mid-to-late fifteenth-century choirbook, were separated out and reassembled in their original order (Fig. 3.2).[7] A great deal of music was missing, since not all the strips had been used in the binding. On close examination, it became apparent that all the various lines were tenor parts, and that some seemed to have been taken from settings of the Gloria. Even more importantly, considering the relative rarity of pre-Reformation repertoire, three of the tenor parts matched those found in Gloria settings from the fourteenth and fifteenth centuries.

All three identifiable pieces preserve only the lowest part of the original composition, and only alternate verses of the Gloria text. The first and third pieces in the reconstructed binding strips correspond with music found in the Old Hall Manuscript.[8] The second Gloria was evidently very popular over a considerable period, since its earliest sources date to the fourteenth century.[9] Perhaps most interestingly, one such concordance is found in a manuscript from St Mary's Abbey in Rufford, Nottinghamshire.[10] This Cistercian house fell within the boundaries of the York diocese, and was not far from East Drayton, the original provenance of the one surviving copy of York's Gradual. Another Gloria setting in the same manuscript concords with a piece from Bolton Priory in Yorkshire, and it could be that the early copies of these Glorias, and the tenors extracted from them later on, were composed in the area of York, or at least within the boundaries of its Use.

All other surviving copies of these three items preserve the music intact, including all the verses. Part books were rare in the fifteenth century, and there is only one plausible reason for the copying of only the lower parts of polyphonic music, that is, for their use as 'squares'. The earliest reference to squares comes from Durham, where, from 1496, the choirmaster was contracted to teach choristers how to use them.[11] Squares were a peculiarly English device, involving the recycling of tenor parts, the lowest lines in older repertory. The new piece would use the melody and rhythm of the original tenor, furnishing it with fresh upper parts to create a new polyphonic composition. Alternate verses might be sung as plainchant rather than expanded into polyphony, a useful way of speeding up the longest

Mass items such as the Gloria and Creed. Example 1a (p. 51), shows the opening of the original three-part polyphonic Gloria, as preserved in the Rufford Manuscript, and Example 1b shows the square found as item 2 in the York binding strips (cf. Fig. 3.2). This can be compared with the first item shown in Fig 3.2. The square in Example 1b misses out alternate sections of the original Gloria, suggesting that they were sung in plainchant. Unfortunately, no specimins survive of how the 'new' compositions would have sounded, and it is possible that they were improvised. They were probably not meant to sound like the fifty-year old compositions from which they had been taken, but rather reflected the developments in improvised choral elaboration specific to the middle of the fifteenth century.

Composing using squares was fairly common in England in the century before the Reformation.[12] Examples of Masses based upon squares are known from institutions across the country, from Durham, where the word is first recorded, to Louth, and from London to Bath. Yet it is relatively rare to find a source that contains only the squares themselves, and they are often identifiable only through the same tenor line cropping up in more than one piece of music.

The York Masses

The third and perhaps most important source of choral music from pre-Reformation York, the 'York Masses', survived as a result of its use as pastedowns in the binding of a volume of consistory court acts. The collection also contains pieces of music composed using squares, though these differ from the squares preserved in the binding strips. Masses II and IV in the York Masses, composed between *c.*1490 and the 1520s, are based upon the tenor square inscribed at the end of the piece and labelled *Custodi nos domine* (see Example 2a, p. 52).[13] Example 2b shows the use of the square as the lowest part of the Gloria of Mass II, and Example 2c demonstrates the variation of the melody found in the Benedictus of Mass IV. Both the polyphonic settings use the square transposed to start on F rather than C, perhaps to suit the range of the bass singer. These examples show that, although there is some decoration of the square, its basic melodic and rhythmic shape remains intact, and it provides a firm harmonic foundation for the parts written above it.

The York Masses contain a wide variety of musical styles, including

Opposite:
Fig. 3.3 Kyrie No.1, York Masses. BIHR MS Mus. 1 f. 1r. (Reproduced from an original in the Borthwick Institute, University of York.)

polyphony in three and four parts for a variety of scorings. One of the most peculiar pieces is the anonymous Kyrie that opens the collection (Fig. 3.3). Only three parts are provided on the page. A rubric at the foot of the page describes instructions for the canonic part:

> Hic sunt quattuor partes contentis in tribus et ego demonstrabo vobis quomodo debetis inventis quartam partem et quarta pars est Bassus primo querite in triplice in prima parte et postea in secundam triplice in parte de Christe et tunc in tenor in ultram parte et sic quartas in venietis partes si bene queratis venietis sex postea semper.

> Here four parts are contained in three, and I shall demonstrate to you how you should find the fourth part; and the fourth part is the bass. First seek [the bass part] in the triplex in the first part [the Kyrie], and afterwards in the second triplex in the part of the Christe, and then in the tenor in the final part [the second Kyrie]. And thus you will find four parts and if you seek well you will always come six [beats] after.

In other words, the complete four-part texture relies on a rather talented bass singer who has to follow all three other parts in turn after six beats rest (see Example 3, pp. 53-5). Each successive section of the Kyrie presents a more complex line for the bass to remember. The composer who wrote this piece, and the scribe who copied it, clearly envisaged a choral group that included a highly musical individual, and it is possible that the composer was writing music to perform himself, in order to demonstrate his performance skills. Canons, pieces with close imitation between parts in the manner of a 'round', were popular in England during this period, but this is the only such piece to have survived from York.

Very little is known about the composers whose music was performed in the city, since most of the music is preserved anonymously. In the York Masses, two composers are named. The second Kyrie in the collection is ascribed to 'Horwod', who may be the William Horwood (†1484) whose music survives in the Eton Choirbook of *c*.1500. The settings in the Eton Choirbook are all elaborate Marian pieces, and the Kyrie in the York Masses is quite conservative in comparison. Only two voices of the Kyrie survive, but they show that Horwood based his setting on a cantus firmus using the plainchant *Rex Clemens,* which migrates from the tenor to another part, presumably the bass, in the second polyphonic Christe. Horwood provided choral polyphony for four sections, leaving the alternate five as plainchant.

There seems to be a particular emphasis in York sources of this sort of alternating arrangement of plainchant and polyphony. Masses II and IV in the York Masses, both paired settings of the Gloria and Creed, give only alternate verses in polyphony, and, as has been seen, the squares in the binding strips also leave out alternate verses despite the fact that the earlier pieces from which they had been copied set the complete Gloria text. This was not the only means by which the Mass could be shortened, as other fifteenth-century composers, such as John Dunstaple (†1453), sometimes 'telescoped' parts of the Mass text, overlapping statements of more than one verse across different vocal parts.[14]

Mass V in the York Masses is the other work to be ascribed to a named composer, 'Johannes Cuke' (John Cook). He may have been the musician of the same name who died in London in 1507, but the name is so common that it is impossible to be certain on this point.[15] Mass V, based on the plainchant antiphon *Venit dilectus meus,* is perhaps the most elaborate and complex music in the York Masses.[16] Parts of the Gloria and Benedictus, and the whole of the Agnus Dei, have survived from this Mass cycle, but the Creed (Credo) has been lost. The number of reduced scorings in Cook's music, duets and trios within the basic four-part texture, are reminiscent of the musical style of compositions found in the Eton Choirbook. The melodic lines, frequently shadowed in thirds and sixths elsewhere in the texture, have a lyrical grace surpassing other music in the York collection, as the duet from the Agnus Dei demonstrates (see Example 4, p. 56). This is a very different musical style from that of Masses I and II, which condensed the music with alternating sections of plainchant and polyphony. In Cook's music, one word of the text might last twenty bars or more; the final phrase, 'dona nobis pacem', is extended over thirty-four bars of music, building from a two-part to a three, and finally four-part texture.

The music discovered in the bindings of documents still held in York is not the only evidence of the city's choral tradition. The surviving copy of the York Gradual includes two pieces of polyphony, a setting of the texts *Veni Creator* and *Deo Gracias.*[17] A York Antiphonal at Arundel Castle contains a setting of the text *Asperges me,* preserved on flyleaves to the main volume.[18] This piece once belonged to the choristers of the Chapel of St Mary and All Angels in York, the chantry college of York Minster. More usually known as St Sepulchre's, the chapel had a staff of prebendaries who were employed to sing Masses for the dead. An inscription in this source reads: 'Iste liber pertinet ad capellam beate marie [virginis] et sanctorum angelorum [et archangelorum ebor]' (this book pertains to the chapel of the Blessed [Virgin] Mary and Holy Angels, York). The chapel, destroyed at the Reformation, was attached to the north wall of the nave of the Minster, where the blocked-up doors are still visible (see Fig. 1.2). The setting of *Asperges me* is in four parts, like all but the final Gloria-Creed pair in the York Masses (which is in three), and probably dates to *c.*1480. It is also known from two further sources, also anonymous.[19] Richard Rastall has explored the two-part music used to accompany some of York's cycle of mystery plays, which, though dating to approximately the 1430s or 1440s, may actually have been copied up to twenty or thirty years later.[20] Finally, records show that choral music was performed and owned by several other churches, such as Holy Trinity, King's Square; St Michael's, Spurriergate and All Saints', North Street.[21]

There was doubtless much more music performed than has survived, especially in York Minster, St Mary's Abbey and St Leonard's Hospital, by far the wealthiest institutions in the city. But it is clear from what has survived that York had a rich musical tradition, closely connected with developments elsewhere, and that it was quite possibly the source of a number of settings which became standard in the repertory.

Music Examples

Gloria

Example 1
a (above): Polyphonic setting of the Gloria. BL Cotton Titus D. XXIV ff. 2–3v.

b (left): Square, BIHR MS Mus. 9 f. Av.

Cus - to - di nos Do - mi - ne

Gloria

Example 2
a (top): Square,
'Custodi nos
domine'. BIHR
MS Mus. 1.
b (centre): Gloria
from Mass II, York
Masses. BIHR MS
Mus. 1.
c (bottom):
Benedictus from
Mass IV, York
Masses. BIHR MS
Mus. 1.

Benedictus

Kyrie

Example 3 Above and on pages 54 & 55.
Kyrie No. 1, York Masses. BIHR MS Mus. 1.

Agnus Dei

Example 4 John Cook, Agnus Dei from Mass V, York Masses. BIHR MS Mus. 1.

4

'Four hundred masses on the four Fridays next after my decease'. The care of souls in fifteenth-century All Saints', North Street, York

P. S. Barnwell

The parish of All Saints

Belief in Purgatory, and in the ability of the actions of the living to aid the souls of the departed in their passage through Purgatory to their ultimate resting-place in Heaven, is one of the defining features of the late middle ages.[1] The strength of Purgatory's hold over men and women is reflected in their wills, usually made when the end of life was in sight, which, in addition to disposing of property, made provision for the funeral, for pious works, and for prayers or Masses to be said in the days or even years following death. The relationship between the living and the dead was more complex than is implied merely by the performance of service by the former for the latter: praying for the dead, or paying others to pray or to say Masses for them, was itself accounted a pious work, ultimately benefiting the living agent as well as the departed soul, while the prayers of those already in Purgatory could reduce the future pains of the living.[2]

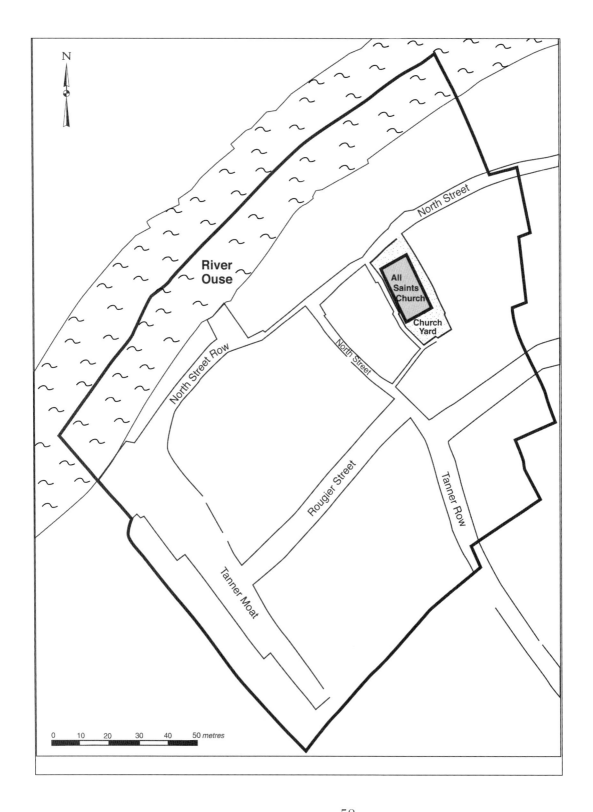

N

River
Ouse

North Street

All
Saints
Church

Church
Yard

North Street Row

North Street

Rougier Street

Tanner Row

Tanner Moat

0 10 20 30 40 50 metres

Much previous scholarship which has attempted to explore the implications of these beliefs has been concentrated upon whole dioceses or towns, usually in the south of England, where the survival of relevant documents is better than further north.[3] Here, by contrast, the focus is on a single parish community — that of All Saints', North Street, York — during the fourteenth and, more particularly, the fifteenth century. The main part of the evidence is contained in the wills made by parishioners between 1390 and 1502, which constitute the largest surviving body of written material specific to the parish.[4] Eighty-eight wills relating to people who desired to be buried in the parish of All Saints, North Street, York, between 1390 and 1502 have been examined, together with twelve made by testators buried elsewhere but who made some gift or other provision relating to the parish. Coverage of the second category, in particular, does not claim to be comprehensive. In addition to discussing the steps taken by testators to ensure the care of their souls, particular attention is devoted to the way in which the provisions of their wills determined the physical development of their church.

The medieval parish of All Saints, North Street, was bounded by the city wall at the south-west, and the River Ouse to the north-west (Fig. 4.1). Some 80 yards north-east of the church was the boundary with the parish of St John the Evangelist, the church of which stands at the junction of North Street and Bridge Street. To the east, All Saints' lay adjacent to the parish of St Martin, Micklegate, while on the south it only extended as far as what is now Station Road, beyond which was the former parish of St Gregory. No part of the parish is more than 250 yards from the church.

Although a number of merchant families were associated with the parish, attracted by the river frontage, All Saints' was not on the fashionable side of town, and it contained one of the main concentrations of artisans, particularly those engaged in the noxious trades of dyeing and, more especially, tanning.[5] Some members of both trades were relatively affluent by comparison with many others of their class, but their wealth rarely compared with that of the merchants.[6] The tanners had a particular reputation for promoting their own interests, and for being troublesome to the city authorities: despite their number and economic position, none held the office of mayor in the period from 1399 to 1507,[7] and their craft was excluded

Opposite:
Fig. 4.1 Parish of All Saints, North Street, York. (© Amanda Daw.)

from those which gained representation under the revised city constitution of 1517.[8]

Assessments of the relative wealth of the parishes of York are imprecise, since late-medieval taxation figures are notoriously slippery, but All Saints' stands in the middle rank in the 1524 Lay Subsidy, owing £3 1s. 1d., and slightly lower than that in terms of the number of taxpayers.[9] These figures relate to the end of the period under consideration, and must be set against the background of the general decline in York's economy during the fifteenth century, with its particular impact on the merchant classes.[10] A hundred years earlier the parish, in common with the rest of the city, was more populous, probably contained greater wealth in absolute terms, and perhaps ranked slightly higher in relation to the rest of the city. The resources of the area in the sixteenth century could be reflected in the fact that it was one of a number of York parishes considered for abolition in 1549, the proposal being to amalgamate it with neighbouring St John's in the same way as St Gregory's was merged with St Martin's, Micklegate. This may, however, have been more a reflection of the modest population of the parishes than of the wealth of individual inhabitants, for the income of All Saints' was relatively high, ranking tenth out of the 26 York parishes recorded in the 1535 *Valor Ecclesiasticus*, despite having suffered a small fall in absolute terms since 1291.[11] In the event the union never took place,[12] perhaps confirming that All Saints' was not as impoverished as some of the parishes which were finally abolished in 1586, but also perhaps partly reflecting the earlier association with the parish of some leading members of the merchant oligarchy of York, including the Blackburns and the Boltons (Fig. 4.2).

The nature of testamentary custom in the northern province of the Church means that it is not possible to use the evidence of wills to refine the picture of the level of wealth within the parish, since reference is not always made to all types of property. Wills were usually restricted to disposing of moveables, the fate of land and houses often being settled earlier in life and in separate instruments which have not survived. Not all moveables, however, were devisable by will, custom dictating that a third was equally divided between surviving children, while another third went to a surviving spouse, leaving only one third to be disposed by will. The result was that written wills tended to be

Fig. 4.2 All Saints',
North Street, York:
exterior.
(© Allan B. Barton.)

made only by the wealthier members of the community, those who had a significant amount of goods of which they could freely dispose, about twenty per cent of the population.[13] Although it is therefore difficult to extract economic data from the wills, it is still possible to use the evidence they contain to gain an insight — albeit not a comprehensive one[14] — into the way in which people sought to provide for the post-mortem care of their souls: while economic circumstances dictated what could be afforded, there is nothing to suggest that beliefs concerning the fate of the soul varied significantly with social class, and it can be assumed that most people aspired to the same kind of provision for its care, even if not everyone could afford the best.

Provision for the funeral

The most pressing matter for the dying was to ensure that their funerals were conducted properly.[15] While there were many variations of detail, the general medieval custom was for the body to be taken to the church the day before the burial, and for the coffin, sometimes draped in a pall, to be surrounded by a timber frame, or hearse, which held candles: the will of one particularly wealthy individual specified that 20s. should be spent on the construction of what was presumably a very elaborate hearse.[16] Late on that same day, was performed the first part of the Office of the Dead, consisting of the Placebo, or Vespers of the Dead, the title of which was derived from the opening words, the Vulgate version of Psalm 116 verse 9: 'I shall please the Lord in the land of men'. An overnight vigil ensued, followed, the next day, by the second part of the Office, the Dirige, the title similarly derived from the opening words of the service, 'Direct my way into your sight, O Lord my God' (Psalm 5 verse 8).[17] Later that day the Requiem Mass was celebrated, after which the body was usually taken out of the coffin for burial.

Arrangements for the basic funeral were well known, and are almost never revealed by the wills (any more than they are in their present-day counterparts), simply being subsumed in donations to the parish priest, clerk and sub-clerk for their services, or, sometimes, a note of the amount which the executors might incur in expenses. Occasionally, however, there are reminders of a few elements of what was involved. The will of John de Richemonde, a chaplain, who died in 1437/8,[18] states that the payment to the parish clerk was for his 'trouble' on the day of burial and a week later, which is revealed by another clergy will, three years later, to include ringing the church bells. Both wills explain that the sub-clerk was responsible for making the grave, while the first one also refers to 4d. bequeathed to the boys who sang in the church — one of several references to church music in the All Saints' wills.[19]

Most parts of the rites could be elaborated to a greater or lesser extent, depending on the circumstances of the testator. Apart from a general wish that the executors pay for the funeral expenses out of the estate, the most common provision amongst the will-making class, found in a quarter of the wills, was for wax for candles to burn around the body while it was in the church, the lights serving to ward off demons as well as to light the soul on its way towards the next life.[20] Some of the candles were retained after the funeral, and used at a specified altar in the church,[21] sometimes only at Easter,[22] and usually at the Elevation of the Host, the most solemn moment of the Mass, at which the bread and wine were believed to be turned into the actual body and blood of Christ (see chapter 7).[23] A few people, such as Nicholas Blackburn, senior, who were buried elsewhere but had an association with All Saints', requested that the lights be transferred to All Saints' from the church where their funeral took place.[24] Other bequests for candles were more modest, and assisted in keeping the lights of St Crux and of the Holy Sepulchre burning, as well as that before the image of the Virgin which, as in every church, adorned the choir.[25]

The passage of the soul from the body to Judgement was a particularly perilous time, the danger of which might be reduced by the number of prayers and Masses said on behalf of the departed. There were a number of ways in which testators could seek to increase the services performed for their assistance. The dead person would expect prayers to be said by his or her relations and friends, but some wills provided an inducement for so doing, by setting aside a sum for their 'calling together', presumably to pay for the funeral feast which might take place either in the house of the deceased or in the nave of the church.[26] Those without immediate family were at a disadvantage in this respect, and it is perhaps significant that one of the clergy wills includes some of the most elaborate provisions of this kind, requesting the Preaching Friars, the Dominicans, whose friary was in the neighbouring parish of St Gregory, to process to All Saints' on the day of burial, thereby acting as a surrogate family, as well as to perform other services there, for which they were to receive 6s. 4d. as well as 3s. 4d. for breakfast. The other orders of friars (the Grey Friars in Castlegate, the Carmelite Friars off Stonebow, and the Austin Friars at Lendal) were to receive smaller donations if their members accompanied the procession.[27]

There were all sorts of ways of trying to ensure that people prayed for the dead on the day of the funeral: while another testator left 20d. to each of the four orders of friars if they attended the funeral,[28] one of the most common methods, particularly among the wealthier classes, was to leave sums for distribution on the day of burial to the poor, sick or those otherwise in trouble, including debtors and prisoners. These acts of charity were 'good works', for which the deceased would gain eschatological credit, but testators hoped that the recipients would express their gratitude by remembering the donor in their prayers that day, though, in contrast to practice in some other places, including Bristol, the aspiration is rarely spelt out.[29] Typical examples of this kind of action are found in the wills of John de Thorlethorpe, a tanner, who died in 1399 leaving 20s. to the poor on the day of his funeral, or of Henry de Bolton, a cooper, who died five years later having made an almost identical provision, while in 1445 John Hipper, a yeoman, left four times that amount to the bedridden poor.[30] Sometimes, the donations are much more precise, as in the will of Richard Toone, tanner, who, in 1448, left 6d. to every Maison Dieu and leper house in York and its suburbs, 12d. to the poor in the Hospital of St Thomas of Canterbury outside Micklegate Bar, and 6d. to the prisoners in each of the city's three jails – that of the king at the castle, that of the archbishop, and that of the city, the Kidcote on Ouse Bridge.[31] In the case of the wealthiest of the testators, who made many bequests of this nature, it is not clear whether all the payments could be made on the day of burial or whether some were made slightly later,[32] but no doubt the testator's instruction to undertake such works of charity would nevertheless have been weighed in the balance at his or her Judgement. In one case — that of Nicholas Blackburn, senior — relatively modest charity was to be distributed on the day of burial, but at both the next Easter and Feast of All Saints (1 November), £100 was to be spent in charitable distributions, including the provision of clothing and fuel for the poor, with a further £60 to be spent at the feast of the Purification of the Blessed Virgin Mary (2 February).[33]

Another kind of pious work where the intention may have gained immediate credit at the time of Judgement, is peculiar to one particular class of testator. Some of the richest merchants, including Nicholas Blackburn, who relied upon good communications to prosecute their business, left money for the maintenance of roads and bridges.[34] Such bequests might, if publicised, assist in promoting the memory of those who made them, but were accounted charitable works, since they were of practical assistance to travellers, and were also seen as symbolic reminders of the journey embodied in the Christian life.[35] It is clear, however, that such works could not be undertaken at once. Some idea of the delay which could be involved is indicated by the will of Margaret Blackburn, who died in 1435, three years after her husband: she left instructions for her own executors to complete the works for which he had left money, and sought to ensure that this would be achieved within four years of her own death.[36] Much more common and accessible to those of modest means were donations to the fabric of religious buildings: the majority of the will-making class left at least a quarter of a mark to the fabric of All Saints' itself, though some people left rather larger sums, while a tile-maker left a quantity of roof tiles and a tanner an amount of lead.[37] A few of those with particular connections further afield also made bequests to the fabric of other churches, in the hope of being remembered in the prayers of their clergy and congregations.[38]

Multiple Masses

Prayers on the day of burial were not the only means of smoothing the path of the soul; more powerful were the effects of the celebration of multiple Masses, though they required the involvement of specialist agents in the form of priests. Such Masses did not have the same function as the High Mass celebrated on Sundays and major feasts, or as the solemn Requiem Mass, when there was greater ceremony and when the laity could, at least theoretically, communicate (though they were only required to do so once a year, at Easter). Instead, Masses for the dead were Low Masses, otherwise known as private Masses or soul Masses, usually said by the priest alone, and not providing the prospect of communion to such congregation as might be present. The performance of such private Masses was seen as an offering, and, in that sense, as a sacrifice, rather than an act of commemoration, thanksgiving, praise and adoration, and paying for them was therefore similar to paying for any other 'good work'. Furthermore, Masses for the dead conferred advantages on the living as well as upon the deceased donor, since it was believed that great benefits flowed from seeing Christ in the form of the transubstantiated Host: the popular fifteenth-century manual for priests written by John Myrc, for example, records that seeing the Host provided protection against hunger, blindness and death for the rest of the day.[39] This meant that the power of the 'good work' operated at several levels and, because anyone witnessing the private Mass might know who had paid for it, the celebration could generate further prayers for the donor. The private Mass could unlock the gates of Purgatory and was perhaps the defining characteristic of late-medieval religion — in the words of the late-medieval *Lay Folks Mass Book*, 'the worthiest thing, most of goodness in all this world, it is the Mass';[40] it was the thing against which sixteenth-century reformers railed most vociferously, Thomas Becon, at one time a chaplain to Archbishop Cranmer, fulminating in post-Purgatorial fervour that it was 'the fountain, well, headspring and original of all idolatry, wickedness, sin and abomination'.[41]

The All Saints' wills are in this respect a mirror of their times. The clearest example is that of Agnes Everingham, who died in 1426/7, leaving 4d. to nine priests to celebrate on her behalf.[42] Many other wills are similar, though some are less explicit, simply recording the bequest of a small sum to each of the chaplains attached to All Saints' in return for the celebration of a Mass.[43] More costly was provision for more elaborate and numerous celebrations, especially trentals (sets of 30 Masses) to be performed either on the day of burial or within the week, the normal rate for which was 5s., or 2d. per Mass, while one will, of 1485, requested no fewer than eight trentals.[44] One of the more unusual requests occurs as part of the highly elaborate provisions made in 1407 by the wealthy mercer, William Vescy, who left money for 'four hundred Masses on the four Fridays next after my decease', for which he left £4, which implies that he meant there to be a hundred Masses each week, at 2½d. each:[45] the will does not make it clear whether they were all to be celebrated in All Saints', at a rate of twenty at each of its five altars,[46] though the fact that he also left a year's stipend for seven chaplains to celebrate in the church suggests that such was his intention.

There are occasional references to rites being performed a week after the burial. One of the most explicit is found in the will of John de Escryke, who died in 1405/6 leaving 4d. to chaplains for the celebration of Mass on both the day of burial and the following week, and 6d. to the parish priest for the same services.[47] In addition to the money for nine chaplains, Agnes Everingham left 20s. for expenses on the day of burial and at its octave;[48] a decade later, in 1437/8, John de Richemonde bequeathed money to the parish clerk for services rendered on the octave as well as on the day of burial, while in 1487/8 William Lonnesdale, tanner, specified that the lights which surrounded his body before his burial were to be used again a week later.[49] The rarity of such references is mirrored by the fact that the nature of the ceremonies is nowhere explained, but their provisions suggest that the funeral was re-enacted after a week, as it could be in an obit performed on its anniversary.[50] References in the wills to such anniversary ceremonies only occur in that of William Vescy, the wealthy mercer, who left 100s. for them, in that of the rich merchant, Robert Savage, and in that of a prosperous tanner, Richard Alne.[51] Both anniversaries and celebrations at the octave may have been more common than this suggests, since it is known that Bristol wills under-represent their incidence.[52] The possibility that there may have been more such anniversaries in All Saints' is underlined by the fact that the will of Adam del Bank, who died in 1410/11, does not refer to an anniversary, though a separate document, relating to the establishment of a chantry, does.[53]

Not all the services requested were to take place in All Saints', even though that was the parish where the deceased was to be buried. In one instance, money was left not only to the chaplains attached to All Saints', but also to those based at the nearby chapel of St William on Ouse Bridge.[54] Another, and more usual, way of obtaining the assistance of extra-parochial agents in addition to the All Saints' clergy was to leave money to one or more of the city's guilds or confraternities, particularly to those to which the testator had belonged while alive. Some nine wills, including four of clerics, incorporate bequests of this nature, almost always to more than one such institution; in all, some ten different organisations are mentioned, the most frequently cited being the great Corpus Christi guild.[55] Such bequests were made in the hope of remembrance at guild festivals as well as of the prayers of the guild chaplains and ordinary guild members. A slightly different strategy, equally popular, was to leave money to one or more of the orders of friars, in the hope of being remembered in their intercessions,[56] or, sometimes, with specific requests that their members celebrate Masses,[57] including trentals.[58] Most bequests not associated with particular services were made to all four orders, while specified services were more usually requested from a single order.[59] Although friaries are the kind of religious community most commonly cited in the wills, there are others. The Priory of Holy Trinity, Micklegate, which owned the advowson (right to nominate the parish priest) of All Saints', is singled out in four wills,[60] but other York houses, such as St Mary's Abbey and the nunnery at Clementhorpe, were mentioned on occasion,[61] as were the recluses who lived within the city, including one who lived in the churchyard of All Saints' itself.[62] The wide connections of two of the wealthiest testators, both mercers and both, significantly, men who left money for bridge works, are reflected in bequests of 5s or more which Robert Colynson distributed as far afield as Carlisle in return for a trental of Masses at each community,[63] and by William Vescy's donations to some twenty religious institutions spread across Yorkshire, explicitly in return for prayers.[64] Vescy's will is unique amongst those from All Saints' in leaving instructions for men to travel to distant churches and shrines in order to make offerings: journeys were to be made within Yorkshire to Beverley, Bridlington, Scarborough, Thorpe Bassett and Whitby; one man was to make a tour to Lincoln, Walsingham, Bury St Edmunds, Canterbury, Bromeholme, St Paul's in London, and Hailes, offering between 1d. and 6d. at each, a figure which, even when all the offerings are added together, was dwarfed by the 20s. expenses allowed for the surrogate pilgrim; and another man was given 7 marks (93s. 4d.) to make a pilgrimage to the house of St James beyond the seas, Santiago de Compostela.

Far-flung bequests were restricted to the mercantile élite, and supplemented other, more systematic and medium to long-term measures which were also adopted by those of lesser means, namely the provision for Masses to be celebrated for as long as possible. One of the most common bequests of this nature was a sum of money, usually 7 marks, to pay the stipend of a chaplain who would say Mass daily for a year, though in one case, where the chaplain was to be the testator's son, the amount was 8 marks. This kind of provision is found in thirteen wills,[65] including those of four clergymen, four tanners, one dyer, one merchant, and one mercer who also put in place longer-term measures. William Lonnesdale, who asked for the lights from his funeral to be reused at the octave, seems not to have been able to afford a full year, for, in 1487, he bequeathed money for a chaplain for a quarter of a year which, at 20s., was lower than a pro rata stipend.[66] By contrast, over three-quarters of a century earlier, in 1400, the widow of another tanner was able to leave 42 marks for the employment of six chaplains, all of whom were to celebrate daily in All Saints' church, presumably for a year each.[67] An alternative to this, which cost the same, was for one chaplain to be paid for a number of consecutive years: in 1391, Margaret de Etton, wife of a merchant, requested her executors to pay a chaplain for two years,[68] in 1394 a dyer left 14 marks for two years' worth of services,[69] while in 1446, a tile-maker left 8 marks for a chaplain for one year, following which another two years were to be paid for at £5, marginally more than the normal 7 marks.[70] In 1502, the same standard rate was still applied when Richard Norwod, a chaplain, endowed a priest for three years:[71] the stability of the 7-mark figure is particularly noteworthy since it was significantly higher than the 5 marks laid down by Statute in 1363, and than 6 marks, the minimum annual pay for a parish priest.[72] The longest fixed-term provision of this kind was made in 1429 when a leading merchant, Reginald Bawtre, instructed his executors to sell his rents in the city and use the proceeds to pay for a chaplain for seven consecutive years.[73] There were other possible variations on the theme, one of which, encountered in 1393, was to instruct that land be sold and the capital be used to pay for a chaplain for as long as it lasted.[74] Perhaps the most intriguing fixed-term provision, though, is that recorded in the will of another leading merchant, Robert Colynson, who died in 1458.[75] He appears to have requested the daily performance of services for three years, including a St Gregory's trental, for which he left £15 — 4s. 4d. more than 7 marks a year — and, in a codicil to the will, added payment for a chaplain to be paid 7 marks for a further eight years. The St Gregory's trental was a highly elaborate form of devotion, believed to be particularly efficacious, which involved the saying of special Masses during the octave of each of the ten major festivals in the liturgical year, and required the celebrant to fast and undertake other works of mortification of the flesh.[76] If Colynson was really asking for the full performance of a St Gregory's trental in addition to daily services, the 4s. 4d. over the 7 mark stipend was not much compensation for the extra trouble involved, particularly as it has already been noted some chaplains received more than that for ordinary services. It is not always explicitly stated where the Masses being funded were to take place, but it is likely that, in the absence of specific instructions, the executors would have ensured that they took place in All Saints', the parish church of the deceased.[77]

Perpetual chantries and their influence on All Saints' Church

For those for whom money was plentiful, generally only the merchants or wealthiest craftsmen,[78] the best form of post-mortem provision was the establishment of a perpetual chantry, the priest of which would celebrate Mass daily for the benefactor, other named individuals and, usually, the souls of all the faithful departed. This was expensive not only because the endowment of a salary in perpetuity required a large capital sum, normally supplied by income from one or more pieces of property, but also because the permanence of the arrangement meant that licence had to be obtained from the Crown to alienate the land in mortmain. Since the establishment of a perpetual chantry was complex and frequently involved landed property, it was often set in hand before the will was made, with the result that the will did not always mention this aspect of the testator's provision for his soul. Despite the best efforts of testators and their executors, the long-term future of a chantry was not always secure, as the means of financial support might wither away, particularly in a period in which the economy both of York as a whole, and of All Saints' parish, was declining. This, at least as much as changes in preference, seems to be reflected in a drop in the number of perpetual chantries founded in York, from a high point of at least 39 in the first half of the fourteenth century to a mere seven in the second half of the fifteenth.[79] In addition, not all chantries which were founded in perpetuity survived until the abolition of the entire system under Edward VI. Particularly vulnerable were those which were managed by the city corporation:[80] as early as 1530, the city obtained an Act of

70

Parliament permitting it to terminate nine chantries and three obits, including some of those in All Saints'.[81]

The oldest chantry in All Saints' for which evidence survives is that founded at the altar of St Mary by John Benge in 1324 (Fig. 4.3). In 1323/4 an inquisition prior to the grant in mortmain was held in York, and in September 1324 the king issued a licence permitting John Benge, chaplain, to establish the chantry with an endowment of one messuage and 58s. of rent.[82] There are no other surviving records

Fig. 4.3 All Saints', North Street, York: chapel of St Mary. (© Allan B. Barton.)

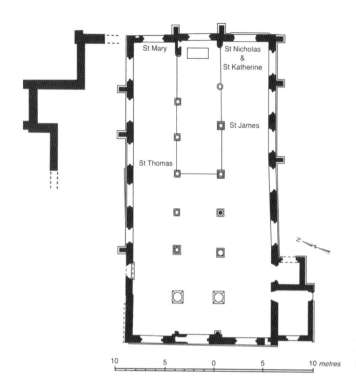

St Mary

St Nicholas & St Katherine

St James

St Thomas

10   5   0   5   10 *metres*

Fig. 4.4 Plan of All
Saints', North Street,
York. After RCHM.
(© Amanda Daw.)

relating to the foundation of this chantry, but it seems from these documents that the altar of St Mary already existed, as would in any case be likely given a rise in devotion to the Virgin during the course of the twelfth century. It is, however, possible that the chapel in which the altar stood was enlarged at about the period when the chantry was founded, perhaps as a direct consequence of its new function. The evidence for this is tentative, and rests on interpretation of the fabric of the church itself. Although the account of the building published by the Royal Commission is in need of revision,[83] particularly in relation to its suggestion that the church assumed a cruciform shape in the thirteenth century,[84] it is conceivable that the buttresses flanking the second bay from the east of the north wall mark the sides of a former transept-like chapel of thirteenth-century date, a position commonly used for Lady Chapels (Fig. 4.4). Any such chapel did not originally extend the full length of the chancel because in 1867 the jambs of apparently thirteenth-century windows were discovered towards the east end of the chancel walls.[85] The tracery in the east window of the present chapel may date from the 1320s, perhaps suggesting that the chapel was enlarged when Benge's chantry was founded.[86]

John Benge's is the only chantry where so direct a link between its foundation and the fabric of the church can be postulated, the other documented chantries having been founded at pre-existing altars. In the 1340s, for example, John Catton, a merchant, transmitted to the Mayor and Commonalty of York, land and tenements in North Street, including property adjacent to the church, to endow another chantry at the altar of St Mary, with the annual stipend of 6 marks.[87] The next documented chantry presents a similar case, for when, in 1409/10, the executors of William Vescy's will established the chantry he requested in a codicil to his will,[88] they did so at a pre-existing altar of St Thomas the Martyr in the north nave aisle (see Fig. 4.4). It is, however, possible, that this foundation precipitated the widening to its present dimensions of what was, by analogy with church development elsewhere, probably a narrower earlier aisle,[89] since the will of the mason Hugh Grantham, who died in 1409/10, refers to sums owed to him for an incomplete window at All Saints'.[90]

The following year, another chantry was established upon the death of the wealthy dyer, Adam del Bank. The arrangements, made some time earlier and only hinted at in his will, were for a perpetual chantry at the altar of St Nicholas,[91] which stood in the south chancel aisle, mirroring that of the Virgin to the north (Fig. 4.5, see also Fig. 4.4). The chapel was already in existence by 1369 when William Savage, mayor of York, was buried there, and may, on the evidence of the glass in its east window, have been complete by the 1340s.[92] The foundation documents reveal that a chaplain with a stipend of 8 marks was to celebrate Masses for Adam, Margaret his wife, and John Bawtre, to chant the offices of the dead, including the Placebo and Dirige, and

Fig. 4.5 All Saints', North Street, York: chapel of St Nicholas and St Katherine. (© Allan B. Barton.)

Fig. 4.6 All Saints',
North Street, York: St
Thomas window.
(© Allan B. Barton.)

to mark the anniversary of Adam's death. Del Bank also stipulated that the chaplain should join his fellows in the church in singing the canonical hours, and at Mass on Sundays and at festivals: although this is the only occasion on which such provisions are recorded in relation to All Saints', it is likely that canonical regulations laid such duties on all chantry chaplains.[93] Despite all Adam del Bank's care, including entrusting the running of the chantry to the city authorities, whose records show that they faithfully paid successive chaplains during the course of the fifteenth century, both his chantry and that of John Catton, who had taken similar measures, were among those dissolved in the 1530s.[94]

If these four perpetual chantries were the only ones in All Saints', it would correspond with the average in even the more prosperous of York's churches.[95] There is, however, evidence that there was at least one further chantry in the church for, in 1509, an inventory was taken of the altar ornaments of some of the chantries for which the city was responsible, one of which was a chantry in All Saints' of John Bolton, son-in-law of Nicholas Blackburn, senior, who was buried in St Saviour's.[96] The later fate of this chantry is not clear: it did not feature in the list of those abolished by the city in the 1530s, and the Chantry Certificates of Henry VIII (1546) and Edward VI (1548) do not mention any chantries at All Saints' since the commissioners responsible for compiling them do not seem to have included foundations in churches which were thought to be about to be closed.[97]

Assuming that by the end of the fifteenth century there were four or five perpetual chantries, and adding to them the large number of fixed-term provisions for the celebration of Masses, the church can be seen to have been home to a great deal of activity on behalf of the departed. Although it is not possible to calculate how many soul Masses there would have been each day, there would have been an absolute minimum of five, which could rise significantly in an exceptional year such as 1407 when William Vescy endowed seven priests. On top of that were the Masses celebrated on or shortly after the day of burial, including the trentals. In addition, many of the less wealthy parishioners who did not make wills may have paid for burial-day Masses, perhaps in significant numbers, as even a trental, which cost 5s., would have been within the means of a significant number of parishioners. In addition to this there were the Requiem Masses on the day of burial and, sometimes, on its anniversaries. The majority of such services were additional to the main business of pastoral care conducted by the parish priest, including the celebration of a daily Mass and the liturgical hours, with more elaboration, including the singing of polyphonal music,[98] on Sundays, feast days and holy days, at all of which the chaplains were expected to assist.

The wills reveal that this activity was distributed between five altars (see Fig. 4.4).[99] The high altar was the preserve of the parish priest, leaving four altars for the chaplains who conducted the majority of soul Masses. That of St Mary was, as noted earlier, in the north chancel aisle, as confirmed by a will of 1502.[100] Immediately to its west, in the north nave aisle, stood the chapel of St Thomas of Canterbury, at which Vescy established his chantry, its position indicated by the iconography of the third window from the east (Fig. 4.6), though the glazing, which contains the arms of the Bawtre family, was not

Fig. 4.7 All Saints',
North Street, York: St
James window.
(© Allan B. Barton.)

installed until after the death of Reginald Bawtre, whose will left 100s. for its completion in 1429.[101] In the south nave aisle was an altar not so far mentioned, dedicated to St James; its position is revealed both by a window of *c*.1440 (now the fourth from the east, but originally the second; Fig. 4.7)[102] and by Adam del Bank's will of 1410, which contains one bequest for the repair of the altar of St James in the south part of the church, and another for a stone window there.[103] This leaves the south chancel aisle for the choir and altar of St Nicholas, which is known to have existed from at least 1369, and where Adam del Bank founded his chantry. The position is complicated, however, by a will of 1406, five years after the first clear reference to the presence of five unspecified altars in the church,[104] which contains a request for burial in the choir of St Katherine.[105] Although this at first sight suggests the presence of a sixth altar, there is a later request for burial in the chancel of the chantry of St Nicholas and St Katherine,[106] perhaps indicating that the altar may have had a double dedication, and that testators could choose the one to which they wished to pay homage: such a double dedication could have existed from the date of construction of the south chancel aisle, but it is also possible to envisage a sequence of development in which each of the two eastern bays at one stage contained separate altars, which were only amalgamated later, perhaps around 1400.

It was the increasing use of the subsidiary altars, primarily for soul Masses, which lay behind much of the fourteenth and fifteenth-century expansion of the aisles.[107] It has already been suggested that the chapel of St Mary may have been expanded when the Benge chantry was founded, and that the north nave aisle may have been widened when Vescy set up his chantry at the altar of St Thomas. Development of the south side of the church is less well documented, but it is likely that it was driven by similar forces, with the chapel of St Nicholas becoming the site of Adam del Bank's chantry, even if it was not purposely built for another one. The increased space thus created was not available for congregational use, for the chapels associated with the altars were screened off from the nave in the same way as was the chancel, into which the laity seldom penetrated. The interior of the church was, therefore, fragmented into a series of semi-private spaces, the main public area being relatively constricted and probably feeling very closed-in on itself by the screens (Fig. 4.8); the absence of a nave clearstorey would have made the chapels seem relatively light by comparison with the nave itself, which would have been further darkened by the presence of wall paintings, and by the tympanum which probably blocked the area above the rood screen. Laymen standing in the nave could see into the chapels with their colourful windows, and would have been able at least to glimpse the pricks of light provided by the flickering candles, the shiny altar vessels and, above all, the Host at its Elevation: the whole created a setting in which the interplay of light and darkness heightened the sense of mystery and expectation.

Memorial gifts

If it was only the relatively wealthy who could afford to fund the multiplicity of Masses which provided benefits for themselves and, by providing increased opportunities to see the Host, for the living, any service held in the church was a vehicle which could be used to benefit an individual's soul. Although the evidence is dominated by the documents of the rich, even people of means too modest for them to have made a will could have afforded lights for their funeral, which could afterwards be transferred for use at one of the altars, particularly as Elevation lights.[108] This was a 'good work', enabling the Host to be illuminated and therefore more readily seen by the congregation, but the light was also seen as a representative of the deceased, bringing his or her name into the very presence of God.[109] A similar dual logic related to the provision of other items for use during the service, such as a legacy to purchase a sacring bell to attract the attention of the laity immediately before the Elevation so that they could kneel down and view the Host.[110] A particularly interesting bequest of this kind, made by Margaret Gateshead in 1442/3, consisted of two twill towels 6½ ells (a little over 8 yards) in length, one to All Saints' and the other to St Edward's. They may have been made into towels for the celebrant, but their length suggests that they could have been intended as houseling cloths, held under the chins of rows of kneeling communicants in order to catch any crumbs which fell from the Host.[111] William Vescy endowed his own new chantry with 100s. for altar ornaments and with two items of silver for conversion into a chalice,[112] while John Tidman, chaplain at Adam del Bank's chantry, in 1458 left a quarter of a mark for the upkeep of the ornaments of his chantry altar.[113]

Many of the clergy, whether parish priests or chaplains, made distinctive bequests of service books to the altars or to individual colleagues: John de Richemonde, a chaplain, left a Missal for use at the

Fig. 4.8a All Saints', North Street, York. Interior as it appears today. (© R. Skingle.)

altar of St Nicholas; Robert Alne, who had worked in the Minster, left a two-volume Legend (book of readings) to the church; James Bagule, parish priest at All Saints', bequeathed a Processional and another volume on condition that they be chained to a stall in the choir, as well as leaving a book of motets to a fellow cleric; Nicholas Clyff, chaplain, left an Antiphoner; Thomas Howren, parish priest, bequeathed to a fellow priest a Troper with the Ordinal according to the Use of York, and another Troper to Christopher Dobley, chaplain for the Bank chantry.[114] The only recorded member of the laity to leave a book to the Church was Isabella Persay, who, though not buried in the parish, left an English Psalter to its priest.[115]

Clergy might also donate their vestments, while a few of the laity were also instrumental in making this kind of gift. The most prominent of the clergy to make such a bequest was John Cliffe, chaplain in the Catton chantry, who left to his brother, Nicholas, also a chaplain in All Saints', a vestment of white fustian with red orphreys (see chapter 2) for use at the altar where John had celebrated, and to his successor at that altar a red vestment of cloth of gold on condition

Fig. 4.8b All Saints', North Street, York. Interior as it might have appeared in the late fifteenth century. (© English Heritage.)

Fig. 4.9 All Saints',
North Street, York:
Blackburn window.
(© Allan B. Barton.)

that John's name was written into the Missal so that other chaplains would remember to pray for him; he also gave other vestments to the altar of St James in return for prayers.[116] Amongst the laity, Vescy, a mercer by trade, not surprisingly left expensive cloth to be made into vestments for his own chantry, supplementing his bequest for the chalice,[117] while the widow of a tanner bequeathed materials to the parish priest for vestments to be worn when he celebrated Mass for her and her late husband,[118] and Richard Alne, himself a tanner, left a white vestment and cope to the church to be used at the feasts of the Blessed Virgin Mary and on other occasions apart from the churching of women.[119]

The inventories of the altar ornaments belonging to the Bolton and Bank chantries made in 1509 give some idea of the cumulative effect of these donations.[120] The property of the former included a Mass book with copper gilt buckles; an eight-ounce chalice of silver gilt; a pair of pewter cruets; a great glass; a small pax (to be kissed by the congregation in place of taking communion);[121] four corporals (cloths for holding the consecrated Host); three towels; eleven altar cloths, two of damask; three painted hangings, two other hangings and a hanging for Lent; and nine sets of vestments of various colours and degrees of elaboration. Adam del Bank's chantry, situated on the opposite side of the church, possessed a Mass book; a twelve-ounce chalice; a pair of pewter cruets; four corporals, and a total of ten altar cloths, four with associated frontals and two with associated curtains; a third frontal; two other curtains; a Lent hanging; and eight vestments of various fabrics including velvet and silk, amongst which were two in red with gold orphreys, and one each of black with red, black with gold, black with white, and grey with red. All of this reminded the chaplains to pray for the benefactors, but, by contributing to the dignity and spectacle of divine service, such donations were themselves a good work since they supported services in the church.

There were, however, yet other forms of memorial to prompt both clergy and laity to intercede for their benefactors. The most obvious, and expensive, memorials found in All Saints' are some of the windows, such as that for which Reginald Bawtre left money in 1429,[122] and the two windows associated with the Blackburns (one now the east window of the south chancel aisle, but originally in the north wall of the church (Fig. 4.9), next to their other window, depicting the Corporal Acts of Mercy (Fig. 4.10)), and others paid for by parishioners.[123] Almost as conspicuous, at least to the clergy, were two gifts of the Gilliots in the second half of the fifteenth century: a seat with a misericord (Fig. 4.11), and the ornate five-bay hammerbeam roof over the chancel and its aisles, with carved bosses and winged angels, some playing musical instruments, others holding emblems, churches or shrines (Fig. 4.12).[124]

Perhaps on account of the relatively small number of really wealthy families associated with the parish, All Saints' appears to have contained no raised or recessed tombs, the most conspicuous type of funerary monument, but many incised floor slabs and indents for brasses survive.[125] Some 85 per cent of the will-making class of All Saints' in the fifteenth century wished to be buried inside the church, the remaining dozen specifically requesting to be laid to rest in the churchyard. Within the church, the chancel was generally regarded as the preserve of the clergy, though the wealthiest men, including

Fig. 4.10 All Saints',
North Street, York:
Corporal Acts of
Mercy window.
(© Allan B. Barton.)

William Marsthall, a merchant, and William Vescy, might obtain permission to be buried there, as near as possible to the high altar, the point of highest ritual status.[126] Other people, including chaplains, sometimes specified in which chapel they wished to rest, those in the chancel aisles attracting many more requests than those in the nave aisles, with six for St Mary and nine for St Nicholas and St Katherine, as opposed to one for St Thomas and none for St James, again on

Fig. 4.11 All Saints',
North Street, York:
misericord donated
by the Gilliots.
(© Allan B. Barton.)

account of their proximity to the high altar.[127] Three of the clergy, however, found alternative means of seeking proximity to the holy: Thomas Howren, parish priest, requested to be buried in the churchyard, opposite the image of Christ crucified which formerly adorned the niche part way up the west face of the tower, and the chaplain Christopher Dobley wished to be buried next to him;[128] Richard de Wakefield, on the other hand, wanted to be buried in the nave, near the pulpit, perhaps because he thought his grave would be noticed there.[129] Incised stones and brasses set in the floor near altars were only routinely seen by the chaplains, not by the greater number of people who used the church (Fig. 4.13).

It was perhaps with this in mind that Adam del Bank, having founded his chantry in the chapel of St Nicholas, one of the most inaccessible and invisible parts of the church, wished his burial to be between the doors in the nave.[130] While this request no doubt contained an element of humility, since those attending the church could not avoid walking over his tomb,[131] it gave del Bank and other,

Fig. 4.12 All Saints', North Street, York: angel roof donated by the Gilliots. (© Allan B. Barton.)

Fig. 4.13 All Saints',
North Street, York:
incised memorial
slabs.
(© Amanda Daw.)
Left: Anonymous slab,
probably dating from
the first half of the
fourteenth century.
Right: Slab com-
memorating a John
Bawtre, probably the
John Bawtre who
died in 1411.

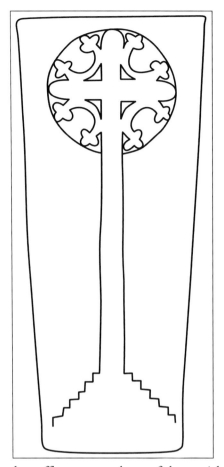

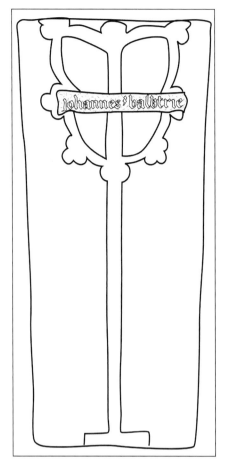

less affluent, members of the parish whose burials and memorials were
prominent in the nave, an additional advantage: their memory was
ever before the parishioners, reminding the living to pray for the souls
of their predecessors, both aiding the deceased and at the same time
reducing their own Purgatorial pains when they joined the mortal
remains of earlier generations in silent supplication beneath the floor
of their parish church.[132]

Table 4.1. Concordance of manuscripts, editions and translations of wills consulted for Chapter 4.[1]

Manuscripts	Editions	Translations	Name of testator	Date of probate
BIHR Prob Reg[2]				
i f. 1v		Shaw[3] 1	William de Oklesthorpe	27 October 1389
i f. 10r		Shaw 2	William de Appilton	1390
i f. 16v		Shaw 3	Alice Pund	20 December 1390
i f. 18r		Shaw 4	Cecilia de Swynford	18 January 1390/1[4]
i f. 22r	*TE*[5] i no. 102		Robert Haunsard	14 February 1390/1
i f. 29v		Shaw 5	Margaret de Etton	27 July 1391
i f. 63v		Shaw 6	Isabel de Oklesthorpe	17 March 1393/4
i f. 66r		Shaw 7	Richard Byrd	18 May 1394
i ff. 70r–71r		Shaw 8	Thomas Strykill	14 July 1394
i ff. 75r–76r		Shaw 9	William Meburn	19 January 1394/5
i f. 85r		Shaw 10	Henry Brynsall	21 August 1395
i f. 87r		Shaw 11	William de Esyngwald	10 September 1395
i f. 90r–v		Shaw 12	John Wardale	30 November 1395
ii f. 8r		Shaw 13	Richard Lyndesay	30 December 1397
ii ff. 11v–12r	*TE* i no. 105		Joanne Colvyll	September 1390
ii 17r	*TE* ii no. 54	Shaw 47	James Bagule	17 March 1440/1
ii f. 33v		Shaw 48	Agnes Clif	22 March 1441/2
ii ff. 52v–53r		Shaw 49	Margaret Gateshead	15 January 1442/3
ii f. 78r		Shaw 50	John Bempton	13 March 1443/4
ii f. 78r		Shaw 51	John Berry	15 April 1444
ii f. 82r–v		Shaw 52	Robert Bilburgh	26 May 1444
ii f. 107v			John Bolton	10 August 1445
ii ff. 114v–115r		Shaw 53	John Hipper	7 November 1445
ii f. 153r–v		Shaw 54	William Marsthall	22 February 1446/7
ii ff. 154v–155r		Shaw 55	John Sharpe	17 March 1446/7
ii ff. 168v–169v			Nicholas Blakburn, jr	8 March 1447/8
ii f. 174v		Shaw 56	Richard Toone	1 July 1448
ii f. 175r		Shaw 57	Richard Mason	15 July 1448
ii f. 183r		Shaw 58	John Ridley	9 December 1448
ii f. 223v		Shaw 59	Richard Killyngholme	11 June 1451
ii ff. 234v–235r		Shaw 60	Richard Hipper	23 October 1451
ii ff. 333v–334r	*TE* ii no. 159	Shaw 61	John Cliffe	9 July 1456
ii f. 334r		Shaw 62	Thomas Ridley	17 August 1456
ii ff. 335v–336r		Shaw 63	Nicholas Clyff	7 September 1456
ii ff. 371v–372r	*TE* ii no. 158	Shaw 64	John Tidman	26 August 1458
ii ff. 378r–380r		Shaw 65	Robert Colynson	3 October 1458
ii f. 411v		Shaw 67	John Haxby	8 August 1459
ii f. 443v		Shaw 68	Robert Faceby	10 May 1461
ii ff. 457v–458r		Shaw 69	Thomas Norman	27 November 1461
ii f. 506r, and YMA[6] MS 2/6(e) f. 3v		Shaw 26	Agnes Everingham	7 March 1426/7

Manuscripts	Editions	Translations	Name of testator	Date of probate
ii f. 511r–v		Shaw 27	Agnes Clyff	7 June 1427
ii f. 511v		Shaw 28	William Rudstan	20 June 1427
ii f. 520r		Shaw 29	Henry de Broughton	1 December 1427
ii ff. 537v–538r		Shaw 30	John Stele	14 October 1428
ii f. 564v		Shaw 31	Thomas Rereby	23 September 1429
ii f. 572r–v		Shaw 32	Reginald Bawtre	21 December 1429
ii f. 603r		Shaw 34	John Selby	March 1431/2
ii ff. 605r–606v	*TE* ii no. 14	Shaw 35	Nicholas Blackburn, sr	10 April 1432
ii f. 610r–v		Shaw 36	Thomas Sutton	10 June 1432
ii ff. 622v–623r		Shaw 37	Peter Leven	20 November 1432
ii f. 662v		Shaw 33	Roger de Allerton	17 January 1429/30
ii f. 682r	*TE* ii no. 53	Shaw 46	Robert Alne	26 December 1440
iii f. 17r–v		Shaw 14	Robert Savage	21 March 1398/9
iii f. 31r		Shaw 15	John de Thorlethorpe	1 December 1399
iii f. 38r–v		Shaw 16	Ellen Wardale	9 June 1400
iii f. 50r–v	*TE* i no. 196		Joanna Hesilrigg	December 1400
iii f. 63r–v	*TE* i no. 199		Isabella Persay	July 1400
iii ff. 66v–67r		Shaw 17	Margaret del Bank	27 November 1401
iii ff. 72(bis)v–73r		Shaw 18	Margaret de Bolton	11 April 1402
iii ff. 107r–108v		Shaw 19	Henry de Bolton	30 May 1404
iii ff. 242v–243r		Shaw 20	John de Escryke	3 February 1405/6
iii ff. 250v–251r		Shaw 21	Robert de Thorlethorpe	24 May 1406
iii f. 264v		Shaw 22	Robert de Nuburgh	17 June 1407
iii ff. 266v–268v		Shaw 23	William Vescy	28 July 1407
iii f. 277r–v		Shaw 24	Nicholas Chaloner	19 July 1407
iii f. 363r–v	*TE* ii no. 20		Adam Wigan	1433
iii ff. 415v–417v	*TE* ii no. 37	Shaw 38	Margaret Blackburn	April 1435
iii ff. 439r–441r	*TE* ii no. 40		Richard Russell	May 1435
iii f. 452r		Shaw 39	Joan Kyllyngholme	4 May 1436
iii f. 452r		Shaw 40	Beatrix Dalton	5 May 1436
iii f. 465r		Shaw 41	Robert Disford	30 August 1436
iii f. 486v		Shaw 42	John Byall	4 May 1437
iii f. 502r		Shaw 43	Robert Benne	26 September 1437
iii f. 510r		Shaw 44	John de Richemonde	7 January 1437/8
iii f. 602v		Shaw 45	John Lyndesay	9 June 1440
iii f. 612v		Shaw 25	Juliana de Cunnesburgh	24 January 1418/9
iv f. 28r–v			John York	25 December 1467
iv f. 135r–v			John Coupland	8 June 1479
iv f. 233r–v		Shaw 70	Thomas Howren	January 1467
v f. 44r			Margaret Clark	24 March 1482/3
v f. 94v			Christopher Dobley	19 January 1480/1
v f. 149r–v			John Burton	27 December 1479
v f. 235v			Thomas Wod	17 September 1484
v f. 240v			John Huetson	13 October 1484
v f. 242v			Agnes Huetson	25 November 1484
v f. 262v			William Pereson	1 October 1485
v f. 271r			Thomas Tailyour	14 January 1485/6
v f. 275r			Thomas Pereson	28 February 1485/6
v f. 310r			Thomas Warthell	18 June 1487

Manuscripts	Editions	Translations	Name of testator	Date of probate
v f. 325v			William Lonnesdale	4 March 1487/8
v f. 331v			Margaret Burton	23 May 1488
v ff. 391r–392r			Richard de Wakefield	4 May 1491
v f. 440r			John Londisdale	28 September 1493
vi ff. 19v–20r			Matilda Newton	28 February 1501/2
vi ff. 23v–24r			Adam Atkynson	16 April 1502
vi f. 57r–v			Richard Norwod	15 March 1502/3

Other sources

YMA MS 2/6(e) f. 3v see BIHR Prob. Reg. ii f. 506r				
YMA MS H2(1)				
ff. 2v–3v			Adam del Bank	21 March 1410/1
YMA MS L2/4				
ff. 154v–155v	*TE* iii no. 10		Hugh Grantham	16 March 1409/10
YMA MS L2/4				
ff. 157r–158r			John Bawtre	
YMB[7] iii pp. 43–4			Richard Alne	May 1409

Notes

[1] In order to facilitate conversion of the manuscript references in the notes into references to editions and translations, the wills are cited in manuscript rather than chronological order.

[2] Borthwick Institute of Historical Research, Probate Registers, cited by volume number and folio.

[3] Partial translation in P. J. Shaw, *An Old York Church. All-Hallows in North Street: its medieval stained glass and architecture* (York, 1908), cited by the number of the will within the Appendix.

[4] Dates from 1 January to 24 March are cited in the form Old Style/New Style.

[5] Edition, sometimes partial, in J. Raine, J. Raine and J. W. Clay (editors), *Testamenta Eboracensia*, 6 vols, Surtees Society, 4, 30, 45, 53, 79, 106 (1836–1902).

[6] York Minster Archive.

[7] M. Sellers and J. W. Percy (editors), *York Memorandum Book*, 3 vols, Surtees Society, 120, 125, 186 (1912–69).

5

A York priest and his parish: Thomas Worrall at St Michael, Spurriergate, York, in the early sixteenth century

Claire Cross

The parish of St Michael Spurriergate

In the last decade Clive Burgess, Beat Kumin and Katherine French among others have used late-medieval churchwardens' accounts, which exist in some numbers for the south of England, to telling effect to re-create the pre-Reformation Church at parish level. Even more recently in *The Voices of Morebath* Eamon Duffy has reconstructed the religious experience of a remote Devon village in the sixteenth century from the accounts kept by its vicar, Christopher Trychay, for over fifty years. The north, however, has fared far less well in the record preservation stakes. Apart from a discontinuous series of annual churchwardens' rolls for the three Hedon parishes of St Augustine, St James and St Nicholas dating from the mid fourteenth to the late fifteenth centuries with two or possibly three rolls for the early sixteenth century, and a fragmentary fourteenth-century list from the York parish of St Margaret, Walmgate, the only consecutive late-medieval churchwardens' accounts to have survived for the entire

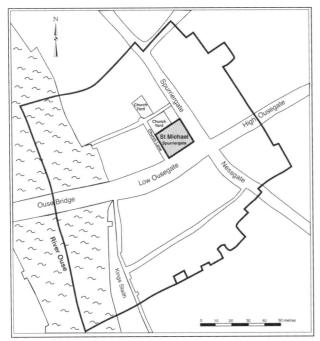

Fig. 5.1 Parish of St Michael, Spurriergate, York. (© Amanda Daw.)

Fig. 5.2 Plan of St Michael's, Spurriergate, York. After RCHM. (© Amanda Daw.)

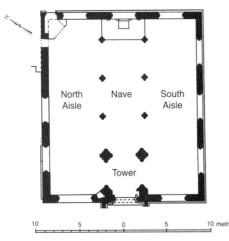

region are those of St Michael, Spurriergate, in York. Covering the period 1518 to 1548, these accounts, published in a full, scholarly edition in 1997, provide a unique means of access to the spiritual life of just one of the forty or so York parishes in the last generation before the break with Rome.[1]

At the heart of a large city, albeit one not nearly as prosperous or as populous as it had been in the high middle ages, the roughly rectangular, very small, parish of St Michael, Spurriergate, could scarcely have been more different from Morebath, a large rural parish on the edge of Exmoor. To the north the parish boundary ran from the Ouse along a now lost lane into Market Street, turned at a right angle below Peter Lane to extend as far as Coppergate, went down Coppergate to Nessgate and then more or less followed the course of the present Cumberland Row back to the river (Fig. 5.1). Two of York's major roads, High and Low Ousegate and Coney Street with its continuation into Spurriergate and Nessgate, divided the parish into four unequal segments which abutted upon St Martin's, Coney Street, to the north, All Saints', Pavement, to the east, St Mary's, Castlegate, to the south, and St John's, Ousebridge, across the river to the west. Though tiny, as a city centre parish, St Michael's attracted large numbers of migrants, even in a time of population stagnation. In 1548 the commissioners surveying chantry foundations for the crown estimated the parish contained some 350 adult communicants which with the inclusion of children would suggest a total population of between 550 and 600: Morebath had no more than about 150 inhabitants in the same period.[2]

90

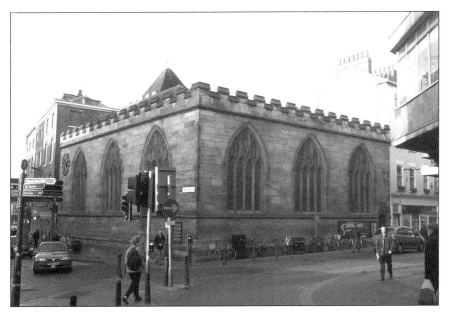

The church

Situated at the centre of the parish, at the intersection of Spurriergate and Ousegate, the church of St Michael the Archangel had undergone extensive structural changes in the mid fifteenth century which had resulted in the raising of arcades along the north and south aisles, the addition of a clearstorey, and erection of the tower (Fig. 5.2). Consequently the church fabric needed little more than routine maintenance in the early Tudor period. Most years the churchwardens spent only a few shillings on replacing roof tiles, repointing the walls or soldering gutters, though repairs to the windows in the tower and to the church porch amounted to over £10 in 1540 and the re-roofing of the north side of the church cost around £14 in 1542.[3]

Like so many other York city churches constricted by its site St Michael's would have seemed unimpressive in the late middle ages in comparison with a great civic church such as St Peter, Mancroft, in Norwich, or St Mary, Redcliffe, in the suburbs of Bristol, or nearer home Holy Trinity, Hull, and St Peter's, Leeds, but its parishioners had not allowed its size to curb their aspirations (Figs. 5.3 and 5.4). As well as the high altar, in the early sixteenth century the church somehow accommodated at least eight other altars dedicated to Jesus, the Holy Trinity, St Mary, St John the Baptist, St Mary Magdalen, St Thomas, St

Fig. 5.4 St Michael's, Spurriergate, York: interior. (© Allan B. Barton.)

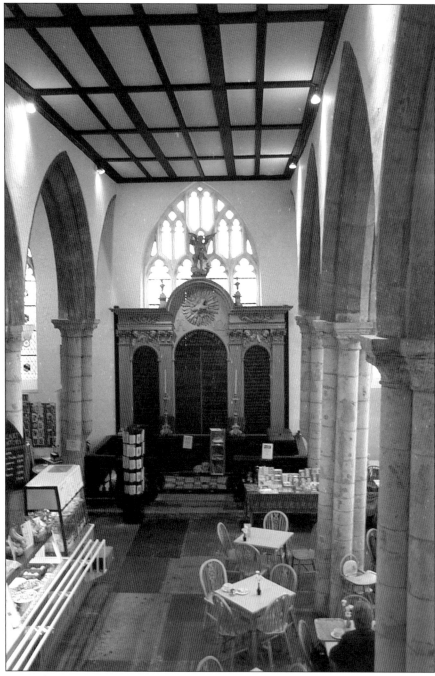

Nicholas and St Margaret, while there was a shrine to St Anne in the churchyard, and perhaps also another altar in her honour in the church itself. As prescribed by canon law, statues of St Mary and the church's

Fig. 5.5 St Michael's, Spurriergate, York: Nine Orders of Angels window. (Reproduced by permission of the Centre for Medieval Studies, University of York.)

patron saint, St Michael, stood on either side of the high altar, and the church certainly also had images of the Virgin and St John before the cross on both the roods, a third image of St Mary in the north aisle, and statues of St John the Baptist, St Nicholas, St Crux, St Agnes and St Sith elsewhere.[4]

By the early Tudor period, parishioners had set up separate funds to maintain lights before the Holy Sacrament and some if not all of these images. In 1525 the parish spent 2d. on paper books 'the one for the rood light and St Sith, the other for to write our implements [deeds] of our houses in'. When the city corporation fell into dire financial straits in 1537 the keepers of the St Sith stock contributed 53s. 4d. 'to the chamber of York to help to bring it out of debt'. At least in the earlier part of the century, in addition to the rood light and St Sith light, there were independent funds for Our Lady's light, St Agnes's light, the Summergame light and 'the light that the childer finds'.[5]

93

Fig. 5.6 St Michael's, Spurriergate, York: Root of Jesse window. (Reproduced by permission of the Centre for Medieval Studies, University of York.)

All the windows in the church had already received their full complement of stained glass by the beginning of the sixteenth century: one appropriately depicted the nine orders of angels (Fig. 5.5), another the tree of Jesse (Fig. 5.6), a third scenes from the life of St John. The churchwardens repaired the 'Root of Jesse' window in 1533 and the St John's window four years later. They also commissioned the painting, or perhaps repainting, of St Christopher on one of the wall spaces between the windows in 1527, and in 1533 the painting of the devil at the nether end of the church, probably part of a doom. The tower housed a ring of at least five bells which involved the parish in the constant expense of renewing clappers, baldrics and bell strings. The church had also made a considerable investment in its music, certainly possessing a pair of organs by 1513 when Thomas Hardsong enjoined his wife to establish for the health of his soul 'a Mass of the commemoration of Our Lady the Virgin every Saturday solemnly to be sung with note of men and children and the organs for ever while the world shall endure'. The parish purchased new organs from a London organ maker in 1536, and had them installed in the choir. In 1542 the church bought yet more organs, this time for the rood loft, from a local craftsman, Gillam of Castlegate.[6]

The music, bells, paintings and images furnished a suitably magnificent setting for the daily sacrifice of the Mass. In addition to the Masses celebrated at the high altar on Sundays, Masses took place at the side altars on every day of the week. Robert de Sallay had founded a perpetual chantry dedicated to the Virgin Mary in the south choir aisle in 1336. Daily Masses were apparently still being offered for his soul at the end of the fifteenth century, as in 1475 Robert Harwod left a house to the chantry to add his soul to the daily supplications, in 1496 Robert Hancock gave another house to the chantry in return for an obit, an annual re-enactment of the funeral Mass, while in 1497 Robert Johnson asked for burial before the altar of this chantry, going on to bequeath 12d. to every 'chantry priest or soul priest' of the church attending his Requiem. In the economic depression of the first half of the sixteenth century, when in 1536 the city corporation obtained a private Act of Parliament to dissolve seven of the nine chantries for which it was responsible on the grounds that the endowments no longer produced sufficient revenue to support the priests, the chantry in St Michael's seems also to have failed. The royal commissioners made no mention of any perpetual chantry in the church in 1548.[7]

Local demand for prayers for the dead, however, continued unabated, and, in place of a permanent chantry, several parishioners set up temporary chantries, a much more secure form of spiritual investment since they could be overseen in person by the testator's executors. In 1502 Thomas Geffrey hired a priest for 14 marks to celebrate for his soul every day in St Michael's for two years after his death. Six years later Maud Hancock paid £10 for an honest priest to perform Mass daily at the Jesus altar for her soul, her husband's soul, and her parents' souls for a similar two years and, as late as 1531, John Roger desired a priest to sing daily for his soul, the souls of his parents and friends in the church for two years. Other parishioners sought an alternative in a weekly Requiem Mass. In addition to Robert Dale's Mass offered in perpetuity at the Jesus altar on Fridays, and Thomas Hardsong's Mass of the Blessed Virgin Mary also celebrated in perpetuity on Saturdays, in 1526 Brian Lorde established a Mass of the Holy Ghost to be sung in the church on Mondays for the space of five years.[8]

On top of all this permanent and semi-permanent provision of Masses there were the annual obits of eminent parishioners such as Janet Carter and Margaret Vicars. Those unable to afford this kind of commemoration could at least contemplate a series of Masses on their deaths. At the cost of no more than 20d. William Foxgale arranged to have five Masses of the Five Wounds said for him on the day of his burial in 1522. The barber-surgeon George Keld paid a similar sum in 1524 for one Mass of Jesus, a second Mass of the Five Wounds, a third of Our Lady, a fourth of burial and a fifth of Requiem. In 1531 Thomas Glasyn set 5s. aside for the performance of half a St Gregory's trental after his death.[9]

Priests at the church

To discharge the terms of these bequests St Michael's, Spurriergate required the services of three or four priests in addition to the incumbent. Between 1500 and 1550 at least three clerics held the rectory which was assessed at £8 12s. 0d. in the *Valor Ecclesiasticus* of 1535, a little above the average for a York city benefice, but still not sufficient to induce career clergy to settle in the parish. Virtually nothing is known about Henry Shafton, rector during the first part of the sixteenth century, who died in 1522; since none of the parishioners mentioned him in their wills he may not have resided in the city. His successor, John Marshall, admitted to the cure in February 1523, had the distinction of being one of the very few graduate clergy instituted to a city living throughout the Tudor period. A bachelor of law from Cambridge, and also vicar of Meldreth in Cambridgeshire, he may well have come to York to practice in the ecclesiastical courts. At all events he appears to have made little impact upon the parish, hiring a deputy to perform his duties, and after ten years he resigned the living in 1532. In marked contrast, his replacement, Nicholas Atkinson, a native of Bishopthorpe ordained priest in York in 1503, had actually served as a chaplain in St Michael's in the early years of the century. He seems to have carried out his pastoral duties in person.[10]

In addition to the rector the parish supported a team of stipendiary priests, some of whom may only have come into the church for special occasions to participate in trentals or obits, but others of whom were employed full time to perform the liturgy. For twenty years between 1507 and 1527 Robert Barker, curate, witnessed parishioners' wills. William Ferne, or Feron, spent three years in the parish immediately before his appointment to a chantry in All Saints', North Street, in 1523; after the loss of his chantry he migrated to St Lawrence's where he died at the end of Mary's reign. Henry Gelsthorpe, having served at the beginning of the century as a chaplain in the neighbouring parish of St Mary, Castlegate, deputised for Marshall throughout his ten year incumbency, reading the bede roll, a list of deceased benefactors, and annually paying for the church to be strewed with rushes, duties which the rector would normally have performed. Towards the end of his life in 1532 he also obtained a chantry, but at the altar of St Andrew in the Minster, not in a city church. Richard Hutchinson made his will as a priest in St Michael's in February 1542, leaving the church a vestment and his fellow priest, Sir Francis Giles, 10s. and a gown furred with black Spanish lamb to say a trental for his soul.[11]

Thomas Worrall

Among all the comings and goings of clergy at St Michael's in the first part of the sixteenth century there remained one priest upon whom the congregation could always depend. Thomas Worrall, one of the two sons of John Wirrall, fishmonger, had been born in the parish in about 1489. In adult life he sang the Jesus Mass each day and had a pair of clavichords in his house on his death, so it seems very probable that he learnt music as well as his letters as one of the children of the choir: the church certainly possessed both a song school and a school house at this date. To gain his working knowledge of Latin he may have needed to attend a grammar school elsewhere in the city, but it seems unlikely that he received any of his education outside York. As a young man he may have served an unofficial apprenticeship with one of the parish clergy, still at this period the usual way of preparing to enter the church. Then in 1512 at the age of 24, the earliest date permitted by canon law, he was ordained deacon in York Minster on 10 April and priest in the Austin Friary in Lendal on 18 December, taking his 'title', a financial guarantee routinely provided by a monastic house, from the Benedictine priory of Holy Trinity across the river in Micklegate.[12]

From Christmas 1512 the new priest would have been in a position to compete for the paid services the townspeople were constantly calling upon the unbeneficed clergy to perform. The York Corpus Christi Guild, the most prestigious guild in the city which attracted members from throughout the county, indeed from the whole of England, required six priests each year to help the master at the annual Corpus Christi procession and to enlist new recruits: Worrall acted as a 'keeper' in the guild in 1514 and 1515. Within the parish itself the daily and weekly round of Masses for the dead together with the annual cycle of obits provided regular opportunities for employment. Given the number of priests needed for the celebration of a trental, he may well have participated in the St Gregory's trental his own father, in July 1517, willed to be done 'in St Michael's church for my soul the day of my burial or else before, the price 10s.' Worrall, however, unlike many of his contemporaries, who had to spend years if not decades in temporary work of this kind, acquired a permanent post within a few years of his ordination, certainly by 1518, becoming stipendiary priest in St Michael's at an annual salary of £5 6s. 8d.[13]

As one of his ancillary duties, from 1518 Worrall compiled a fair copy of the churchwardens' accounts each year for three decades without a break. At almost exactly the same date on his appointment as vicar of Morebath, Christopher Trychay embarked on the same task. Yet despite writing at the same time and necessarily conforming to the same genre, they produced very different accounts. As vicar of Morebath Trychay had sole charge of the spiritual welfare of his flock; Worrall never gained this responsibility in St Michael's. Secure in his parson's freehold, and probably also the most literate man in the village, Trychay could use the Morebath accounts as a means of addressing, exhorting, cajoling and at times rebuking his parishioners. Worrall enjoyed nothing like the same status: as a paid employee he had no choice but to obey the 'church masters', the wealthy, influential and educated lay members of the parish. The contrast between the two clerics explains why the Spurriergate accounts contain virtually none of the personal remarks with which the Morebath accounts abound. Worrall accepted his place in the parish hierarchy and the parish responded by continuing to favour a local boy made good. A special entry he inserted into the accounts in 1522, only a decade after his

Fig. 5.7 Grant of a chamber rent free to Sir Thomas Worrall for life, 1522. BIHR PRY/MS4 f. 25r. (Reproduced from an original in the Borthwick Institute, University of York.)

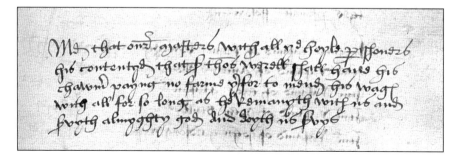

98

ordination, implicitly acknowledges this relationship:

> Memorandum that our masters with all the whole parishioners is contented that Sir Thomas Werell shall have his chamber, paying no farm [rent] therefore, to mend his wages withall for so long as he remaineth with us and serveth Almighty God and doth us service (Fig. 5.7).[14]

The obligations the parish expected Worrall to fulfil can be glimpsed, though often only darkly, from his annual statements of income and expenditure. First and foremost came his participation not only as a priest but also as a chorister in the liturgy over the course of the year. During the penitential season of Advent he noted the purchase of pounds of wax for the candles at Christmas 'to burn in the murk mornings'. At High Mass every Sunday the rector or his deputy customarily read out an abbreviated version of the bede roll of the parish's benefactors, exhorting the congregation to pray for their souls, and once a year many parishes celebrated a general Requiem at which the priest recited the bede roll in its entirety. Every year Worrall recorded the gift of a pair of gloves to the under clerk 'for singing of A Mind of Me' on the twelfth day of Christmas, and St Michael's may just possibly have held its commemoration on this date.[15]

In Lent custom prescribed that the rood should be veiled; at St Michael's in 1538 Worrall listed payments 'for helping of the Lenten cloth, ... for white incle and rings to it' and 'for a cord to draw it with to and fro'. Every year he oversaw the purchase of sacks of charcoal for the fire on Easter eve before the ceremonies at the Easter sepulchre on Easter day. Affluent parishes took a particular pleasure in procuring mechanical devices for their churches in the late middle ages. In London in 1473, for example, the chief men of St Botolph by Billingsgate set down instructions for operating their recently acquired 'Billingsgate George', which, at their annual patronal festival, by means of an intricate system of pulleys was made to slay the dragon and snatch the maiden from the monster's lair. St Michael's, Spurriergate, apparently had a holy sepulchre something along these lines: in 1546 Worrall recorded that John Carver had spent a day and a half in the church among other things 'mending of St Pulchre house and for helping of the angels' wings ...', and the following year included a payment 'for soap to the parish clerk to anoint the St Pulchre gear that the image went in at the Resurrection'.[16]

At St Michael's as elsewhere popular customs, partially Christianised, filled the quiet period after the celebrations for Whitsuntide, Holy Trinity and Corpus Christi. Bequests to the Summergame light suggest that even in this most urban of parishes the young people had found a space for their summer festivities. Then in the autumn the parishioners held their patronal feast. Worrall revealed little about the Michaelmas festivities apart from the expense incurred in 1540 'for sweeping in Coney Street against the church of St Michael's even'.[17]

Over and above his commitment to assist at parish worship, Worrall had the special responsibility for singing the Jesus Mass, or the Mass of the Five Wounds, at the Jesus altar daily which augmented his salary by 6s. 8d. each year. He was invariably present at obits which occurred in the church almost every month, and each attendance brought him an additional fee of 4d. amounting to about a noble, 3s.4d., over the course of the year. In 1542, for example, he participated at the obit for Master Robert Hancock on the Saturday before the feast of St Valentine, at that for Master John Ralf in the third week of Lent, at the obit of Matthew Balladine in the Trinity octave, at the obit for William Wallay and Margaret his wife around the feast of St Augustine the Great in August, at the obits for Master Thomas Harrison, for Master Thomas Barton, and for Master John Harrison and Ellen his wife at unspecified dates later in the year, at the obit for Master John Gelder about the feast of St Edmund King and Martyr in November and lastly at the obit for John Roger and his wife Margaret at the Conversion of St Paul on 25 January.[18]

Apart from Thomas Barton who died in 1461, Worrall had probably known most of the inhabitants whose funeral ceremonies he re-enacted each year. Robert Hancock had survived until 1496, his widow Maud till 1508 while John Roger, fishmonger, whose death did not take place until 1532, would have been a near contemporary. Other parishioners remembered the priest by name when they came to make their wills. The wealthy merchant, Brian Lorde, in his will of 1526 left 20d. each to his curate, Henry Gelsthorpe, and Thomas Worrall, but only 12d. a head to the other parish clergy, Robert Barker, John Wilson and John Stapleton. As early as 1524 John Marshall of the neighbouring parish of St Mary, Castlegate, made Worrall one of the feoffees of a house in Hemingbrough in the East

Riding the revenues from which were to support a daily Mass in perpetuity in the Grey Friars' church for his soul, his wife's soul, the souls of his father and mother, and all his good friends' souls, the priest receiving the sizeable sum of 10s. for his pains. Thomas Glasyn in 1531 and Richard Savage in 1543 both appointed Worrall the supervisor of their wills. He witnessed the will of John Easingwold in 1527, that of Agnes Hardsong, widow, in 1538, and that of Thomas Dawson alias Bartram the following year.[19]

While most inhabitants of St Michael's put their loyalty to their parish church first among their priorities, some had also formed close ties with local monasteries, nunneries, friaries, and other extra-parochial institutions. Worrall's own father paid 3s. 4d. to the Grey Friars in Castlegate to conduct his body to his parish church and to offer prayers for his soul and that of his wife. Besides a bequest of 20s. to the prioress and convent of Clementhorpe the incomer Anthony Middleton commissioned a trental for the souls of his mother and father at his birthplace of Kirkby Lonsdale in Westmorland. Both Margaret Vicars and Alice Blakey showed a special devotion to the York Carmelites, the latter leaving her great brass pot to Our Lady of the White Friars in 1525. Alice Blakey also gave Our Lady in St William's chapel on Ouse Bridge a sheet and a towel and every priest there 4d., while in 1531 John Roger presented a cloth to the chapel to make an alb for the Morrow Mass priest.[20]

Very unusually, in 1535 Alderman John Beisbey, who had moved to York from Barton on Humber, wished his body to be interred outside the parish. Having bequeathed, as convention required, 5s. 'to my curate the parson of my parish church of St Michael aforesaid for tithes and oblations forgotten', another 5s. to the church works 'and towards the mending of vestments there', and 4d. 'to the said parson or to his parish priest for the time being yearly during 20 years next ensuing ... to pray for my soul amongst other on the Sundays in his bede roll', he bestowed all his lands and tenements in the city and suburbs upon the Grey Friars in return for burial before the altar of the Resurrection in the Franciscan church, for the offering of five Masses by five priests at the Scala Celi altar, and for the celebration in perpetuity of a daily Mass at the half hour between six and seven in the morning 'for the soul of me ... John Beisbye, the souls of my wives, parents, friends, good doers and all Christian souls'.[21]

Worral's responsibility for church property

In spurning the services of his parish clergy Beisbey was acting quite contrary to the accepted practice of most York parishioners in the Tudor period for whom charity began and often ended at home. Through their endowment of temporary chantries and obits in their parish church, St Michael's, Spurriergate, had in fact accumulated a very considerable amount of property by the early sixteenth century, overseen with various degrees of efficiency until the late 1530s by a succession of parish clerks. For a short time in mid career Thomas Worrall had toyed with the idea of spreading his wings, and, though still continuing as a stipendiary priest in his home parish, in October 1528 had acquired a chantry in St Mary's, Castlegate. He resigned the chantry, however, after only five years in August 1533. Then perhaps partly to compensate for this loss of income, in 1538 he took on a quite new assignment: the administration of the St Michael's estate.[22]

Through copying the accounts for the churchwardens over the previous twenty years Worrall had become very familiar with the particulars of the church's assets. Now in addition to supervising all the work on the church he assumed the onerous position of housing manager for the parish. By the early sixteenth century the church possessed some 26 messuages and tenements in Spurriergate, Low and High Ousegate and Water Lane. Outside the parish it owned two houses in Walmgate, two more in Micklegate, one in Clementhorpe and one in Gillygate. These properties varied greatly in value, with Robert Barker and Thomas Applegarth at the one extreme leasing their mansions for an annual 46s. 8d. and 40s. respectively, while at the other Elizabeth Junkin and John Thornton paid no more than 16d. or 20d. for their hovels in the slums. Most years the whole estate produced between £12 and £16, out of an annual parish income, excluding special fund raising, of between £14 and £18.[23]

Urban landlords found it increasingly hard to let their properties during the prolonged depression of the first part of the sixteenth century, and it may be because of the difficulties the parish clerk had been encountering that the churchwardens turned to Worrall. Yet not even he could prevent tenants vanishing in the night to seek their fortune in 'the south country' and in his very first year at the helm the parish had to write off a total of £3 4s. 11d. in rent arrears 'for that they [the tenants] were poor people and had nought, and some of them be dead, and therefore by the consent of all the parishioners we have remit and forgiven them'. The problem of how to cope with a destitute underclass persisted throughout the decade, and time and again Worrall reported that he could not extract any rent from a tenant 'because he was a very poor man and had nothing to pay'. In the desperate economic climate disaster might strike even hitherto prosperous members of the community like Miles Haxby, who had leased a substantial house in Walmgate at an annual rent of 10s. for several years until a change in circumstances forced him to move out. In 1545 the parish forgave him his rent arrears because 'he was a poor man and fallen in poverty'.[24]

Worrall's duties extended far beyond merely collecting the rents at Whitsun and Martinmas and much of his time appears to have been taken up with acting as clerk of the works. Unlike the church, the parish houses seem to have been in constant need of repair, indeed sometimes of an almost complete rebuilding. The refurbishment of John Wilkinson's house in 1544, for example, required two loads of lime, 20 loads of sand, a bushel of plaster, 500 roofing tiles, two louvres, one for the kitchen and one for the kiln, and four men's labour for tiling and pointing for eight days. The total cost amounted to 26s. 7d., 3s. 3d. more than the tenant's annual rent. Each year Worrall devoted more than half his accounts to the rental, the purchase of building supplies and the hire of men to work upon the properties.[25]

Despite this constant outlay on the parish estate, and payments to the stipendiary priests and parish clerks, in most years the churchwardens contrived to balance their books, and still to have cash in hand to embellish the church. The parish spent well in excess of £8 on the organs for the choir in 1536, and incurred similar charges over the installation of new organs in the rood loft in 1543, but experienced no difficulties in clearing its debts on either occasion. Quite unlike Morebath where it took 20 years of fund raising before Christopher Trychay could obtain the set of black vestments on which he had set his heart, St Michael's normally had money in hand to buy expensive vestments whenever the need arose, in 1523, for instance, spending £3 10s. 8d. in London on '9 yards of flowered damask to make the white copes upon'. Even in a time of recession there was more wealth to be tapped in an urban than a rural parish and the wardens could still count on the generosity of benefactors, as they had done in the past. In 1526 Richard Olyffe presented the church with a hanging candlestick of 'oversea work'; Mistress Hardsong bequeathed an altar cloth in 1538; in 1543 the wardens had a new alb made 'that Mistress Watson gave to sing Lady Mass with'.[26]

While the inhabitants of St Michael's never had to have recourse to church ales, the normal means of raising funds for the church in the countryside, at which money-making and revelry went hand in hand, they still occasionally took part in communal feastings, though they owed these to the generosity of individuals and not to the parish. Anthony Middleton left his neighbours 6s. 8d. in 1519 'in the way of recreation to make merry withall'. In 1526 Brian Lorde gave 10s. to be spent on a similar wake at his death for 'the neighbours of the parishing'. Thomas Glasyn arranged a funeral breakfast for his neighbours in 1531, in 1539 Thomas Dawson provided a funeral dinner, while in 1543 Richard Savage (using the courtesy title 'Sir' to refer to his priest) required that 'there be an honest dirige made for me the day of my burial to all the parishioners both rich and poor after the discretion of my wife and Sir Thomas Wirall' and also 'that there be made a dinner to my neighbours and priests and clerks of the church and ... that thirteen poor men be at the dinner and every one of them to have 1d.'[27]

Through a cash donation by Thomas Tanfield, St Michael's had already acquired one charity to support aspirant parish entrepreneurs by the beginning of the Tudor period. This fund administered by the churchwardens lent small sums at interest annually to young men about to set up in trade. Promotion of commerce by these means seems to have particularly appealed to the mercantile elite: Worrall commented appreciatively on the creation of a second such fund in 1538:

Memorandum that we received of William Hardsong for agreement of the house in Ousegate that we had no right to, but of his gentleness, which is not in our account, for this intent: that every Saturday the priest [who] sings the Lady Mass shall take a proper collect in his Mass and to pray for the soul of Thomas Hardsong and for all his parent souls and all Christian souls, and he so doing to have yearly upon the churchwardens 8d. And so we are all agreed that the said 40s. shall go about in parishioners' hands after the form and custom of Tanfeld stock, and so to [be] named and called Hardsong stock. 40s.[28]

A priest of 'honest qualities'

Assisting in parish worship, singing his Jesus Mass daily, writing the churchwardens' accounts, superintending the parish estate, keeping track to the last penny of the interest on loan money, Worrall had proved his competence in an impressive number of spheres by his late middle age. Yet the Chantry Commissioners on their visit to York in 1548 considered him nothing out of the ordinary, judging him like so many other priests in the city to be 'of honest qualities and conditions, and of indifferent learning'.[29]

With an estimated annual income of a little over £9, well above that of many York beneficed priests, Worrall had attained a comfortable standard of living by 1548. As well as his clavichords, his hall, with a curtain and wall hangings contained a table and cupboard, a chair, stool and three cushions, a great standing bed and a trundle bed, together with three lockers and a little table to set by the fire. In addition to two corporal cases and a corporal, some towels, two old altar cloths and a Chrisom, all relating specifically to his priestly activities, he possessed an abundance of linen, napkins, tablecloths, sheets, pillowcases, a shaving cloth and a night cap. There were some books on the shelves in his study, not itemised, together with a locker for writings. In one chamber adjoining the hall he had a clothes cupboard, a chair, cushion, three forms, two chests, a basin, bottle and pot, an altar and holy water vat; in the other chamber six carpet-work cushions and a needlework cushion, a white coverlet and a red coverlet, a curtain for the window and more wall hangings. Besides jackets, doublets, caps, shoes, boots and hose, Worrall's clothes included a riding cloak, a frieze gown faced with rabbit, a black gown faced with say, and two superior mosterdeviles gowns. He also had more than £5 in ready money at the time of his death. His cash and goods combined amounted to a total sum of £20 9s. 6d (Fig. 5.8).[30]

Thomas Worrall died, it seems intestate, aged about 61 before the end of August 1550. He had lived just long enough to record in his accounts the removal of the lights, the images and the side altars. Both in the parish and the church at large his death marked the end of an era. With its abolition of Masses for the dead and new emphasis on sermons rather than sacraments, the Protestant regime of Edward VI had little room for the old school of clergy to which Worrall belonged. Apart from the glass, of all the possessions of St Michael,

Fig. 5.8 Inventory of the goods of Sir Thomas Worrall. BIHR D&C Original Wills 1550. (Reproduced from an original in the Borthwick Institute, University of York.)

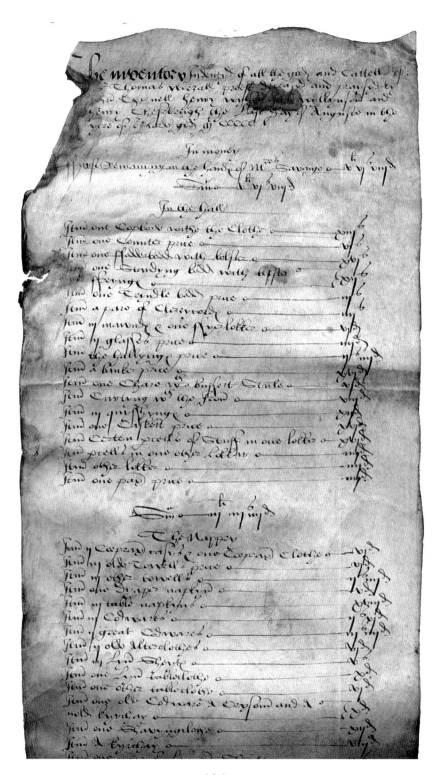

Spurriergate – altars, statues, vestments, paintings – only his accounts survive to commemorate the services one priest performed for his parish in the final decades of the medieval Catholic Church in England.[31]

6

Endings and beginnings

Claire Cross

Changes under King Henry VIII

In the mid sixteenth century York, along with the rest of the nation, mirrored the contradictory policies of successive English governments which over the course of two generations rejected papal authority, introduced Protestantism, returned to the Roman obedience, and then finally and permanently committed the country to Protestantism once more. In 1530 the seemingly ageless Latin liturgy was being celebrated with great elaboration and splendour in both the Minster and the parish churches: fifty years later worship in the city had been totally transformed. Although in parts of England some of the clergy and laity anticipated and positively welcomed these innovations, the citizens of York, upholding the old ceremonies to the very end, conformed only with reluctance.

Martin Luther's attack upon the system of papal indulgences in Wittenberg in 1517 attracted few supporters in the north of England. Even fewer agreed with his subsequent assertion that 'there was no Purgatory in the Old Testament, nor in the New Testament at the time of the apostles, nor long thereafter'. While many of the inhabitants of German Imperial cities responded with enthusiasm to the message that salvation came through faith in the merits of Christ alone, for the next three decades York clergy and laity clung to their belief in good works and in particular the efficacy of Masses for the dead.[1]

An Augustinian canon and an academic, Luther appealed in England in the first instance to small groups of reforming theologians at the universities of Cambridge and to a lesser extent Oxford. A little later despite the hostility of the crown and the leading churchmen his teachings began to take root among some sections of the population of London and other southern towns, but York, the administrative centre of the northern province, continued resolute in its loyalty to the old ways.

This, however, did not mean that the city remained untouched by movements for reform within the Catholic Church. In 1496, after an eminent career in Cambridge, one of the most prominent humanists of the age, William Melton, had become chancellor of the Minster, where he resided fairly regularly until his death some thirty years later. A passionate advocate of the better education of the clergy, Melton never deviated from the path of Catholic orthodoxy. In addition to works of the Fathers, the pagan classics, and modern writers like Mirandola, Erasmus and More, his splendid library included a defence of the Mass and a confutation of Luther by his former pupil, John Fisher.[2]

Under such leadership the city remained a bastion of the traditional faith, and the only York inhabitant to be found guilty of heresy in the first half of Henry VIII's reign was a 'Dutchman', Gilbert Johnson of Holy Trinity, King's Court, not a native. Among much else Johnson had accused the clergy of being worse than Judas, since Judas had betrayed 'Almighty God for 30d.', while 'priests will sell God for half a penny'.[3]

Consequently the York representatives who went down to London to attend a new parliament in the autumn of 1529 must have been totally unprepared for the religious upheaval to which the country was about to be subjected. Having failed to obtain an annulment of his marriage to Catherine of Aragon through diplomacy, Henry VIII at first attempted to use parliament to pressurise the papacy into granting the divorce, and it was only after this stratagem also miscarried that he moved on to challenge the legitimacy of papal jurisdiction in England and turned to a purely English tribunal. His new archbishop of Canterbury, Thomas Cranmer, pronounced the union void, Henry married Anne Boleyn in January 1533, and early in 1534 parliament settled the succession on the children of this marriage and required all male adults throughout the kingdom to swear to uphold the act. In June 1534 the crown issued a proclamation that the bishop of Rome should no longer enjoy the prayers of the English people. Then in November of the same year parliament passed the Act of Supremacy, formally recognising the king as the head of the Church in England.

Such a change of allegiance demanded a massive programme of re-education and the government immediately dispatched emissaries to disseminate news of the royal supremacy throughout the length and breadth of the country. With his evangelical chaplain, Thomas Garret, Sir Francis Bigod of Settrington in the East Riding, a very early convert to Lutheranism, arrived in York to superintend events in the summer of 1535. He informed Thomas Cromwell that Archbishop Lee had duly promulgated the monarch's powers over the Church before a large congregation in the Minster. As intended, details of these developments percolated down to the city parishes: in their accounts for the year the churchwardens of St Michael's, Spurriergate, recorded spending 5d. 'for ale when Master Bigod was at the preaching'. All the York clergy accepted the royal supremacy without any outward protest, but Bigod did encounter some resistance at Jervaulx Abbey where a monk, George Lazenby, interrupted Garret's sermon to defend the papal supremacy. On his persistent refusal to accept the king's jurisdiction over the Church, Lazenby was tried for treason at the Yorkshire Assizes, found guilty and executed in York on 6 August.[4]

From this time onwards more and more directives from Westminster rained down upon the localities. In urgent need of new sources of money to finance his foreign wars, early in 1535 Henry had sent out commissioners to evaluate the possessions of the Church, who in less than twelve months produced the *Valor Ecclesiasticus*. This immensely detailed survey made it possible for the state to impose an unprecedented annual tax of ten per cent of their income upon all the secular clergy. It also provided the information for the implementation of the Act of 1536 permitting the confiscation of all monasteries with revenues of less than £200 a year.

Several poorly endowed York priories fell within the scope of this measure and yet more officials descended upon the city in the summer of 1536. On 29 July Richard Speght and his community were constrained to surrender Holy Trinity Priory, valued at £169 a year, to the crown. While the commissioners had discretion to grant a pension to the prior, his eight monks merely received dispensations to take up livings in the secular church. They then moved on to Clementhorpe nunnery, worth a mere £55 a year, which Isabel Ward vacated with her eight nuns on 31 August. While the prioress obtained a meagre pension, her nuns were faced with the choice of transferring to another house of their order or returning to their families.[5]

Everything seemed to be in a state of flux. In an attempt to improve its precarious financial position in the spring of 1536 the corporation had secured a private act of parliament to appropriate the revenues of certain civic chantries. In the following August Cromwell announced the abolition of numerous holy days, condemned superstitions relating to pilgrimages and images and ordered the parish clergy to expound the Lord's Prayer, the Creed and the Ten Commandments in English.[6]

These innovations provoked widespread resentment. A performance of the play of St Thomas culminated in a riot in August, another serious quarrel erupted in the Merchant Adventurers Hall in September, and there seems to have been considerable unrest in York even before the outbreak of the Pilgrimage of Grace in Beverley at the beginning of October. On 9 October Lord Darcy commanded the mayor to take up arms to defend the city, but his order arrived too late and the people rose on 11 October. Deserted by the archbishop, the mayor capitulated to the rebels, and on 16 October their great captain, Robert Aske, marched through York to the Minster. There he posted up an order restoring the monks and nuns to the houses from which they had so recently been expelled. The prior of the York Augustinian friars, John Aske, and John Pickering, the prior of the York Dominicans, both threw their weight behind the revolt.[7]

Robert Aske spent three days in York before moving south. Then on 20 October Sir Thomas Percy, the younger brother of the earl of Northumberland, at the head of a band of 10,000 men rode through the city to great public acclaim. In December a York delegation attended the meeting between the Duke of Norfolk and the rebels in Pontefract which concluded the first part of the rising. The city played no part in the revolts which broke out afresh in the East Riding early in the new year and sealed the fate of Robert Aske. As a warning to the local populace, after his trial in London, Aske was sent back to be executed in York on 12 July 1537. Since he had not joined in the second rising, his namesake, John Aske, escaped punishment and remained as prior of the Austin Friars, but the Dominican prior, John Pickering, the author of verses in support of the insurrection, died at the stake in May.[8]

With the taint of treason hanging over the city, the archbishop and corporation now needed above everything else to demonstrate their obedience to the crown. There were no open protests in the city in 1538 when the king demanded a valuation of the goods belonging to the parish churches prior to their confiscation. Accepting the inevitable, the churchwardens of St Michael's, Spurriergate, called in a goldsmith to weigh their chalices and other jewels.[9]

The dissolution of the monasteries, interrupted by the Pilgrimage of Grace, also resumed in 1538. The York Dominican, Franciscan and Carmelite friaries were dissolved on 27 November and the Austin friary the following day. While still in the city, government officials also accepted the surrender of St Andrew's priory. As mendicants the 59 York friars did not qualify for any compensation, but under the new government policy the prior of St Andrew's received a pension of £10 a year and the three surviving members of his community pensions of £4 a head.[10]

Having first dealt with the poorest and weakest houses, and left the richest and most powerful to the last, the commissioners suppressed St Mary's Abbey in November 1539, allocating the abbot a substantial pension of 400 marks, the sub-prior a much smaller but still sizeable pension of 20 marks and the 48 other members of the community pensions of between £10 and £5 according to seniority. Monasticism finally came to an end in the city on 1 December 1539 with the submission of St Leonard's Hospital, the pluralist master, Thomas Magnus, obtaining a grant of the hospital's dwelling house and Beningborough grange in lieu of a pension, the eight brothers pensions of between £6 13s. 4d. and £5, and the four sisters £4 6s. 8d. a head.[11]

The expulsion of around 150 monks, friars and nuns must have caused much individual suffering in York and its environs, though some of the wealthier houses had the means to soften the blow for some of their members. St Mary's Abbey, which had possessed appropriations in East Anglia as well as Yorkshire, now placed Guy Kelsaye and Thomas Marse in its Norfolk livings of Wilby and

Hargham, and Richard Barwicke, Thomas Baynes and John Thompson in St Saviour's, St Mary's, Castlegate, and St Michael le Belfrey in York. William Gryme, a monk of Holy Trinity priory, stayed on to serve as rector of the parish church, where Richard Speght, the pensioned former prior, continued to officiate as an unbeneficed priest. Between 1544 and 1550 two brothers of St Leonard's Hospital, Edward Smyth and Richard Hall, in succession occupied the Hospital's rectory of St Denys in Walmgate. The Gilbertine, John Hodgeson, acquired the living of St Mary, Bishophill, Junior.[12]

Having far more limited access to patronage, the friars fared far less well than the monks and only one, the Austin, George Bellerby, gained a city living, that of the very poor parish of St Wilfrid. At least a dozen others, both monks and friars, had to content themselves with the posts of chantry or stipendiary priests. Yet other former religious, who were sufficiently well pensioned not to need new employment, chose to settle in the city. Thomas Clint, the former sub-prior of St Mary's, lived in the parish of St Martin, Micklegate, until his death in 1550, William Vavasour, the last warden of the York Franciscans, in the parish of St Mary, Bishophill, Junior, while Isabel Ward, the former prioress of Clementhorpe, made her home in Trinity Lane in Micklegate, where she died a woman of some substance in 1569.[13]

Though the Government had dissolved the monasteries primarily for economic reasons, by destroying institutions bound to make perpetual intercession for the souls of their founders and benefactors it had also in the most dramatic way possible brought into question the validity of prayers for the dead. Cranmer had indeed criticised the doctrine of Purgatory as early as 1534 and as the decade advanced reformers felt increasingly confident in attacking a whole range of 'popish superstitions'. In September 1538 Archbishop Lee endorsed Cromwell's second set of injunctions which forbade the burning of lights before images, commanded the purchase of English Bibles, and exhorted congregations to pray in English after their priests. The following year the Spurriergate wardens recorded the 'taking down of St Syth's candlesticks and other candlesticks' in St Michael's church.[14]

Having been threatening to visit the north of England ever since the defeat of the Pilgrimage of Grace, Henry at last reached York in September 1541, and in a spectacular display of repentance the archbishop, the lord mayor and all the local dignitaries sought the king's forgiveness on their knees. In October the dean and chapter acquiesced in the destruction of the St William's shrine, using part of the proceeds raised from the sale of plate and precious stones to buy Bibles for some city churches. The Minster also lost six of its most valuable prebends to the crown at this time.[15]

Having exhausted the financial potential of the monasteries, the king moved on to the chantries, authorising a nationwide survey of their endowments in 1546. This had implications for virtually every church in the land and the churchwardens of St Michael's, Spurriergate, were certainly not alone in seeking legal advice 'when the chantries and church lands was presented to the king's council'. Despite the disappearance of some late medieval institutions in the first quarter of the sixteenth century and the municipal dissolution of 1536, the Yorkshire commissioners still found over 100 chantries operating in the city, about 70 in the Minster and around 40 in the parish churches.[16]

King Edward VI and the abolition of the Mass

While Henry VIII had whole-heartedly approved of the expulsion of the pope and the nationalisation of the English Church, and condoned assaults on superstitious practices, he had never permitted any questioning of the central doctrine of the Catholic faith, the real presence of Christ in the Mass, and, apart from readings from the English Bible and the litany in English, the traditional Latin services continued almost unaltered in both cathedrals and parish churches until the end of the reign. Everything changed on Henry's death and the accession of Edward VI in January 1547. The second chantries Act of December 1547 contained a direct attack upon the 'vain opinions of Purgatory and Masses satisfactory to be done for them which be departed', and within the year the crown had pensioned off the priests and absorbed the endowments of all chantry foundations. The abolition of the chantries brought about a permanent reduction in clerical manpower in York, halving the total of clergy in the parish churches at the very least, and decreasing the number of vicars choral in the Minster, who had been supplementing their incomes by serving a chantry, from 21 in 1530 to only ten in 1558.[17]

Archbishop Holgate had been complaining about the lack of preaching in the Minster as early as March 1547. At their visitation the following October the royal commissioners commanded all other services to cease when sermons were being delivered. Having limited the celebration of Masses to one a day, they instructed the priests to devote the time saved to studying the word of God, and ordered the dean and chapter to set up a library containing the works of the Fathers and 'good' modern authors.[18]

With the abolition of traditional ceremonies and the new emphasis on preaching the government considered the Minster no longer had any need for many of its ancient treasures. Over the course of the reign whole cartloads of gold and silver chalices, censors, basins, pyxes, crosses, candlesticks, superaltars, cups, bowls, holy water pots, almost 50 red and purple copes, dozens of green, blue, white and black copes and sets of vestments, altar cloths, curtains, hangings, canopies, mitres, cloths of tissue, turkey carpets, and precious stones left York to augment the state's coffers.[19]

At least one city parish anticipated this appropriation of Church goods to save something for themselves. In 1547, as they were dismantling the roods, the great St Sepulchre candlestick, the images and the retables above the altars, and replastering and whitewashing the walls, the wardens of St Michael's, Spurriergate, sold for the benefit of the church their silver cross head and other plate at the rogationtide market in Beverley. Apart from a single chalice, all the plate and the jewels remaining in the parish churches, as well as the shrine of the very wealthy Corpus Christi guild, were confiscated by the state later in the reign.[20]

When he died in the spring of 1548 Nicholas Atkinson, the parson of St Michael's, had still expected to have five pounds of wax burnt about his body and five Masses of 'the Five Wounds of our Lord Jesu' said for his soul and all Christian souls on his burial day. Within little more than a year with the imposition of the Book of Common Prayer all these traditional practices came to an end.[21]

Already alienated by the government's decision to allow the laity to communicate in both kinds from Easter 1548, Robert Parkyn, the curate of Adwick le Street, near Doncaster, recalled his reaction to the new form of service. After the feast of Pentecost 1549 no priests could

> celebrate or say Mass in Latin, or minister any sacrament in Latin words ...,
> but only in English .... And so the holy Mass was utterly deposed throughout
> all this realm of England ..., and in place thereof a communion to be said in

English without any elevation of Christ's body and blood under form of bread and wine, or adoration, or reservation in the pyx ....[22]

Deploring the fact that in the past 'there hath been great diversity in saying and singing in churches within this realm, some following Salisbury use, some Hereford use, some the use of Bangor, some of York, and some of Lincoln', the Prayer Book now prescribed that 'from henceforth all the whole realm shall have but one use'. To clear the field for the new form of worship, in January 1550 Archbishop Holgate sent a commission 'unto all the deaneries within Yorkshire straightly commanding that all ecclesiastical books, as Mass books, grails, antiphoners, couchers, processioners, manuals, portuses and primers etc. should be conveyed unto the Bishop's Palace in York, and there to be defaced and put out of knowledge'.[23]

Traditional attitudes, however, could not be so easily erased. Having discovered to their consternation that conservatives were contriving to interpret the 1549 communion service as a kind of English Mass, late in 1552 Cranmer and his fellow Reformers brought out an indisputedly Protestant form of prayer. Parkyn could not contain his indignation at the sacrilegious treatment of the Mass in this second Edwardian Prayer Book.

> The table ... was had down into the body of the church in many places, and set in the mid alley among the people, the ends whereof stood east and west, and the priest on the north side, his face turned toward the south, upon which table ... a loaf of white bread (such as men uses in their houses with meat) and a cup of wine was set without any corporal. And part of the loaf was cut off and laid either upon the loaf or by it, and after words of consecration was said, the minister break the same bread, and ate thereof first his self, and then gave to every person that would be partakers a part or piece thereof in to their own hands, saying thus to every one of them, 'Take and eat this in remembrance that Christ died for thee, and feed of him in thy heart by faith with thanksgiving'. That done, the priest or minister did give unto them also the chalice or cup into their own hands, saying, 'Drink this in remembrance that Christ blood was shed for thee and be thankful', straightly forbidding that any adoration should be done thereto, for that were idolatry (said the book) and to be abhorred of all faithful Christians.[24]

For a priest like Parkyn the good old ceremonies were being cast down and nothing of spiritual value put in their place, but at least in the Minster, where scriptural texts adorned the spaces above the high altar where the images had stood, Holgate was making a constructive attempt to advance the Protestant cause. Having directed all the Minster clergy to attend the newly established theology lectures, he imposed upon the deacons and younger vicars choral the weekly task of learning a chapter from the letters of St Paul, beginning with the Epistle to the Romans. To distance the new form of worship even further from the old, he banned the playing of organs entirely during divine service, also decreeing that 'there be none other note sung or used in the said church at any service there to be had, saving square note, plain, so that every syllable may be plainly and distinctly pronounced and understood, and without any reports or repeatings, which may induce any obscureness in the hearers'.[25]

Holgate had greatly offended his more conservative clergy by marrying a Yorkshire gentlewoman early in 1550. Seven of the prebendaries and three vicars choral also abandoned their vows of celibacy during the reign, but significantly none of the city clergy followed their lead. All the parish clergy conformed to the new forms of service, but there is no evidence of any Protestant teaching outside the Minster.[26]

Catholicism under Queen Mary

The death of Edward VI in July 1553 halted all these efforts at Protestant evangelism. On 18 August Mary issued a proclamation permitting the use of the old Latin liturgy and Parkyn recorded that Mass was being sung or said in most Yorkshire parish churches from the beginning of September. 'Holy bread and holy water was given, altars were re-edified, pictures or images set up, the cross with the crucifix thereon ready to be borne in procession, and with the same went procession. And in conclusion all the English service of late used in the church of God was voluntarily laid away and the Latin taken up again ...' The following year the queen repudiated the royal supremacy, called for the suppression of heresy, and ordered the deprivation of married priests.[27]

Archbishop Holgate, dispatched to the Tower in October 1553, was among the first of the men to be affected by the change of regime. After re-converting to Catholicism, disavowing his marriage and paying a huge fine, he eventually obtained his release in January 1555. On the deprivation of the married prebendaries and vicars choral, the new archbishop, Nicholas Heath, took particular pains to fill the chapter with priests committed to Catholic renewal.[28]

Slowly the Minster began to look and sound Catholic again. In 1556 Alderman George Gale left the high altar a purple, red and blue velvet front cloth depicting the Resurrection. In 1557 Sir Leonard Beckwith, a considerable local beneficiary from the dissolution of the monasteries, gave a red and green silk canopy to be held over the blessed sacrament during processions. In the same year the Minster bought new plate including censers for the services in the choir and paid for the repainting of the high altar and the setting up of statues of Our Lady and St John.[29]

At the very minimum the government also expected parish churches to re-erect the rood and acquire all vessels and vestments necessary for the proper celebration of the Mass, and in the city priests appear to have reverted to the old ways with alacrity. In 1556 Lawrence Harrison, vicar of St George, Fishergate, gave two half pounds of wax to be burnt before the blessed sacrament on the day of his burial and commissioned a half trental of Masses to be said for his soul and all Christian souls, if so many priests could be had. In the same year the rector of Holy Trinity, Micklegate, William Gryme, bequeathed his 'two great books of the Bible to the church use and an ordinary in Latin' together with 'four beads of silver and double gilt to hang at the sacrament upon principal days'. The dispossessed chantry priest of St Crux, Miles Walshforth, left St Nicholas's church outside Walmgate Bar 'a table of alabaster with case', his 'best surplice and two half year portuses'. Another former York chantry priest, William Pinder, donated a parchment Mass book of the York Use, a green silk vestment with a red cross and a pax to the chapel of St Thomas's Hospital, and a Missal and a second green vestment with a red velvet cross to St Crux. In October 1558 yet another former chantry priest in St Saviour's, William Kirby, expecting 'to be prayed for there', presented St John's, Ouse Bridge with a parchment Mass book, a covering of white damask, three silk cods, a ratchet, and a surplice with a pocket.[30]

The York laity showed considerably more caution than their priests. At their death a number provided for lights to be burnt in their parish church, but only three testators made a more lasting contribution towards the revival of Catholic practice. Alderman Richard White supplied St Michael le Belfrey with a lamp to burn before the pyx in

August 1556; two years later William Henlayke, corn merchant, returned a chest to St Mary, Castlegate, and Alison Feldewe bequeathed her best candlestick to her parish church of St Cuthbert. Although the family of Alderman George Gale besought the faithful to 'say one Pater Noster and one Ave for their souls', only one gentleman, Thomas Vavasour of Copmanthorpe, risked investing in an obit.[31]

While priests and parishioners seem to have wanted to revert to all the ceremonies which had flourished in the city in the first half of Henry VIII's reign, the very different teachings of the Counter-Reformation were beginning to take effect in the Minster. In December 1555 at the synod of Westminster Cardinal Pole had particularly stressed the importance of education in re-creating the Catholic Church in England. With the express intention of combating heresy with sound morality and sacred learning the dean and chapter responded by founding a seminary for 50 boys in York in 1557.[32]

Protestantism under Queen Elizabeth

The accession of Elizabeth on 17 November 1558 ended all these hopes for a Catholic revival. Despite the united opposition of the Marian bishops, the first parliament of the reign approved legislation returning the country to the Protestant fold. The new Act of Supremacy once more recognised the queen as the supreme governor over the English Church, and renounced papal authority for the second time. The Act of Uniformity then went on to reimpose the second Edwardian Prayer Book, slightly modified to imply the spiritual presence of Christ at the eucharist which both Calvinist and more conservative Protestants could allow. This Prayer Book became the only legal form of service throughout the country from midsummer 1559.[33]

The royal commissioners appointed to superintend the removal of altars and images and the suppression of Catholic ceremonies reached the Minster on 6 September 1559, where they heard one of their members preach the 'sincere doctrine of Jesus Christ' to a large congregation. The following day they called upon the prebendaries to acknowledge the royal supremacy. Some now for the first time placed their loyalty to the papacy before their allegiance to the crown, and their refusal to swear the oath of supremacy resulted in the most substantial purge in the Minster's history with about half the chapter losing their offices over the course of the next two years. This presented the queen's advisors with a unique opportunity for installing Protestants in their stead.[34]

In the absence of Nicholas Wotton, who until his death in 1567 contrived to combine the deanery of York with the deanery of Canterbury, the new chancellor, Richard Barnes began the campaign of Protestant evangelism, preaching against the 'absurd doings' of the papacy in 1561. Five years later Barnes gained a much needed ally on Matthew Hutton's appointment as dean. Within months of his arrival the chapter paid for workmen to whitewash the places where the altars had stood and sanctioned the purchase of Geneva psalm books, first 'set forth' in 1562 'and allowed to be sung in all churches of all the people together'. By the seventeenth century the Minster was renowned for the singing of metrical psalms before the sermon by the whole congregation together with the choir.[35]

Unlike the prebendaries, all the city clergy accepted the royal supremacy, and retained their posts, but most of these priests had neither the ability nor the inclination to advance the Protestant gospel. When he died early in 1566 Thomas Layther, the rector of St Saviour's and former monk of Watton, consigned his soul 'to Almighty God, my creator and redeemer, and to our blessed Lady Saint Mary and to all the holy company of heaven'. Five years later the one time chantry priest, Robert Norham, instituted to the living of St Mary, Bishophill, Junior, in 1541, expressed a similar confidence in the efficacy of the prayers of the Virgin and the saints. Despite the injunctions at the beginning of the reign, in 1571 St Mary, Bishophill, Senior, had still not acquired a pulpit or decent communion table or defaced its stone altar and table of images.[36]

Like their priests, the York laity at first showed little real understanding of the new Protestant services. Just before Mary's death the London alderman, Sir Martin Bowes, had informed the corporation of his decision to endow an annual dirge and Requiem Mass in St Cuthbert's together with a weekly bread dole for the poor of five loaves in honour of the Five Wounds. In 1561 the lord mayor, clearly preferring adaptation to any radical break, informed Bowes of the modifications made to his foundation 'since the late change'. Having substituted the service of evensong for the Dirige, and that of

Holy Communion for the Requiem, the council had used the money intended for holy bread to buy communion bread and wine, given to the poor the income meant for lights upon the altar, and were now offering intercession for their benefactor's 'good estate' in place of prayers for the dead.[37]

The Rebellion of the Earls in the autumn of 1569 brought home to the queen's advisors, if not the queen herself, the dangers of a politically and religiously disaffected north of England, and the need for far closer central control. In Edmund Grindal, Young's successor as archbishop of York, and the earl of Huntingdon, Sussex's replacement as president of the Council in the North, the government gained precisely the agents it sought, and these two men applied all their efforts to the full implementation of the Elizabethan religious settlement, starting with the city of York.

For some time Dean Hutton had been trying to remove popish elements in the medieval Mysteries the corporation insisted upon staging year after year. Grindal called in the text of the plays for closer examination in 1572, and never permitted their performance again. Prompted by the Council in the North, the corporation next issued a series of ordinances requiring attendance at sermons in the Minster on Sundays and holidays. Very gradually, as the old priests died and a new generation of ministers took over the reins, congregations also began to have more frequent sermons in their parish churches.[38]

Slowly this Protestant preaching had an effect. After having heard Henry More, the rector of St Martin's, Micklegate, attack abuses in 1568, Mistress Harrison upbraided a former monk and his fellow priests for not doing the same years before. Some of the parishioners of St John's, Ouse Bridge, were also beginning to show a similar change of heart. Before her death in 1579 the 'religious, devout and godly' centenarian Margaret Metcalfe 'sore repented of her former life, idly spent and evil ... and was heartily sorry that she was so superstitiously and popishly bent in times past'. Having 'lived in God's fear', the butcher Robert Harrison died 'in the true faith of Jesus Christ' in 1580. At the turn of the century the elderly Andrew Watson, 'who was religious in his knowledge and frequented the church very diligently', made an equally devout end.[39]

The wills of influential St John's parishioners also began to exhibit this new Protestant piety. John Warriner, dyer, expressed the hope in 1572 that God 'for his mercy's sake set forth in the death and precious bloodshedding of his dear son Jesus Christ, mine only saviour and redeemer ... will receive my soul into his glorious kingdom'. John Lademan of Cawood, lying sick in the house of John Lademan in St John's parish in 1584, commended his soul 'into the hands of Almighty God, my maker and redeemer, in whom and by the merits of whose blessed passion my whole trust is of clear remission and forgiveness of my sins'. In 1589 Robert Wilcocke hoped 'to be saved only through the blood and passion of my saviour and redeemer, Jesus Christ, and by no other merits'.[40]

Very conscious of the persistence of pockets of Catholic recusancy in parts of the city, in 1585 the lord president persuaded the corporation to set up a city lectureship to supplement the preaching in the Minster and the parish churches, and this persistent Protestant indoctrination had transformed worship in the city by the end of the sixteenth century with preaching and communal psalm singing replacing the Mass and prayers for the dead. When the citizens assembled to give thanks for the queen's escape from assassination in August 1586, they celebrated in the morning with a sermon and a general communion in the Minster and in the afternoon and evening 'every man supped in the said streets at his own door ... with great rejoicing and singing of psalms, and ringing of bells'. A primarily sacramental form of Christianity had given way to the religion of the Word, and the York Use had been quite forgotten.[41]

The Requiem Mass in the Use of York

7

An introduction to the Requiem Mass in the Use of York

P. S. Barnwell, Allan B. Barton and Ann Rycraft

Introduction to the Mass

The most important single element of the pre-Reformation liturgy, as in the Roman Catholic Church today, was the Mass, which could either be performed on its own or be supplemented by rites specific to particular occasions such as baptisms, marriages and funerals.[1] At the core of the Mass is the fulfilment of Christ's command to his disciples to commemorate the Last Supper, elaborated by the belief that the bread and wine were actually transformed into the body and blood of Christ himself. Such belief in transubstantiation was made an official Doctrine of the Church at the Fourth Lateran Council in 1215. The section of the Mass which contained this most sacred and mystical part of the liturgy was known as the Canon or Still Mass. It was followed by prayers that the communion benefit those present, and then by the communion itself, the consuming of the bread and wine. Before the Canon came the Ordinary of the Mass, which began with the Confession and Absolution of sins, followed by the Gloria celebrating Man's redemption, and a series of declarations of faith expressed in the New

Fig.7.1 Procession of ministers into the church. (Although the taperers in this and subsequent figures are female, that would not have been permitted in the middle ages.) See p. 147.
(© Allan B. Barton.)

Testament readings of the Epistle and the Gospel and in the Nicene Creed. Then, towards the end of the Ordinary, came the beginning of the ritual, the Offertory, during which the priest prepared the bread and wine, the offering, for blessing in the Canon. The Ordinary ended with two statements of praise, the Sanctus and the Benedictus.

At various points during the service, particularly in the Ordinary, there were Propers, or passages which varied so that the message was appropriate to the specific occasion on which the Mass was celebrated. Hence, for example, the Epistle, the Gospel and the prayer known as the Collect all varied according to the kind of service (for instance a Requiem or a Nuptial Mass) or to accord with specific Church feasts, including Christmas, Easter, and particular saints' days. Similarly, the Gradual and Tract, sentences said or sung between the

128

Fig. 7.2 Altar before the service. See p. 147.
(© Christopher Daniell.)

reading of the Epistle and Gospel, differed, as did the Communion and Postcommunion, said or sung during and after the communion itself. In addition to the Propers, parts of the ceremonial also varied with the specific occasion. There were, for example, entire additional sections of

Fig. 7.3 The Confession. See p. 147.
(This and all similar illustrations are edited versions of illustrations in
P. Dearmer (editor), *Dat Boexken vander Missen*: see Chapter 2 note 12.)

Fig. 7.4 The Introit.
See p. 148.
(© Allan B. Barton.)

Below:
Fig. 7.5 The Epistle.
See p. 149.
(© Christopher
Daniell.)

liturgy appropriate to particular occasions, such as marriages and funerals, which were performed before or after the normal Mass with its Propers.

The performance of High Mass on Sundays, feasts and special days, required the services of assistants in addition to the priest who conducted the main liturgy. None of the assistants was a priest; they occupied lesser clerical orders, though many became priests later in life. The most senior assistants were the deacon and subdeacon, who helped to prepare the altar, the bread and the wine; they were sometimes called the 'gospeller' and 'epistoller', since the deacon sang the gospel and the subdeacon the epistle. At the start of the service, clergy and their assistants processed into the church, led by the choir which included any chantry priests. Then came taperers bearing their candles, followed by the parish clerk or acolyte, who directed the ceremonial of the Mass. Next came the thurifer (incense bearer) with his censer or thurible, in front of the subdeacon, deacon and priest.

In the late middle ages, direct participation in the service by the congregation was very slight, as the

Fig. 7.6 The Gospel.
See p. 150.
(© Christopher
Daniell.)

emphasis was on the sacrifice performed at the altar by the priest and upon the prayers said by him and the other ministers. The liturgy was conducted almost entirely in the chancel, which was physically divided from the people in the nave by the rood screen. Relatively little of what the priest said was intended to be heard even by his assistants, and what might have been audible in the body of the church would have been largely unintelligible to the laity, since it was in Latin.

The separation between the activities of the lay folk and those of the clergy is apparent from the late-medieval *Lay Folks Mass Book*, which contains instructions for the conduct of the laity. From that, and from other sources, it is apparent that at High Mass they were expected to behave decently, and to recite the rosary. If literate, they followed the service in Primers, Books of the Hours of the Blessed Virgin Mary; if, not, they followed pictures in them. At only a few points did clerical and lay activity coincide. The most important came immediately after the consecration when the bread and wine were turned into the body of Christ. At that moment a small bell, the

Above:
Fig. 7.7 The start of the Offertory. See p. 151.
(© Allan B. Barton.)

Below:
Fig. 7.8 The Offertory.
See p. 152.

Above:
Fig. 7.9 The Preface.
See p. 154.

'sacring bell', was rung to attract the attention of those in the nave, who were supposed to kneel and behold the Body of Christ (the transformed Host) which the priest raised above his head in the rite called the Elevation of the Host.[2] After that, the priestly and lay devotions again diverged. The priest himself took communion, but lay folk were allowed to receive communion on only a few occasions in the year, and even then were given only the Host for fear they might

Fig. 7.10 Start of the
Canon of the Mass.
See p. 156.

Fig. 7.11 Blessing the Sacrament. See p. 157.

Fig. 7.12 Elevation of the Host. See p. 158 (© Allan B. Barton.) ..

Fig. 7.13 Elevation of the chalice. See p. 158.

spill the wine. In place of communion, the laity were allowed to kiss a 'pax' or 'paxbred', a wooden or metal disk bearing holy symbols, which the priest himself had kissed after first kissing the paten on which the Host had rested and the chalice. Finally, after the Mass, a loaf of bread donated by a parishioner and blessed beforehand by the priest was divided amongst the laity.[3]

Fig. 7.14 The breaking of the Body. See p. 162.

135

Fig. 7.15 The
Communion. See p. 163.

The Use of York

Although the basic structure of the Mass, and of the Offices and
liturgies for particular occasions, was the same throughout pre-
Reformation Catholic Europe, some places had their own variants.
The use of particular words or phrases, the readings and some of the
Propers could vary, as could parts of the ceremonial, and details such
as the colour of the vestments appropriate for occasions in the Church

Fig. 7.16 The Ablutions.
See p. 164.

..

Fig. 7.17 Departure from the altar. See p. 166. (© Christopher Daniell.)

Below:
Fig. 7.18 Coffin in the chancel, surrounded by candles. See p. 167. (© Christopher Daniell.)

year or for different types of service. The most widespread variant, or 'Use', in medieval England was the Use of Sarum, which was associated with the eleventh-century regulations established by St Osmund for use at Sarum, the early name for Salisbury.[4] Before the Reformation, several other cathedrals, notably Hereford, Lincoln and York, retained their own Uses, all of which were to some extent influenced by Sarum. Unless the cathedral was a monastery, as at Canterbury or Durham, parishes usually followed the practice of the cathedral of their diocese; in dioceses with monastic cathedrals, parishes in the Province of Canterbury tended to adopt the Use of Sarum and in the Province of York that of York Minster. The main differences between the Uses of York and Sarum, in addition to the Propers, lay in the calendar of observance of saints' days, and certain details of ceremonial.

Fig. 7.19 Censing the corpse. See p. 167. (© Christopher Daniell.)

Each Use was recorded in a number of books, which enabled all the services with their Propers, music and ceremonial to be to be conducted appropriately. In summary, the most important of the books were as follows. The Mass book or Missal contained the liturgy of the Mass. The plainchant for all the chanted scriptural passages, the Propers, was contained in a separate book, the Gradual. Forms for occasional services, including the Absolutions for the Dead, were in the Manual, and specific instructions for processions were in a Processional. The daily Offices were contained in the Breviary. Either within the Breviary or as separate books were the Legend or Lectionary (a book of lessons for each day), the Antiphonal (containing antiphons, psalms or sentences said or chanted by the choir and priest, or by different priests alternately), the Psalter and the Hymnal. The ceremonial, or rites, for the various services were in another volume, the Customary or Consuetudinary. Directions for celebrating services on the correct days throughout the year, both feasts that were fixed, such as Christmas, or moveable, such as Easter, were contained in an Ordinal or Pica.[5] Complicated though all this was (and it attracted specific condemnation at the Reformation, in the Book of Common Prayer),[6] every parish church needed to possess at least one copy of most of these books. In 1250 Archbishop Gray of York required every parish to possess a Missal, Gradual, Manual, Legend, Antiphonal, Psalter, Ordinal and Troper (containing musical elaborations and extensions). Although the vast majority of medieval service books were destroyed at the Reformation, at least one copy of each, apart from a Customary, survives for the Use of York.[7]

The Text

The text printed here is that of the Mass, together with the Propers for a Requiem, followed by the Absolutions for the Dead, after which the corpse was immediately removed to the churchyard for burial. Since they formed an important part of almost every other kind of Mass, and their omission would have limited the usefulness of the text as a whole, the Gloria and Creed have been included even though they did not form part of the Requiem Mass.

Fig. 7.20 Mourners after the service.
(© Christopher Daniell.)

In order to produce a version which is both readily intelligible and practical for actual use, the text presented here has drawn freely on all the published variants. It does not constitute a new edition, but is based upon the standard editions (produced in the nineteenth century) of the Missal, for the Mass, and of the Manual, for the Absolutions for the Dead. The Missal, in particular, is known from a number of manuscripts, but they do not always agree, particularly in the case of the rubrics, the instructions for ceremonial.

The lack of a Customary for the York Use means that the rubrics are particularly difficult to establish with certainty. The different versions of the Missal assist to some extent, but, in order that the reader can readily visualise the action of the Mass, some additional material has been inserted from the Use of Sarum, and a few other directions have been added for clarification: both kinds of addition are clearly indicated in the text. It is not always easy to establish which parts of the liturgy were spoken by the priest quietly to himself, loudly enough for his assistants in the chancel to hear, or in full voice which could be heard by the laity in the nave. In the text given below, where the readily available sources contain no specific instructions, a tentative interpretation has been made based upon comparable passages where the degree of audibility is indicated. This has proved more difficult for the Absolutions for the Dead than for the Mass itself. For these reasons, no claim is made for the precision of the reconstruction of all details of either the text itself or the ceremonial. It was also decided to make the translation fairly literal, rather than using the sometimes imprecise, though more elegant and familiar, phrases of the usual liturgy in English.

The text is that used at a reconstruction Requiem Mass held at All Saints', North Street, York, on 20 April 2002 in honour of Nicholas Blackburn junior, a merchant of the parish who died in 1448. Together with photographs taken at the reconstruction service it is hoped that the meaning of the liturgy will be conveyed, and that something of the experience of medieval parishioners attending Mass in their local church may be recaptured.

8

A note on the reconstructed Requiem Mass held at All Saints', North Street, York, on 20 April 2002

John Hawes with Lisa Colton

Reconstructing a pre-Reformation service requires not only the establishment of a suitable text and rubrics, but also an understanding of those parts of the ceremonial which were not written down, or for which written instructions have not survived. In the particular case of the Use of York, the fact that no Customary survives compounds the difficulties in relation to ceremonial, and necessitates supplementing the rubrics contained in the Missal with material derived from other sources.

The reconstruction held at All Saints', North Street, York, on 20 April 2002 was of a Requiem Mass according to the Use of York, and was held in memory of Nicholas Blackburn junior, a merchant of the parish, who died in 1448. The text of the Mass was essentially that given in the next section of this book and derived, according to the principles outlined in Chapter 7, from the standard printed edition of the York Use Missal, while the Absolutions for the Dead were taken from the printed edition of the Manual. Also as discussed in chapter 7, the rubrics were supplemented by reference to those known from the Use of Sarum. For matters of greater detail, however, the medieval materials were supplemented by illustrations (such as those in chapter 7) and by handbooks produced in the nineteenth and early twentieth centuries as part of the revival of traditional ceremonial in the Church of England. This newer literature supplements the medieval sources, attempting to fill the gaps in previous knowledge from the practical experience of conducting services.

Interest in reviving traditional ceremonial in the Church of England in the middle years of the nineteenth century was associated with both the Oxford Movement and the Cambridge Camden Society. It was mirrored by similar trends in the Roman Catholic church, which produced one of the earliest serious works of scholarship on medieval ceremonial, Daniel Rock's *The Church of Our Fathers as seen in St Osmund's Rite for the Cathedral of Salisbury,* which still provides one of the most comprehensive attempts to understand medieval liturgical practice.[1] It was not until half a century later, however, that a fully practical guide to ceremonial was produced, with the publication of Percy Dearmer's *The Parson's Handbook.*[2] Dearmer's aim was to prove that the early reformers had always intended continuity in ceremonial, and to demonstrate how appropriate pre-Reformation practices were to the Anglican church: this second element meant that the book had to be severely practical. Although the liturgy and its attendant ceremonial are simpler than those of the pre-Reformation church, and some aspects, such as the Elevation of the Host (specifically proscribed in the Book of Common Prayer), are omitted, Dearmer's work is the essential starting point for attempts at reconstruction.

From 1901 to 1916 Dearmer was vicar of St Mary the Virgin, Primrose Hill, which had, and still has, a tradition of maintaining the Sarum ritual. The All Saints' reconstruction drew extensively on experience gained at Primrose Hill over the last hundred years, as well as on the traditions of St Olave's, Marygate, York, and All Saints' itself, where, in the first half of the twentieth century, Patrick Shaw instituted practices similar to those at Primrose Hill (the tradition is described in P. J. Shaw, *An Old York Church*).[3]

The liturgical traditions of these churches have resulted in the acquisition, particularly at Primrose Hill, of many pre-Reformation vestments and ornaments, and of replicas of others, some of which were kindly made available for the All Saints' reconstruction and can therefore be seen in the illustrations to chapter 7. The choice of vestments was conditioned both by availability and by the uncertainty of what was appropriate for a mid fifteenth-century Requiem Mass according to the York Use, which may have resulted in some inaccuracies. The priest, deacon and subdeacon were provided with matching vestments of dark blue velvet made, according to medieval models, for Dearmer, and still used at Primrose Hill for Requiem services. The clerk, directing the ceremonial, was vested in a black tunicle of similar provenance and carried a processional cross made in about 1480, probably in London, and altered in the twentieth century. The processional lights borne by the taperers were, like the vestments, made for Dearmer, and the censer was a 1930s copy of the fourteenth-century Ramsey Censer, made as a memorial to Dearmer.

The All Saints' reconstruction included three pieces of polyphonic music. Since the death of Nicholas Blackburn junior predated the copying of the York Masses, the choir sang anonymous settings of the Sanctus, Benedictus and Agnus Dei, which were taken from the Old Hall Manuscript. This decision was made in order to reflect the kind of music current in York in the mid fifteenth century, which included squares from slightly older repertory known from Old Hall and elsewhere. In the fifteenth century, the choir would have performed the lowest part from the music, the 'square', and either have improvised two or three-part polyphony above, or used specially composed settings. Since the practice of using squares has died out, it was considered more appropriate to use the early fifteenth-century repertoire as it appeared in the Old Hall Manuscript than to try to create something new, with the attendant danger of anachronism. Although it is not known exactly what sort of music was originally performed in memory of Nicholas Blackburn junior, his standing in the community suggest that the use of polyphonic music from this prestigious source was entirely appropriate.

The Requiem Mass: text and translation

Compilers/translators:
P. S. Barnwell, Allan B. Barton and Ann Rycraft

Rubrics, which are in red type, are taken from manuscripts or pre-Reformation printed versions of the Use of York. They are drawn from several variants in order to create instructions which are readily performable, rather than reflecting any particular manuscript or edition.

In addition, in our English translation of the rubrics, further material, placed in square brackets, has been inserted from the Use of Sarum, as have some clarifications. In a few places we have omitted irrelevant material from the rubrics, such as specific instructions for major festivals; these omissions are indicated by an ellipsis in square brackets, thus […].

Instructions in blue are by the compilers.

Roman text is used for the words spoken or chanted by the Priest, italic for those of the Choir.

Places where the priest makes the sign of the cross are marked +.

The Propers are indicated by asterisks, ★.

The Gloria and Creed do not form part of the Requiem, but are used in most other forms of the Mass. They have been placed at the end, and their position indicated in the main text in square brackets.

Ordinary of the Mass

Sacerdos introiens ad altare, procedentibus in ordine ministris, dicat versiculum:

Priest to Ministers
Confitemini Domino quoniam bonus: quoniam in saeculum misericordia ejus.
Confessio.

Priest to Ministers
Confiteor Deo, beatae Mariae, omnibus sanctis, et vobis, fratres, quia ego peccator peccavi nimis corde, ore, opere, omissione, mea culpa: ideo precor gloriosissimam Dei genetricem Mariam et omnes sanctos Dei et vos orare pro me.

Misereatur vestri omnipotens Deus, et dimittat vobis omnia peccata vestra; liberet vos ab omni malo; conservet et confirmet in omni opere bono; et perducat vos ad vitam aeternam. Amen.

Priest to Ministers
Absolutionem et remissionem omnium peccatorum vestrorum, spatium verae paenitentiae, emendationem vitae, gratiam et consolationem Sancti Spiritus, tribuat vobis omnipotens et misericors Dominus.
Choir
Amen.
Factaque ante gradus altaris confessione, ascendat ad altare, dicens:

Priest in secret
Deus, tu conversus vivificabis nos;

Et plebs tua laetabitur in te.
Ostende nobis, Domine, misericordiam tuam.

The priest, approaching the altar (Fig. 7.1), with the ministers going in order before him (Fig. 7.2), is to say the versicle:

We confess to the Lord for [he is] good: for his mercy [is] everlasting.
[Then the priest is to say the] Confession, [the deacon assisting him on the right, and the subdeacon on the left](Fig. 7.3).

I confess to God, blessed Mary and all the saints, and to you brothers, because I, a sinner, have sinned exceedingly in heart, in mouth, in what is done, in what is left undone, by my fault; therefore I beseech Mary, the most glorious mother of God, and all the saints of God, and you, to pray for me.
[The deacon and subdeacon respond:]
May almighty God have mercy on you, and forgive you all your sins, deliver you from every evil, preserve and strengthen you in every good work and bring you to everlasting life. Amen.
[The deacon and subdeacon are then to make their confession in the same manner as the priest, and the priest is to respond in the same form as above.]
[The priest is to absolve them of their sins with a blessing:]

May the almighty and merciful God grant you absolution and remission of all your sins, space for true repentance, amendment of life, the grace and consolation of the Holy Spirit.

Amen.
And, the confession ended before the altar steps, he is to go up to the altar [with the deacon to his right and subdeacon to his left] saying:

O God, when you are turned [to us], you will give us life;
And your people will rejoice in you.
Show us, O Lord, your mercy.
And grant us your salvation.

Et salutare tuum da nobis.
Sacerdotes tui induantur justitiam
Et sancti tui exultent.
Domine, Deus virtutum, converte nos.
Et ostende faciem tuam, et salvi erimus.
Domine, exaudi orationem meam.
Et clamor meus ad te veniat.
Priest to Ministers
Dominus vobiscum.
Choir to Priest
Et cum spiritu tuo.
Inclinatus ad altare dicat:
Priest to Ministers
Oremus.
Aufer a nobis, Domine, omnes iniquitates nostras,
ut ad sancta sanctorum mereamur puris mentibus
introire. Per Christum Dominum nostrum.
Erectus signet se, et in dextro cornu altaris dicat
Officum.

Priest to all and Choir
*Requiem aeternam dona eis, Domine: et lux perpetua
luceat eis.
*Te decet hymnus, Deus, in Sion: et tibi reddetur votum
in Hierusalem: exaudi orationem meam: ad te omnis
caro veniet.

Kyrie Eleison, Kyrie Eleison.
Christe Eleison, Christe Eleison.
Kyrie Eleison, Kyrie Eleison.

Et postea incenset altare.

[Gloria]
Postea conversus sacerdos ad populum dicat:

Let your priests be clothed with righteousness
And let your saints rejoice.
O Lord, God of hosts, change us.
And show us your face, and we shall be saved.
Lord hear my prayer.
And let my cry come to you.

The Lord be with you.

And with your spirit.
Bowing to the altar he is to say:

Let us pray.
Take away from us, O Lord, all our iniquities, so
that with pure minds we may be worthy to enter
into the holy of holies. Through Christ our Lord.
Standing upright he is to sign himself [with the
cross], and at the right corner of the altar he is to
say the Office [or Introit appropriate for the day.
The deacon and subdeacon are to stand in line
behind him (Fig. 7.4). The Office done, he says
and the choir sings the Kyrie Eleison:]

*Eternal rest, grant to them, O Lord:
and let perpetual light shine upon them.
*A hymn is due to you, O God, in Sion: and to you
shall prayer be duly offered in Jerusalem: hear my prayer:
to you shall all flesh come.
[Psalms lxiv (lxv), verses 1-2.]
*Lord have mercy, Lord have mercy.
Christ have mercy, Christ have mercy.
Lord have mercy, Lord have mercy.*
[The deacon is to place incense in the censer, and
is to kiss the priest's hand.] And then [the priest]
is to cense the altar, [first on the right side, then
the midst, then on the left side. Then the priest
himself is to be censed by the deacon; and after
this, the priest is to kiss the text of the Gospel,
which the subdeacon is to bring to him. At a
Requiem Mass, after censing the celebrant, the
deacon goes down into the choir and censes the
corpse.]

Afterwards [signing himself on the face, the priest
is to return to the middle of the altar and the

Priest to all
Dominus vobiscum.
Choir to Priest
Et cum spiritu tuo.
Priest to Ministers
Et reversus dicat:
Oremus.
Cum Collecta
.Priest to Ministers

★Inclina, Domine, aurem tuam ad preces nostras, quibus misericordiam tuam supplices deprecamur, ut animam famuli tui, quam de hoc saeculo migrare jussisti, in pacis ac lucis regione constituas, et sanctorum tuorum jubeas esse consortem. Per Dominum nostrum Jesum Christum Filium tuum, qui tecum vivit et regnat, in unitate Spiritus Sancti Deus per omnia saecula saeculorum. Amen.

Dum legitur Epistola et canitur Graduale et Alleluya vel Tractus vel Tropus, sedeat cum ministris usque ad Evangelium legendum.

Minister to all
Lectio libri Machabaeorum:

In diebus illis, vir fortissimus Judas, collatione facta, duodecim millia drachmas argenti misit Ierosolymam, offerri pro peccatis mortuorum sacrificium, bene et religiose de resurrectione cogitans (nisi enim eos, qui ceciderant resurrecturos speraret, superfluum videretur, et vanum orare pro mortuis) et quia considerabat quod hi qui cum pietate dormitionem acceperant, optimam haberent repositam gratiam. Sancta ergo et salubris est cogitatio pro defunctis exorare, ut a peccatis solvantur.

Choir sing
★Requiem, aeternam dona eis, Domine: et lux perpetua luceat eis.

deacon and subdeacon are to stand in line behind him.] The priest having turned to the people is to say:

The Lord be with you.

And with your spirit.

And turning back to the altar he is to say:
Let us pray.
With the Collect

★Incline, O Lord, your ear to our prayers, by which we humbly beg your mercy that you will grant that the soul of your servant, which you have commanded to depart from this world, may dwell in the land of peace and light, and bid it be a companion of your saints. Through our Lord Jesus Christ your Son, who with you lives and reigns in the unity of Holy Spirit, throughout all ages. Amen.

While the Epistle is being read and the Gradual chanted, and an Alleluia, or a Tract or a Trope, [the priest] is to sit with the other ministers up to the reading of the Gospel.

[The subdeacon is to chant the Epistle] (Fig. 7.5):

A reading from the Book of Maccabees:
And in those days, the hero Judas, having made a collection, sent twelve thousand drachmas of silver to Jerusalem, to be offered, a sacrifice for the sins of the dead, thinking rightly and piously on the resurrection (for if he had not hoped that they who had died would be resurrected, it would seem vain and superfluous to pray for the dead) and also because he considered that they who accepted death with piety would have great grace in store. Therefore it is a holy and sound thought, to pray for the dead, that they may be delivered from sins.
[2 Maccabees, xii. 43-6.]
[After chanting the Epistle, the choir is to sing the Gradual]:

★Eternal rest grant to them, O Lord:
And perpetual light may shine upon them.

Absolve, Domine, animas eorum ab omni vinculo delictorum.

De profundis clamavi ad te, Domine: Domine, exaudi vocem meam.
Fiant aures tuae intendentes in orationem servi tui.
Si iniquitates observaveris, Domine: Domine, quis sustinebit?
Quia apud te propitiatio est: et propter legem tuam sustinui te, Domine.

Dum petit diaconus benedictionem, respondeat sacerdos, dicens:
Priest to Minister
Dominus aperiat tibi os ad legendum et nobis aures ad intelligendum sanctum Evangelium Dei pacis. In nomine Patris et Filii et Spiritus Sancti. Amen.
Et diaconus dicat:
Minister to Priest
Da mihi, Domine, sermonem rectum et benesonantem in os meum, ut placeant tibi verba mea et omnibus audientibus propter nomen tuum in vitam aeternam. Amen.

Minister to all
Secundum Johannem:
In illo tempore, dixit Martha ad Jesum; Domine, si fuisses hic, frater meus non fuisset mortuus: sed et nunc scio, quia quaecunque poposceris a Deo, dabit tibi Deus. Dicit illi Jesus: resurget frater tuus.

Free, O Lord, their souls from every bond of sins.

[and the Tract:]
Out of the depths I have cried to you, O Lord: O Lord, hear my voice.
O let your ears be attentive to the prayer of your servant.
If you will observe sins, O Lord: O Lord, who shall endure it?
For there is reconciliation with you, and because of your law I have upheld you, O Lord.
[Psalms, cxxix (cxxx) 1-4.]
[While the Gradual, Alleluia or Tract are being chanted the subdeacon is to take the bread, wine and water with the chalice, and prepare them for the Mass; the blessing of the water is first to be asked of the priest, the priest in the meantime sitting.
Then the deacon, before he goes and chants the Gospel, is to cense the middle of the altar only, for the lectern is never censed either at Mass or Matins before the Gospel. At a Requiem the deacon goes to the choir and censes the corpse.
Then he is to take the text, the book of the Gospels, and bowing to the Priest standing before the altar, turning his face south, request a blessing.]
When the deacon asks for a blessing, the priest is to answer, saying:

May the Lord open for you a mouth to read, and for us ears to understand, God's holy Gospel of peace. In the name of the Father and the Son and the Holy Spirit. Amen.
And the deacon is to say:

Put into my mouth, O Lord, a proper and well-sounding speech, that my words may please you and may profit all hearers on account of your name [and bring them] to eternal life. Amen.
[The deacon chants the Gospel:](Fig. 7.6)

According to John:
At that time Martha said to Jesus, 'Lord, if you had been here, my brother would not have died, and now I know that, because whatever you will ask of God, God will give it you.' Jesus says to her,

Dicit ei Martha: Scio, quia resurget in resurrectione in novissimo die. Dixit ei Jesus: Ego sum resurrectio et vita: qui credit in me, etiam si mortuus fuerit, vivet: et omnis qui vivit et credit in me non morietur in aeternum. Credis hoc? Ait illi: Utique Domine, ego credidi, quia tu es Christus, Filius Dei vivi, qui in hunc mundum venisti.

Post lectum Evangelium dicat sacerdos secrete:

Priest in secret
Benedictus qui venit in nomine Domini.
Postea osculetur textum.

[Creed]
Post conversus sacerdos ad populum dicat:

Priest to all
Dominus vobiscum.
Choir to Priest
Et cum spiritu tuo.
Et reversus dicat:
Priest to Ministers
Oremus.
Et canat cum suis ministris Offertorium.

Priest and Ministers together
★Domine Jesu Christe, rex gloriae, libera animas omnium fidelium defunctorum de manu inferni et de profundo lacu: libera eas de ore leonis, ne absorbeat eas tartarus, ne cadant in obscura tenebrarum loca: sed signifer sanctus Michael repraesentet eas in lucem sanctam, quam olim Abrahae promisisti et semini ejus.

★Sacerdos ad altare incipiat:
Priest to Ministers
★Hostias et preces tibi Domine, offerimus.
★ Chorus prosequatur:
★*Tu suscipe pro animabus illis quarum hodie memoriam agimus: fac eas, Domine, de morte transire ad vitam. Quam olim Abrahae promissisti.*

'Your brother will rise again.' Martha says to him, 'I know because he will rise again in the resurrection on the last day.' Jesus said to her, 'I am the resurrection and the life: he who believes in me, even though he were dead, shall live: and all who live and believe in me shall not die for ever. Do you believe this?' She says to him, 'Certainly, Lord, I have believed that you are Christ, son of the living God, who has come into this world.'
[John, xi. 21-7.]
After the Gospel has been read the priest is to say, in secret:

Blessed is he who comes in the name of the Lord. After this he is to kiss the text [of the Gospels, which the subdeacon offers him and then carries away pressed against his breast].

Afterwards the priest, having turned towards the people (Fig. 7.7), is to say:

The Lord be with you.

And with your spirit.
And, having turned back [to the altar], he is to say:

Let us pray.
And he is to chant the Offertory with his ministers.

★O Lord Jesu Christ, King of Glory, deliver the souls of all the faithful departed from the hand of hell, and from the deep pit: deliver them from the lion's mouth, lest hell swallow them up, lest they fall into the dark region of the shadows; but let St Michael the standard-bearer restore them to the holy light which you promised in time past to Abraham and his seed.
★Let the priest, at the altar, begin:

★We offer sacrifices and prayers to you, O Lord.
★ Let the choir continue:
★ *We offer sacrifices and prayers to you, O Lord. Accept them on behalf of those souls of whom we make memorial today; cause them, O Lord, to move from death to the life which you promised of old to Abraham.*

151

Postea lavet manus, et componat Hostiam super corporales pannos, et dicat:

Priest in secret
Suscipe, Sancta Trinitas, hanc oblationem, quam ego miser et indignus peccator offero in honore tuo, et beatae Mariae et omnium sanctorum tuorum, pro peccatis et offensionibus meis: et pro salute vivorum et requie fidelium defunctorum. In nomine Patris et Filii et Spiritus sancti. Amen.

Item calicem cum vino et aqua, et dicat:

Priest in secret
Acceptum sit omnipotenti Deo sacrificium istud. In nomine Patris et Filii et Spiritus Sancti. Amen.

Lavet manus, et dicat:
Priest in secret
Lavabo inter innocentes manus meas et circumdabo altare tuum, Domine.
Et hymnum.
Priest in secret
Veni, Creator Spiritus
Mentes tuorum visita
Imple superna gratia
Que tu creasti pectora.
Qui Paraclitus diceris
Donum Dei altissimi
Fons vivus, ignis, caritas
Et spiritalis unctio
Tu septiformis munere
Dextre Dei tu digitus
Tu rite promisso Patris

[As the deacon hands the host and chalice and paten to the priest let him kiss his hand.]
Then [the priest] is to wash hands (Fig. 7.8), and lay the Host on the corporal cloths and say:

Accept, O Holy Trinity, this oblation which I, miserable and unworthy sinner, offer in your honour and [in that] of the blessed Mary and of all your saints, for my sins and offences, and for the salvation of the living and repose of the faithful departed. In the name of the Father and the Son and the Holy Spirit. Amen.
Item the chalice with wine and water, and he is to say:

May this sacrifice be acceptable to Almighty God. In the name of the Father and the Son and the Holy Spirit. Amen.
[The priest is to kiss the paten and place it under the corporal to the right of the Host. This done, he is to take the censer from the deacon and cense the sacrifice three times, making the sign of the Cross over it; then round the chalice and Host; then between himself and the altar, saying 'Let my prayer go forth, O Lord, as incense, in the sight of your majesty'. After this the priest is to be censed by the deacon and the subdeacon is to bring him the text to kiss. At a requiem Mass the deacon censes the corpse directly after censing the priest.]
[The priest] is to wash hands and say:

I will wash my hands among the innocent and I will encircle your altar, O Lord.
And the hymn.

Come, Creator Spirit
Visit the minds of your people
Fill with heavenly grace
The hearts you have created.
You who are called the comforter,
The gift of God most high,
The living spring, fire, love
And spiritual anointing.
You are seven-form in gift,
You the finger of God's right hand,
You by the Father's promise duly

Sermone ditans guttura.
Accende lumen sensibus
Infude amorem cordibus
Infirma nostri corporis
Virtute firmans perpetuum
Hostem repellas longius
Pacemque dones protinus
Doctore sic te previo
Vitemus omne noxium
Per te sciamus, da Patrem
Noscamus atque filium.
Te utriusque spiritum
Credamus omni tempore
Deo Patri sit gloria
Et Filio qui a mortuis
Surrexit ac Paraclito
In saeculorum saecula.

Postea ante medium altaris inclinatus dicat:

Priest in secret
In spiritu humilitatis et animo contrito
suscipiamur a te, Domine, et sic fiat sacrificium
nostrum, ut a te suscipiatur hodie, et placeat tibi,
Domine Deus meus.

Et ingrediendo osculetur altare, et signet
sacrificium dicendo:

Priest in secret
Sit signatum+, ordinatum+, et sanctificatum +
hoc sacrificium nostrum.
Postea versus ad populum dicat:
Priest to all
Orate, fratres et sorores, pro me peccatore, ut
meum pariterque vestrum Domino Deo
acceptum sit sacrificium.
Chorus respondeat:
Choir to Priest
Exaudiat te Dominus in die tribulationis;
Protegat te nomen Dei Iacob.
Mittat tibi auxilium de sancto,
Et de Sion tueatur te.
Memor sit omnis sacrificii tui,
Et holocaustum tuum pingue fiat.

Endowing our mouths with speech.
Kindle light for our senses,
Pour love into our hearts,
Making firm forever by your strength
Our body's infirmities.
Drive far away the foe and
Grant us peace forthwith.
With you, our guide, thus before,
May we avoid all harm.
Grant that we, through you, may know the Father
and recognise the Son.
May we at all time believe
You the Spirit of them both.
To God the Father be glory
And the Son, who from the dead
Arose, and to the Comforter
For all ages.
[The priest is to return to the altar and the
ministers stand behind him.]
After this, bowing before the middle of the altar,
he is to say:

In the spirit of humility and with a contrite mind
may we be accepted by you, O Lord, and may our
sacrifice be so offered that it may be accepted by
you this day, and may it please you, O Lord, my
God.
And, having approached it, he is to kiss the altar,
and sign the sacrifice [with the sign of the cross],
saying:

May this our sacrifice be signed+, well-ordered+,
and sanctified+.
After this, turning to the people, he is to say:

Pray, brothers and sisters, for me, a sinner, that my
sacrifice and equally yours may be acceptable to
the Lord God.
The choir is to respond:

May the Lord hear you on the day of distress;
May the name of the God of Jacob protect you.
May he send help to you from the holy place,
And may he look upon you from Sion.
May he remember all your sacrifice,
And may your burnt offering be fat.

Post versus ad altare dicat Secretas:

Priest in secret
*Absolve, quaesumus, Domine, animam famuli tui ab omni vinculo delictorum, ut in resurrectionis gloria inter sanctos et electos tuos resuscitatus respiret.
Et concludat:
Priest in secret
Per Dominum nostrum Jesum Christum Filium tuum, qui tecum vivit et regnat in unitate Spiritus Sancti Deus,
Et dicat cum alta voce:
Priest to all
Per omnia saecula saeculorum.

Et sequator Praefatio quae pertinet ad diem:

Priest to Ministers
Dominus vobiscum.
Choir to Priest
Et cum spiritu tuo.
Priest to Ministers
Sursum Corda.
Choir to Priest
Habemus ad Dominum.
Priest to Ministers
Gratias agamus Domino Deo nostro.
Choir to Priest
Dignum et justum est.
Priest to Ministers
Vere dignum et justum est, aequum et salutare, nos tibi semper ut ubique gratias agere, Domine, sancte Pater, omnipotens aeterne Deus.
*Et te, Domine, suppliciter exorare, ut gregem tuum, pastor aeterne, non deseras, sed per beatos apostolos tuos continua protectione custodias: ut eisdem rectoribus gubernetur, quos operis tui vicarios eidem contulisti praeesse pastores.

*Et ideo cum angelis et archangelis, cum thronis et dominationibus cumque omni militia caelestis

Afterwards, turning to the altar, he is to say the Mysteries:

*Free, we beg you, O Lord, the soul of your servant from the chain of sins, so that he may, revived, live again in the glory of the resurrection among your saints and your chosen ones.
And he is to conclude:

Through our Lord Jesus Christ your Son, who lives and reigns with you, in the unity of the Holy Spirit, God,
And he is to say in a loud voice:

Throughout all ages.
[The subdeacon is to take the paten and the offertory veil from the deacon, and he is to give them to the clerk to hold until the Lord's Prayer. The clerk meanwhile is to stand behind the subdeacon.]
And the Preface which is proper to the day is to follow (Fig. 7.9):

The Lord be with you.

And with your Spirit.

Lift up your hearts.

We lift them up to the Lord.

Let us give thanks to the Lord our God.

It is fitting and right.

Truly it is fitting and right, just and for salvation to give thanks at all times and in all places to you, O Lord, holy Father, almighty eternal God.
*And to beseech you humbly, O Lord, not to abandon your flock, eternal shepherd, but to guard [it] through your apostles, with continual protection, so that it may be governed by those same rulers, whom you have appointed to be in authority, substitute shepherds of your work.
*And so with angels and archangels, with thrones and dominations and with all the company of the

exercitus hymnum gloriae tuae canimus, sine fine dicentes:

Hic erigat parum per sacerdos brachia sua, et jungat manus usque ad verbum in nomime Domini; tunc signet se in facie sua, et sic faciat in omnibus Missis per annum.

Choir
Sanctus, sanctus, sanctus, Dominus Deus Sabaoth, pleni sunt caeli et terra gloria tua. Hosanna in excelsis.
Bene+dictus qui venit, in nomine domine. Hosanna in excelsis.

heavenly host we sing a hymn of glory, saying without end:

Here the priest is to raise his arms for a brief time and to put hands together until the phrase 'in the name of the Lord'; then he is to sign himself [with the cross] on his face and he is to do so in all Masses throughout the year.

Holy, holy, holy, Lord God of Sabaoth, heaven and earth are filled with your glory. Hosanna in the highest.
Bles+sed is he who comes in the name of the Lord. Hosanna in the highest.

The Canon, or Still Mass

Junctis manibus sacerdos inclinetase se, dicens:

Priest in secret

Te igitur, clementissime Pater, per Jesum Christum Filium tuum Dominum nostrum, supplices rogamus ac petimus uti accepta habeas et benedicas
Hic faciat sacerdos tres cruces super calicem et panem, ita dicens:
Priest in secret

haec do+na, haec mu+nera, haec san+cta sacrificia illibata,
Hic elevet manus, dicens:
Priest in secret

imprimis quae tibi offerimus pro ecclesia tua sancta catholica, quam pacificare, custodire, adunare, et regere digneris toto orbe terrarum, una cum famulo tuo papa nostro N., et antistite nostro N., et rege nostro N.. Et omnibus orthodoxis atque catholicae et apostolicae fidei cultoribus.
Hic oret pro vivis.
Priest in secret

Memento, Domine, famulorum famularumque tuarum N. et omnium circumstantium atque omnium fidelium Christianorum quorum tibi fides cognita est et nota devotio; pro quibus tibi offerimus vel qui tibi offerunt hoc sacrificium laudis, pro se suisque omnibus, pro redemptione animarum suarum, pro spe salutis et incolumitatis suae, tibique reddunt vota sua aeterno Deo vivo et vero.
Priest in secret

Communicantes et memoriam venerantes, inprimis gloriosae semper virginis Mariae,
Hic parum inclinatus dicat ad istam septem verba sequentia:
Priest in secret

genetricis Dei et Domini nostri Jesu Christi, sed et beatorum apostolorum ac martyrum tuorum, Petri, Pauli, Andreae, Jacobi, Johannis, Thomae,

[As soon as the ministers have said the Sanctus and Benedictus, the deacon and subdeacon are to stand behind the priest.] With hands together the priest is to bow (Fig. 7.10), saying:

Therefore we suppliants ask you, O most merciful Father, through Jesus Christ, your Son, our Lord, and beg to you receive and bless

Here the priest is to make three crosses over the chalice and the bread, saying this:

these gi+fts, these offer+ings, these ho+ly undefiled sacrifices,
Here he is to raise the hands, saying:

firstly we offer to you for your holy catholic church, which you deign to keep in peace, to guard, to join together and to govern, throughout the whole world; together with your servant our Pope N., and our Archbishop N., and our King N., and all right believers and maintainers of the Catholic and Apostolic faith.
Here he is to pray for the living.

Remember, O Lord, your servants male and female, and all standing here, and all faithful Christians, whose faith is recognised and devotion known by you; for whom we offer to you, or who themselves offer to you, this sacrifice of praise, for themselves and all theirs, for the redemption of their souls, for the hope of their salvation and safety, and are rendering their vows to you, eternal God, living and true.

In communion with and venerating the memory, first, of the glorious and ever-virgin Mary,
Here let him, bowing slightly, say to her the following seven words:

mother of our God and Lord Jesus Christ, also of your blessed Apostles and Martyrs, Peter, Paul, Andrew, James, John, Thomas, James, Philip,

Jacobi, Phillippi, Bartholomaei, Matthaei, Simonis et Thaddaei, Lini, Cleti, Clementis, Sixti, Cornelii, Cypriani, Laurentii, Chrysogoni, Johannis et Pauli, Cosmae et Damiani, et omnium sanctorum tuorum, quorum meritis precibusque concedas, ut in omnibus protectionis tuae muniamur auxilio. Per eundem Christum Dominum nostrum. Amen.

Hic respiciat Hostiam cum veneratione, dicens:

Priest in secret

Hanc igitur oblationem servitutis nostrae, sed et cunctae familiae tuae, quaesumus, Domine, ut placatus accipias, diesque nostros in tua pace disponas, atque ab aeterna damnatione nos eripi, et in electorum tuorum jubeas grege numerari. Per Christum Dominum nostrum.
Amen.

Supra calicem:

Priest in secret

Quam oblationem tu, Deus omnipotens, in omnibus, quaesumus

Hic benedicatur ter tam super Hostiam quam super calicem, dicendo:

Priest in secret

bene+dictam, ascri+ptam, ra+tam, rationabilem, acceptabilemque facere digneris, ut nobis

Hic separatim signetur super Hostiam, dicendo:

Priest in secret

cor+pus

Hic super calicem:

Priest in secret

et san+guis fiat dilectissimi filii tui Domini nostri Jesu Christi.

Hic erigat sacerdos manus et conjungat: postea tangat digitos, et elevat Hostiam, dicens:

Priest in secret

Qui pridie quam pateretur, accepit panem in sanctas ac venerabiles manus suas, et elevatis oculis in caelum,

Hic elevet oculus, dicens.

Priest in secret

ad te Deum patrem suum omnipotentem,

Hic inclinet, dicens:

Bartholomew, Matthew, Simon and Thaddeus, Linus, Cletus, Clement, Sixtus, Cornelius, Cyprian, Lawrence, Chrysogonus, John and Paul, Cosmas and Damian, and of all your saints: To whose merits and prayers grant that we may in all things be defended by the help of your protection, through the same Christ, our Lord. Amen.

Here he is to look upon the Host with veneration, saying:

Therefore this offering of our service, as also of your whole household, we beseech you, O Lord, that being reconciled, you will accept, and will order our days in your peace, and command that we be delivered from eternal damnation and numbered in the flock of your chosen ones; through Christ our Lord. Amen.

Over the chalice:

Which oblation, we beseech you, O God Almighty, see fit to render altogether

Here a blessing is to be made three times over the Host and chalice (Fig. 7.11), saying:

bles+sed, appro+ved, con+firmed, reasonable and acceptable, that it may become for us

Here a separate sign is to be made over the Host, saying:

The Bo+dy

Here over the chalice:

and Blo+od of your most beloved Son, our Lord Jesus Christ.

Here the priest is to raise hands and join them; then touch fingers and elevate the Host, saying:

Who on the day before he suffered took bread into his holy and venerable hands, and his eyes raised up towards heaven,

Here he is to raise the eyes, saying:

to you, O God, his Father Almighty,

Here he is to bow, saying:

157

Priest in secret
Tibi gratias agens
Hic signet Hostiam, dicens:
Priest in secret
bene+dixit ac fregit
Hic tangat Hostiam, dicens:
Priest in secret
deditque discipulis suis, dicens, Accipite et
manducate ex hoc omnes.
Priest to all
Hoc est enim corpus meum.

Et debent ista verba proferri tam sub uno spiritu
quam sub una prolatione, nulla pausatione
interposita. Post haec verba inclinet se sacerdos ad
Hostiam et elevet eam supra frontem ut possit a
populo videri: nec nimis diu teneat elevatum, nec
aliqua parte sui corpus Christi tangi debet nisi
tantum digitis ad hoc specialiter consecratis.
Deinde reverentur illud reponat ante calicem in
modum crucis per idem factae, et tunc
discooperiat calicem et teneat inter manus suas,
non disjugendo pollicem ab indice nisi dum faciat
benedictionem, ita dicens:

Priest in secret
Simili modo posteaquam cenatum est, accipiens et
hunc praeclarum calicem in sanctas ac venerabiles
manus suas,
Hic inclinat se, dicens:
Priest in secret
item tibi gratias agens, bene+dixit, deditque
discipulis suis, dicens, Accipite et bibite ex eo
omnes.
Hic calicem parum levet, dicens:
Priest in secret
Hic est enim calix sanguinis mei novi et aeterni
testamenti, mysterium fidei, qui pro vobis et pro
multis effundetur in remissionem peccatorum.

Hic elevet calicem usque ad caput, dicens:

Priest in secret
Haec quotiescunque feceritis, in mei memoriam
facietis.

giving thanks to you
Here he is to sign the Host, saying:

he bles+sed and broke [it]
Here he is to touch the Host, saying:

and gave it to his disciples, saying, 'Take, all of you,
and eat of this.'

'For this is my Body.'
[The acolyte is to ring a small bell.]
And these words are to be said both with one
breath and in one delivery, no pause being
inserted. After these words the priest is to bow to
the Host and to raise it above the head so it can
be seen by the people (Fig. 7.12). He is not to
hold it aloft too long, nor should the Body of
Christ be touched by any part of his person,
except the part with the fingers specially
consecrated for this. Then he is to replace it
reverently in front of the chalice, in the manner of
a cross made by the same and then he is to
uncover the chalice and hold it in both hands,
without separating thumb from forefinger, except
when he is to pronounce the blessing, saying this:

In like manner after supper, taking also this most
excellent cup into his holy and venerable hands,

Here he is to bow, saying:

again giving thanks to you, he blessed it and gave
to his disciples, saying, 'Take, all of you, and drink
from this.'
Here he is to raise the chalice a little, saying:

For this is the cup of my Blood, of the new and
everlasting covenant, a mystery of faith, which
shall be shed for you and for many for the
remission of sins.
[The bell is rung again.] Here he is to raise the
chalice to head height (Fig. 7.13), saying:

As often as you do these things, you are to do
them in memory of me.

Hic reponat calicem et fricat digitos ultra calicem propter micas, et cooperiat, et elevet brachia in modum crucis junctis digitis usque ad haec verba, de tuis donis et datis, ita dicens:

Priest in secret
Unde et memores, Domine, nos tui servi, sed et plebs tua sancta ejusdem Christi Filii tui Domini Dei nostri tam beatae passionis, necnon et ab inferis resurrectionis, sed et in caelos gloriosae ascensionis, offerimus praeclarae maiestati tuae de tuis donis ac datis,

Hic tres cruces faciat super Hostiam et calicem, dicens:
Priest in secret
Hostiam pu+ram, Hostiam sanc+tam, Hostiam immac+ulatam,
Hic super Hostiam:
Priest in secret
panem sanc+tum vitae aeterne,
Hic super calicem:
Priest in secret
et calic+em salutis perpetuae. Supra quae propitio ac sereno vultu respicere digneris, et accepta habere sicut accepta habere dignatus es munera pueri tui justi Abel, et sacrificium patriarchae Abrahae, et quod tibi obtulit summus sacerdos tuus Melchisedech, sanctum sacrificium, immaculatam hostiam.

Hic inclinet corpus et manibus cancellatis ad modum crucis, dicat:
Priest in secret
Supplices te rogamus, omnipotens Deus, jube haec perferri per manus sancti angeli tui in sublime altare tuum, in conspectu divinae majestatis tuae, ut quotquot
Hic osculetur a dextris sacrificium.
Priest in secret
ex hac altaris participatione,
Osculetur altare a dextris sacrificii.
Priest in secret
sacrosanctum Filii tui
Hic signet super Hostiam, dicens:
Priest in secret
Cor+pus

Here he is to replace the chalice and rub the fingers together over the chalice because of crumbs, and cover [it] and raise the arms in the form of a cross with fingers together, until these words, 'of your gifts and presents', saying this:

Wherefore also we your servants, O Lord, as also your holy people, callers to mind of the blessed passion of the same Christ, your Son, our Lord God, as of his resurrection from the depths, and also of his ascension into the glorious heaven, do offer to your excellent majesty, of your gifts and presents,
Here he is to make three crosses over the Host and chalice, saying:

a pu+re sacrifice, a ho+ly sacrifice, an unde+filed sacrifice,
Here, over the Host:

the ho+ly bread of eternal life,
Here, over the chalice:

and the cha+lice of everlasting salvation. Upon which do you see fit to look with favourable and gracious countenance, and hold them accepted, as you saw fit to hold accepted the offerings of your righteous servant Abel, and the sacrifice of our forefather Abraham, and the holy sacrifice, the undefiled offering, which your high priest Melchizedek offered to you.
Here he is to bow the body and with hands crossed in the manner of a cross, is to say:

We suppliants ask that you, almighty God, command these things to be carried by the hands of your holy angels to your altar on high, in the sight of your divine majesty, so that as many as
Here he is to kiss the sacrifice from the right.

from this participation at the altar,
He is to kiss the altar from the right of the sacrifice.
your Son's holy
Here he is to make a sign over the Host, saying:

Bo+dy

Et super calicem.

Priest in secret

et san+guinem sumpserimus

Hic signet seipsum, dicens:

Priest in secret

omni bene+dictione caelesti et gratia repleamur. Per eundem Jesum Christum Dominum nostrum. Amen.

Hic oret pro mortuis.

Priest in secret

Memento etiam, Domine, famulorum famularumque tuarum N. et N., qui nos praecesserunt cum signo fidei, et dormiunt in somno pacis; ipsis, Domine, et omnibus in Christo quiescentibus locum refrigerii, lucis, et pacis ut indulgeas deprecamur. Per eundem Christum, Dominum nostrum. Amen.

Hic sacerdos percututiat pectus aliquantum altius dicens:

Priest to Ministers

Nobis quoque peccatoribus famulis tuis, de multitudine miserationum tuarum sperantibus, partem aliquam et societatem donare digneris, cum tuis sanctis apostolis et martyribus, cum Johanne, Stephano, Matthia, Barnaba, Ignatio, Alexandro, Marcellino, Petro, Felicitate, Perpetua, Agatha, Lucia, Agnete, Caecilia, Anastasia, et cum omnibus sanctis tuis, intra quorum nos consortium non aestimator meriti, sed veniae, quaesumus, largitor admitte. Per Christum, Dominum nostrum. Amen.

Priest to Ministers

Per quem haec omnia, Domine, semper bona creas,

Hic signet ter tam Hostiam quam calicem, dicendo:

Priest to Ministers

sancti+ficas, vivi+ficas, bene+dicis, et praestas nobis.

Postea discooperiat calicem et signet cum Hostia quinquies, primo ultra calicem ex utraque parte, dicens:

Priest to Ministers

Per ip+sum

secundo calici aequale, dicens:

And over the chalice.

and bl+ood shall consume

Here he is to sign himself, saying:

may be filled with every heavenly blessing and grace. Through the same Jesus Christ, our Lord. Amen.

Here he is to pray for the dead.

Remember also, O Lord, your servants both male and female N. and N., who have gone before us with the sign of faith, and sleep the sleep of peace; to them, O Lord, and to all resting in Christ, we entreat you to grant a place of refreshment, light, and peace. Through the same Christ, our Lord. Amen.

Here the priest is to beat the breast saying somewhat more loudly:

To us sinners also, your servants, hoping in the multitude of your mercies, deign to grant some part and fellowship with your holy apostles and martyrs, with John, Stephen, Matthias, Barnabas, Ignatius, Alexander, Marcellinus, Peter, Felicity, Perpetua, Agatha, Lucy, Agnes, Cecilia, Anastasia, and with all your saints, into whose company we beseech you admit us, not as one weighing our merits, but as pardoner, freely, of our sins. Through Christ, Our Lord. Amen.

By whom, O Lord, you ever create good things,

Here he is to sign both the Host and the chalice three times, saying:

sanc+tifiy, fill + with life, bles+s, and bestow upon us [these things].

Then he is to uncover the chalice and sign it with the Host five times, the first above the chalice on each side, saying:

Through hi+m

the second level with the chalice, saying:

Priest to Ministers
et cum ip+so
tertia infra calicem, dicens:
Priest to Ministers
et in ip+so
quarto ut primo, dicens:
Priest to Ministers
est tibi Deo Patri omni+potenti in unitate
quinto ante calicem, dicens:
Priest to Ministers
Spiritus + Sancti omnis honor et gloria

Hic reponat Hostiam super corporale, et cooperiat calicem sacerdos, et teneat manus super altare usque Pater Noster, et dicat excelsa voce:

Priest to all
Per omnia saecula saeculorum.
Oremus.
Praeceptis salutaribus moniti, et divina institutione formati, audemus dicere:
Hic levet manus.
Priest to all
Pater noster, qui es in caelis: sanctificetur nomen tuum: adveniat regnum tuum: fiat voluntas tua, sicut in caelo, et in terra. Panem nostrum quotidianum da nobis hodie: et dimitte nobis debita nostra, sicut et nos dimittimus debitoribus nostris. Et ne nos inducas in tentationem.
Hic sacerdos tacita voce, dicat:
Priest in secret
Amen.
Hic accipiat diaconus patenam a manu subdiaconi [...] et stet a dextris sacerdotis, patena discooperta, usque da propitius pacem [...]

Priest in secret
Libera nos, quaesumus, Domine, ab omnibus malis, praeteritis, praesentibus, et futuris: et intercedente pro nobis beata et gloriosa semper virgine Dei genetrice Maria et beatis apostolis tuis Petro et Paulo atque Andrea, cum omnibus sanctis,
Hic committat diaconus patenam sacerdoti osculans manum ejus, et postea ponat ad sinistrum oculum, deinde ad dextrum. Postea faciat crucem cum patena ultra caput, et tunc reponat eam in locum suum, dicens:

and with hi+m
the third below the chalice, saying:

and in hi+m
the fourth as the first, saying:

to you, God the Father Al+mighty, in the unity
the fifth in front of the chalice, saying:

of the Holy + Spirit, all honour and glory belong to you
Here the priest is to replace the Host on the corporal and cover the chalice and hold hands over the altar until 'Our Father' and say or chant in a raised voice:

Throughout all ages.
Let us pray.
Admonished by soul-saving precepts and formed by divine instruction, we are bold to say:
Here he is to raise the hands.

Our Father, who is in heaven: may your name be sanctified: may your kingdom come: let your will be done as in heaven so on earth. Give us this day our daily bread: and forgive us our debts, as we forgive our debtors. And do not bring us into temptation.
Here the priest is to say, in a low voice:

Amen.
Here the deacon is to receive the paten from the hand of the subdeacon [...] and to stand on the right of the priest, with the paten uncovered, until 'favourably grant peace' [...]

Deliver us, we beg you, O Lord, from all evils past, present and to come; and by the interceding for us of the blessed and glorious ever-virgin mother of God, Mary, and your blessed apostles Peter and Paul and Andrew with all the saints,
Here the deacon is to hand the paten to the priest, kissing his hand, and then place it before his left eye, then his right. Then he is to make a cross with the paten above the head, and then replace it in its place, saying:

da propitius pacem in diebus nostris, ut ope misericordiae tuae adjuti, et a peccato simus semper liberi, et ab omni perturbatione securi.

Hic discooperiat calicem et sumat corpus Christi cum inclinatione transponens in concavitatem calicis retinendo per pollices et indices, et frangat in tres partes, prima fractio verum dum dicit:

Priest in secret

Per eundem Dominum nostrum Jesum Christum Filium tuum qui tecum vivit regnat in unitate Spiritus Sancti, Deus,

Hic teneat duas fracturas in sinistra manu, et tertiam fracturam in dextra manu in summitate calicis, dicens:

Priest to all

Per omnia saecula saeculorum.

Pax Dom+ini sit sem+per vo+biscum.

Ad Agnus Dei dicendum accedat diaconus ad sacerdotem, scilicet a dextris ejus, et dicat privatim:

Priest in secret

*Agnus Dei, qui tollis peccata mundi, dona eis requiem.

Agnus Dei, qui tollis peccata mundi, dona eis requiem.

Agnus Dei, qui tollis peccata mundi, dona eis requiem sempiternam.

Hic deponat tertiam partem Hostiae in sanguine, dicens:

Priest in secret

Haec sacrosancta commixtio corporis et sanguinis Domini nostri Jesu Christi, fiat nobis et omnibus sumentibus salus mentis et corporis; et ad vitam aeternam capessendam preparatio salutaris. Per eundem Dominum nostrum Jesum Christum Filium tuum, qui tecum vivit et regnat, in unitate Spiritus Sancti Deus, per omnia saecula saeculorum. Amen.

Deinde osculetur corporalia in dextra parte, et postea tangat summitatem calicis infra cum Hostia, et tunc deosculetur calicem, et postea diaconum, et dicat:

Priest to Ministers

Habete vinculum pacis et caritatis, ut apti sitis sacrosancti mysteriis Dei.

favourably grant peace in our days, that we, aided by the help of your mercy, may be always free from sin, and safe every trouble.

Here he is to uncover the chalice and, bowing, take the Body of Christ, moving it over into the bowl of the chalice, holding [it] between thumbs and forefingers, and break it into three parts (Fig. 7.14), the first break [being made] while he says:

Through the same, our Lord, Jesus Christ your Son, who lives and reigns with you, in the unity of the Holy Spirit, God,

Here he is to take two broken pieces in the left hand and a third broken piece in the right had, on the rim of the chalice, saying:

Throughout all eternity.

The peace of the Lo+rd be alw+ays with y+ou.

At the saying of the 'Lamb of God' the deacon is to go to the priest, that is to say on his right, and say to himself:

*O Lamb of God, you who take away the sins of the world, grant them rest.

O Lamb of God, you who take away the sins of the world, grant them rest.

O Lamb of God, you who take away the sins of the world, grant them eternal rest.

Here he is to place the third part of the Host in the Blood, saying:

May this most holy mingling of the Body and Blood of our Lord Jesus Christ be for us and for all who receive it, salvation of mind and body, and a saving preparation for laying hold on eternal life. Through the same, our Lord, Jesus Christ your Son, who with you lives and reigns in the unity of the Holy Spirit, God, throughout all ages. Amen.

Then he is to kiss the corporals on the right side, and next touch the top of the inside of the chalice with the Host, and then kiss the chalice and after that the deacon, and say:

Receive the bond of peace and charity that you may be fit for the mysteries of God most holy.

Diaconus a dextris sacerdotis pacem recipiat ab eo, et det primo praelato si praesens fuerit, deinde aliis ministris [...]. In Missis vero pro defunctis nulla pax detur, sed sacerdos deosculetur corporalia in dextra parte et summitatem calicis ut supra.

Post pacem datam dicat sacerdos orationes sequentes privatim antequam se communicet, tenendo Hostiam duabus manibus, ita dicens:

Priest to Ministers
Oremus.
Priest in secret
Domine, sancte Pater, omnipotens aeterne Deus, da nobis hoc corpus et sanguinem Filii tui Domini Dei nostri Jesu Christi ita sumere ut mereamur per hoc remissionem peccatorum nostrorum accipere et tuo Sancto Spiritu repleri; quia tu es Deus et praeter te non est alius, nisi tu solus. Qui vivis et regnas Deus, per omnia saecula saeculorum.
Priest to Ministers
Oremus.
Priest in secret
Perceptio corporis et sanguinis tui, Domine Jesu Christe, quam indignus sumere praesumo, non mihi veniat ad judicium nec ad condemnationem, sed pro tua pietate prosit mihi ad tutamentum animae et corporis. Qui cum Deo Patre et Spiritu Sancto vivis et regnas Deus, Per omnia saecula saeculorum.
Priest to Ministers
Oremus.
Priest in secret
Domine Jesu Christi, Fili Dei vivi, qui ex voluntate Patris, cooperante Spiritu Sancto, per mortem tuam mundum vivificasti; libera me, per hoc sacrosanctum corpus et sanguinem tuum ab omnibus iniquitatibus et universis malis meis; et fac me tuis obedire praeceptis, et a te nunquam in perpetuum separari permittas. Qui cum Deo Patre et eodem Spiritu Sancto vivis et regnas Deus, per omnia saecula saeculorum. Amen.

Hic sumat corpus, cruce prius facta cum ipso

The deacon on the right of the priest is to receive the peace from him, and give first to the prelate, if he is present, then to the other ministers [...]. But in Masses for the Dead no peace is given, but the priest is to kiss the corporals on the right side and the top of the chalice, as above.

After the peace has been given, [the deacon and subdeacon again standing in line behind the celebrant,] the priest is to say the following prayers to himself, before he takes communion, holding the Host in two hands, saying this:

Let us pray.

O Lord, holy Father, Almighty everlasting God, grant us so to receive this Body and Blood of your Son our Lord God Jesus Christ, that we may be worthy hereby to receive remission of our sins and to be filled by your Holy Spirit; for you are God, and beside you, there is no other, but you alone. Who lives and reigns God, throughout all ages.

Let us pray.

May the taking of your Body and Blood, O Lord Jesus Christ, which I unworthily presume to receive, come to me neither as judgement nor as condemnation, but for your mercy's sake may it be profitable to me for the protection of soul and body. Who with God the Father and the Holy Spirit lives and reign God, throughout all ages.

Let us pray.

O Lord Jesus Christ, Son of the living God, who by the will of the Father, and with the co-operation of the Holy Spirit, has by your death given life to the world; deliver me by this your most holy Body and Blood from all my iniquities and my entire wickednesses; and make me obey your commandments, and never for all time allow me to be separated from you; who with God the Father and the same Holy Spirit lives and reigns God, throughout all ages. Amen.
Here he is to receive the Body (Fig. 7.15), having

corpore ante os, deinde ad sanguinem, dicens:

Corpus Domini nostri Jesu Christi sit mihi remedium sempiternum in vitam aeternam. Amen.

Sanguis Domini nostri Jesu Christi conservet me in vitam aeternam. Amen.

Ante perceptionem corporis et sanguinis Domini dicatur haec oratio:

Corpus et sanguis Domini nostri Jesu Christi custodiant corpus meum et animam meam in vitam aeternam. Amen.

Hic sumat sanguinem.

*Lux aeterna luceat eis, Domine: cum sanctis tuis in aeternum, quia pius es.
*Requiem aeternam dona eis, Domine: et lux perpetua luceat eis. Cum sanctis tuis in aeternum, quia pius es.

[Sanguine] sumpto eat sacerdos ad dextrum cornu altaris cum calice inter manus, adhuc digitis junctis sicut prius; et accedat thurifer, et tradat subdiacono fiolam cum vino ut ipse calici infundat, et resinceret manus suas sacerdos, ne reliquiae aliae corporis et sanguinis remaneant in digitis vel in calice. [...] et post primam ablutionem sequatur oratio hoc modo:

Quod ore sumpsimus, Domine, pura mente capiamus; et de munere temporali fiat nobis remedium sempiternum in vitam eternam. Amen.

Hic lavet digitos suos in concavitate calicis cum infusione vini a subdiacono. Quo hausto sequatur oratio:

Haec nos, Domine, communio purget a crimine, et caelestis remedii faciat esse consortes. Per Christum Dominum nostrum. Amen.

first made the cross with that Body, before his face, them towards the Blood, saying:

May the Body of our Lord Jesus Christ be to me an everlasting healing, bringing eternal life. Amen.

The Blood of our Lord Jesus Christ preserve me for everlasting life. Amen.

Before the receiving of the Body and Blood of the Lord, this prayer is to be said:

May the Body and Blood of our Lord Jesus Christ preserve my body and spirit for eternal life. Amen.

Here he is to receive the Blood.
[The priest is to say and the choir to chant the Communion:]

*May eternal light shine on them, O Lord, with your saints for ever, for you are compassionate.
*Grant eternal rest to them, O Lord, and may perpetual light shine upon then, with your saints for ever, for your are compassionate.

[The Blood] having been received, the priest is to go to the right corner of the altar with the chalice in his hands, the fingers still joined as previously, and the thurifer is to approach and hand to the subdeacon the cruet with the wine in it, so he may pour it into the chalice, and the priest is to rinse his hands, so that no remnants of the Body or Blood may remain on the fingers or in the chalice [...] and after the first washing a prayer is to follow, thus:

What we have taken with the mouth, O Lord, may we receive with a pure mind; and from a worldly gift may it become for us an everlasting remedy bringing eternal life. Amen.

Here he is to wash his fingers in the bowl of the chalice with the infusion of the wine from the subdeacon (Fig. 7.16). With this completed, a prayer is to follow:

May this communion, O Lord, cleanse us from guilt, and make us to be sharers of the heavenly healing. Through Christ our Lord. Amen.

Hic similiter infundat subdiaconus vinum in calicem; quo hausto eat sacerdos in medium altaris, et reponat calicem super patetam, et inclinet se, et dicat:

Priest in secret

Gratias tibi ago, Domine, sancte Pater, omnipotens aeterne Deus, qui me refecisti de sacratissimo corpore et sanguine Filii tui Domine nostri Jesu Christi, et precor ut hoc sacramentum salutis nostrae quod sumpsi indignus peccator non veniat mihi ad judicium neque ad condemnationem pro meritis meis, sed ad perfectum corporis mei et animae saluti in vitam aeternam. Amen.

Et cum oratione eat sacerdos ad dextrum cornu altaris, ut ipse thurifer det sacerdoti aquam in sacrario, ceroferario tenente pelves, et dum fiant, diaconus replicet corporalia, et postea ad dextrum cornu altaris librum portet. Deinde accipiat diaconus calicem jacentem super patenam, et si quid infusionis in ea remanserit ori sacerdotis venientis a dextro cornu altaris porrigat resumendum: et postea involvat calicem in aquilonari parte altaris, et superponat corporalia et tradat subdiacono vel acolytho [...]. Post perceptionem sacramenti et ablutionem manuum, vertat se sacerdos ad dextrum cornu altaris versus populum, et dicat Communionem et cetera.

Priest in secret

★Annue nobis, Domine, ut anima famuli tui remissionem quam semper optavit, mereatur precipere peccatorum. Per Dominum nostrum Jesum Christum Filium tuum, qui tecum vivit et regnat in unitate Spiritus Sancti Deus,

Priest to all

Per omnia saecula saeculorum.

Choir to all

Amen.

Finita Missa, sacerdos, corpore inclinato, junctis manibus, tacita voce coram medio altaris, dicat hanc orationem:

Priest in secret

Placeat tibi, Sancta Trinitas, obsequium servitutis

Here as before the subdeacon is to pour wine into the chalice; this being done, the priest is to go to the middle of the altar and replace the chalice on the paten, and he is to bow, and say:

I thank you, O Lord, holy Father, almighty eternal God, who has restored me by the most holy Body and Blood of your Son our Lord Jesus Christ, and I pray that this sacrament of our salvation which I, an unworthy sinner, have received, may not come to me as a judgement nor condemnation on account of my deserts, but for the perfection of my body and the salvation of my soul for eternal life. Amen.

And with the prayer, the priest is to go to the right corner of the altar, so that the same thurifer may give water to the priest in the sacrarium, the taperer holding the basins, and while they are doing [this] the deacon is to fold the corporals and then carry the book to the right corner of the altar. Then the deacon is to take the chalice, lying on the paten, and if any of the infusion remains in it, present [it] to the mouth of the priest coming from the right corner of the altar, for drinking again, and then he is to cover up the chalice on the north side of the altar, and place the corporals over it, and hand [it] to the subdeacon or acolyte [...]. After the receiving of the sacrament and washing of hands, the priest is to turn himself towards the right corner of the altar, facing the people, and he is to say the Communion, etc.

★Grant us, O Lord, that the soul of your servant may be worthy to receive the remission of sins which he always desired. Through our Lord Jesus Christ your Son who lives and reigns with you in the unity of the Holy Spirit, God,

Throughout all ages.

Amen.

The Mass ended, the priest, with bowed body, hands joined, is to say this prayer in a low voice, at the middle of the altar:

May the reverence of my service be pleasing to

meae, et praesta ut hoc sacrificium quod oculis tuae majestatis indignus obtuli, tibi sit acceptabile, mihique et omnibus pro quibus illud obtuli, sit, te miserante, propitiabile. Qui vivis et regnas Deus per omnia saecula saeculorum. Amen.

you, Holy Trinity, and grant that this sacrifice which I, unworthy, have offered to the eyes of your majesty, may be acceptable to you, and by your mercy conciliatory for me and all for whom I have offered it, O you who live and reign God throughout all ages. Amen.

[All three ministers are to go to the altar, bow to it, and then leave in order (Fig. 7.17).]

The Absolutions of the Dead (Fig. 7.18)

Post Missam sacerdos in albis et capatus solus capa serica cum suis in albis aspergat et incenset corpus.

Interim cantetur Responsorium:

Choir

Subvenite sancti Dei; occurite, angeli Domini, suscipientes animam eius offerentes eam in conspectu altissimi. Suscipiat te Christus qui vocavit te, et in sinu Abrahae angeli deducant te.

Choir

Kyrie Eleison.
Christe Eleison.
Kyrie Eleison.

Choir

Pater Noster, qui es in caelis: sanctificetur nomen tuum: adveniat regnum tuum: fiat voluntas tua, sicut in caelo, et in terra. Panem nostrum quotidianum da nobis hodie: et dimitte nobis debita nostra, sicut et nos dimittimus debitoribus nostris. Et ne nos inducas in tentationem. Amen.

Priets to Ministers

Oremus:

Priest in secret

Non intres in judicum cum servo tuo, Domine, quoniam nullus apud te justificabitur homo, nisi per te omnium peccatorum suorum tribuatur remissio. Non ergo eum, quaesumus, tua judicialis sententia premat, quem tibi vera supplicatio fidei Christianae commendat, sed gratia tua illi succurrente mereatur evadere judicium ultionis, qui dum viveret insignitus est signaculo Sanctae Trinitatis. Per Christum Dominum nostrum. Amen.

Corpus thurificetur, dum canitur Responsorium:

Choir

Antequam nascerer, novisti me: ad imaginem tuam, Domine, formasti me. Modo reddo tibi creatori animam meam. Commisa mea pavesco, et ante te erubesco: dum veneris judicare, noli me condemnare.

After Mass the priest in albs and cloaked only with a silk cope with his [ministers] in albs is to asperge and cense the corpse.

Meanwhile the Responsory is to be chanted:

Bring help, O saints of God, speed, angels of the Lord, bearing his soul, offering it up in the sight of the most high. May Christ who called you receive you, and may angels lead you to the bosom of Abraham.

Lord have mercy.
Christ have mercy.
Lord have mercy.

Our Father who is in heaven: may your name be sanctified: may your kingdom come: let your will be done, as in heaven so on earth. Give us this day our daily bread: and forgive us our debts, as we forgive our debtors. And do not bring us into temptation. Amen.

Let us pray:

Enter not into judgement with your servant, O Lord, for with you shall no man be justified, except he be granted through you the remission of all his sins. We beg you therefore to grant that the verdict of your judgement may not weigh heavy upon one whom the fervent supplication of Christian faith commends to you, but by your grace he may deserve to escape the judgement of retribution, [he] who while he lived was signed with the sign of the Holy Trinity. Through Christ our Lord. Amen.

The corpse is to be censed (Fig. 7.19), while the Responsory is chanted:

Before I was born you knew me: you formed me, O Lord, in your image. Now I return my soul to you the creator. I am appalled at my faults and I blush before you. When you come to judge do not condemn me.

Choir

Choir

Kyrie Eleison.
Christe Eleison.
Kyrie Eleison.

Lord have mercy.
Christ have mercy.
Lord have mercy.

Choir

Pater Noster, qui es in caelis: Sanctificetur nomen tuum: adveniat regnum tuum: fiat voluntas tua, sicut in caelo, et in terra. Panem nostrum quotidianum da nobis hodie: et dimitte nobis debita nostra, sicut et nos dimittimus debitoribus nostris. Et ne nos inducas in tentationem. Amen.

Our Father who is in heaven: may your name be sanctified: may your kingdom come: let your will be done, as in heaven so on earth. Give us this day our daily bread: and forgive us our debts, as we forgive our debtors. And do not bring us into temptation. Amen.

Priest to Ministers

Oremus.

Let us pray.

Priest in secret

Deus, cui omnia vivunt, et cui non pereunt moriendo corpora nostra sed mutantur in melius, te supplices deprecamur, ut quicquid anima famuli tui vitiorum tuaeque voluntati contrarium, fallente diabolo et propria iniquitate atque fragilitate, contraxerit, tu pius et misericors abluas indulgendo, eamque suscipi jubeas per manus sanctorum angelorum tuorum deducendam in sinibus patriarcharum tuorum Abraham scilicet amici tui et Isaac electi tui atque Jacob dilecti tui, quo aufugit dolor et tristitia atque suspirium, fidelium quoque animae plena felicique jocunditate laetantur, ut in novissimo magni judicii die inter sanctos et electos tuos eam facias perpetuae gloriae percipere portionem, quam oculus non vidit nec auris audivit nec in cor hominis ascendit, quam praeparasti diligentibus te. Praestante Domino nostro Jesu Christo, qui tecum vivat et regat in unitate Spiritus Sancti Deus, per ominia saecula saeculorum. Amen.

O God, for whom all things live, and for whom our bodies, when they die are not destroyed, but are transformed into a better [estate]: we suppliants beseech you that whatsoever wrong and defiance of your will the soul of your servant may have conceived, through deception of the devil and by its own iniquity and frailty; that you being just and merciful may wash away in forgiveness and bid that [his soul] be carried by the hands of your holy angels to be placed in the bosoms of your patriarchs, that is to say of Abraham your friend, and Isaac your chosen, and Jacob your beloved, where grief flees and sorrow and sadness, and where the souls of the faithful, filled with joy and happiness, rejoice, so that on the last day of the great judgement you will cause [his soul] to receive, among your saints and chosen ones, the portion of eternal glory, which eye has not seen nor ear heard, nor has it entered into the heart of man, which you have prepared for those who love you. Through Jesus Christ our glorious Lord, who lives and reigns with you in the unity of the Holy Spirit, God, for all eternity. Amen.

Corpus incensetur, dum cantatur Responsorium:

The body is to be censed, while the Responsory is chanted:

Choir

Heu mihi, Domine, quia peccavi nimis in vita mea! Quid faciam miser? Ubi fugiam, nisi ad te Deus meus? Miserere mei, dum veneris in novissimo die. Anima mea turbata est valde: sed tu, Domine, succurre ei dum veneris in novissimo die.

Woe is me, O Lord, for I have sinned exceedingly in my life! What shall I, a wretch, now do? Whither shall I fly, if not to you, my God? Have mercy on me, when you come on the last day. My soul is greatly troubled: but you, O Lord, succour it when you come on the last day.

168

Choir

Kyrie Eleison.
Christe Eleison.
Kyrie Eleison.

Choir

Pater Noster, qui es in caelis: sanctificetur nomen tuum: adveniat regnum tuum: fiat voluntas tua, sicut in caelo, et in terra. Panem nostrum quotidianum da nobis hodie: et dimitte nobis debita nostra, sicut et nos dimittibus debitoribus nostris. Et ne nos inducas in tentationem. Amen.

Priest to Ministers

Oremus.

Priest in secret

Fac, quaesumus, Domine, hanc cum servo tuo N. defuncto misericordiam, ut factorum suorum in paenis non recipiat vicem, qui tuam in votis tenuit voluntatem: ut sicut hic eum vera fides junxit fidelium turmis, ita cum illic tua miseratio societ angelicis choris. Per Christum Dominum nostrum. Amen.

Choir

Kyrie Eleison.
Chiste Eleison.
Kyrie Eleison.

Hic roget circumstantes orare pro eo. Sine nota:

Choir to Priest

Pater Noster, qui es in caelis: sanctificetur nomen tuum: adveniat regnum tuum: fiat voluntas tua, sicut in caelo, et in terra. Panem nostrum quotidianum da nobis hodie: Et dimitte nobis debita nostra, sicut et nos dimittimus debitoribus nostris. Et ne nos inducas in tentationem. Amen.

Priest to all

Requiem aeternam dona eis, Domine:

Choir to Priest

Et lux perpetua luceat eis.

Priest to all

Credo videre bona Domini:

Choir to Priest

In terra viventium.

Priest to all

A porta inferi:

Choir to Priest

Erue, Domine, animas eorum.

Lord have mercy.
Christ have mercy.
Lord have mercy.

Our Father who is in heaven: may your name be sanctified: may your kingdom come: let your will be done, as in heaven so on earth. Give us this day our daily bread: and forgive us our debts, as we forgive our debtors. And do not bring us into temptation. Amen.

Let us pray.

Show, we beg you, O Lord, this mercy towards your departed servant N. that he should not receive requital of his deeds, who in his prayers kept your will, so that, just as here true faith joined him to the army of the faithful, so in the other [world] your mercy may ally him with the angelic choirs. Through Christ our Lord. Amen.

Lord have mercy.
Christ have mercy.
Lord have mercy.

Here he is to ask those standing round to pray for him. Without music:

Our Father who is in heaven: may your name be sanctified: may your kingdom come: let your will be done, as in heaven so on earth. Give us this day our daily bread: and forgive us our debts, as we forgive our debtors. And do not bring us into temptation. Amen.

Eternal rest grant to them O Lord:

And let light perpetual shine upon them.

I believe [I shall] see the good [works] of the Lord:

In the land of the living.

From the gate of hell:

Deliver their souls, O Lord.

Priest to all
Dominus vobiscum
Choir to Priest
Et cum spirtu tuo.
Priest to all
Oremus.

Priest to all
Miserere, quaesumus, Domine, animabus omnium benefactorum nostrorum defunctorum, et de beneficiis quae nobis largiti sunt in terris praemia aeterna consequantur in caelis. Per Dominum nostrum Jesum Christum. Amen.
Hic aspergatur corpus et incensetur ter et efferatur ad sepulchrum.

The Lord be with you

And with your spirit.

Let us pray.
[For benefactors of the church the following prayer is used:]

Have mercy, we beg you, O Lord, on the souls of all our deceased benefactors, and from the benefits which have been bestowed on us on earth, may eternal rewards follow in heaven. Through our Lord Jesus Christ. Amen.
Here the corpse is to be asperged and censed three times and taken to the grave.

The Gloria
(not part of the Requiem)

The Gloria
In medio altaris erectis manibus incipiat:

Standing at the middle of the altar, with uplifted hands, [and with the deacon to his right and subdeacon to his left], he is to begin [saying or singing:]

Priest to all
Gloria in excelsis Deo.

Glory to God in the highest.
[And the choir is to continue while the priest, with the deacon and subdeacon, go to the right corner of the altar, the deacon standing to his right and the subdeacon to his left, where they shall say the Gloria in a low voice:]

Priest and Ministers in secret. Chanted by Choir
Et in terra pax hominibus bonae voluntatis. Laudamus te, benedicimus te, adoramus te, glorificamus te. Gratias agimus tibi propter magnam gloriam tuam, Domine Deus, rex caelestis, Deus Pater omnipotens. Domine Fili unigenite, Jesu Christe, Domine Deus, Agnus Dei, Filius Patris, qui tollis peccata mundi, miserere nobis. Qui tollis peccata mundi, suscipe deprecationem nostram. Qui sedes ad dexteram Patris, miserere nobis. Quoniam tu solus sanctus, tu solus Dominus, tu solus altissimus, Jesu Christe, cum Sancto Spiritu, in gloria Dei Patris. Amen.

And on earth peace to all men of good will. We praise you. We bless you. We worship you. We glorify you. We give thanks to you for your great glory. Lord God, King of heaven, God the Father Almighty. O Lord, the only Son, Jesus Christ; Lord God, Lamb of God, Son of the Father, who takes away the sins of the world, have mercy on us. Who takes away the sins of the world, receive our prayer. Who sits at the right of the Father, have mercy on us. For you alone [are] Holy, you alone [are] the Lord, you alone [are] the most high, Jesus Christ, with the Holy Spirit, in the glory of God the Father. Amen.

The Creed
(not part of the Requiem)

The Creed
Statim sacerdos in medio altaris symbolum fidei
incipiat excelsa voce:

Priest to all
Credo in unum Deum,

Choir
*Patrem omnipotentem, factorem caeli et terrae, visibilium
omnium et invisibilium. Et in unum Dominum Jesum
Christum, Filium Dei unigenitum, Et ex Patre natum
ante omnia saecula: Deum de Deo, lumen de lumine,
Deum verum de Deo vero, genitum, non factum,
consubstantialem Patri, per quem omnia facta sunt. Qui
propter nos homines et propter nostram salutem
descendit de coelis. Et incarnatus est de Spiritu Sancto
ex Maria virgine, et homo factus est. Crucifixus etiam
pro nobis sub Pontio Pilato, passus et sepultus est. Et
resurrexit tertia die secundum scripturas, et ascendit in
coelum, sedet ad dexteram Patris, et iterum venturus est
cum gloria judicare vivos et mortuos: cuius regni non erit
finis. Et in Spiritum Sanctum, Dominum et
vivificantem, qui ex Patre Filioque procedit, qui cum
Patre et Filio simul adoratur et conglorificatur, qui
locutus est per prophetas. Et unam sanctam catholicam
et apostolicam ecclesiam. Confiteor unum baptisma in
remissionem peccatorum, et exspecto resurrectionem
mortuorum, et vitam venturi saeculi. Amen.*

Notandum est quod Credo dicitur generaliter
omnibus Dominicis diebus per totum annum.

Dum canitur Credo, subdiaconus cum textu et
acolythus cum thuribulo chorum circumeant.

Immediately the priest at the centre of the altar,
[with the deacon and subdeacon in line behind
him,] is to begin the statement of the faith with a
loud voice:

I believe in one God,
[and the choir is to continue:]

*the Father Almighty, maker of heaven and earth, of all
things seen and unseen. And in one Lord Jesus Christ,
the one and only born Son of God, born of the Father
before all ages. God from God, light from light, true God
from true God, born, not made, of one substance with
the Father, through whom all things were made; who for
us men and for our salvation came down from heaven
and was incarnate by the Holy Spirit of the Virgin Mary
and was made man. For our sake also he was crucified
under Pontius Pilate: he suffered death and was buried.
And he rose again on the third day in accordance with
the scriptures, and ascended into heaven, and sits at the
right hand of the Father, and he shall come again in
glory to judge the living and the dead. Of his kingdom
there shall be no end. And [I believe] in the Holy Spirit,
the Lord and giver of life, who proceeds from the Father
and the Son; who together with the Father and the Son
is worshipped and glorified; who has spoken through the
prophets. And [I believe] in one holy, catholic and
apostolic Church. I acknowledge one baptism for the
forgiveness of sins. And I await the resurrection of the
dead and the life of the world to come. Amen.*
It should be noted that the Creed is said without
exception on all Sundays throughout the whole
year.
While the Creed is being chanted the subdeacon
with the text [of the Gospels] and the acolyte
with the censer are to go around the choir.

Further Reading

The suggestions made for Further Reading are intended to provide a guide to the essential literature for the principal subjects covered in the various chapters, but avoid duplication between sections. Full references to the primary sources (published and manuscript) and secondary literature for each chapter are found in the relevant detailed notes. In a few cases the Further Reading includes background literature which is not specifically cited in the notes to each chapter.

Chapter 1

The best introduction to the place of the Mass in the later middle ages is J. Bossy, 'The Mass as a social institution, 1200–1700', *Past and Present*, 100 (1983), pp. 29–61. J. Martos, *Doors to the Sacred: A Historical Introduction to Sacraments in the Christian Church* (London, 1981), provides an accessible account of all the sacraments in their historical context, while E. Duffy, *The Stripping of the Altars: Traditional Religion in England, 1400–1580* (New Haven and London, 1992), provides a guide to religious practice immediately before and after the Reformation. For other aspects of devotional life, see R. Swanson, *Religion and Devotion in Europe, c. 1215–c. 1515* (Cambridge, 1995), and R. Swanson, *Catholic England: Faith, Religion and Observance before the Reformation* (Manchester and New York, 1993), a collection of translated sources. The development of rites connected with the Host is elucidated by M. Rubin, *Corpus Christi: The Eucharist in Late Medieval Culture* (Cambridge, 1991), and the evolution of thinking concerning Purgatory is discussed in J. Le Goff, *The Birth of Purgatory* (Chicago, 1984).

The most recent short history of York is P. Nuttgens (editor), *The History of York from Earliest Times to the Year 2000* (Pickering, 2001). Much more detailed considerations of the church in late medieval York are contained in P. M. Tillot (editor), *The Victoria History of the Counties of England. A History of Yorkshire: The City of York* (London, 1961), and G. E. Aylmer and R. Cant (editors), *A History of York Minster* (Oxford, 1977). All these works are indebted to the seminal antiquarian history of York, F. Drake, *Eboracum* (London, 1736), which includes transcripts of many original documents. The best modern edition of the York cycle of mystery plays is R. Beadle (editor), *The York Plays* (London, 1982), while the indispensable historical source for their performance in the city is A. F. Johnston and M. Rogerson (editors), *Records of Early English Drama, York*, 2 vols (Toronto, 1979).

Chapter 2

Much of the literature relevant to this chapter was influenced by, if not actually part of, the revival of ceremonial in the late nineteenth century. Although the revivalists were scholarly, it must be remembered that they often wrote with the specific purpose of demonstrating continuity with pre-Reformation ceremonial, and with an eye to what could practically be used in the Anglican Church of their own day.

The best work on the setting of the altar is F. Bond, *The Chancel of English Churches* (Oxford, 1916), while P. Dearmer, *Fifty Pictures of Gothic Altars,* Alcuin Club Collection 10 (London, 1910), is an invaluable source of visual reference. For the altar itself, C. E. Pocknee, *The Christian Altar in History and Today,* Alcuin Club Tract 33 (London, 1963), provides an accessible account. Testers, reredoses, screens and other aspects of furnishing are discussed in J. C. Cox and A. Harvey, *English Church Furniture*, 2nd edn (London, 1908), J. C. Cox, *English Church Fittings, Furniture and Accessories* (London, 1923), F. E. Howard and F. H. Crossley, *English Church Woodwork* (London, 1917), and F. Bond, *Screens and Galleries in English Churches* (London, 1908). J. T. Micklethwaite, *The Ornaments of the Rubric,* Alcuin Club Tract 1

(London, 1901), is a mine of information on the hangings and other accessories of the altar.

A readable introduction to clergy vestments is P. Dearmer, *The Ornaments of the Ministers* (London, 1908). Other discussions are in C. E. Pocknee, *Liturgical Vesture - Its Origins and Development,* Alcuin Club Tract 30 (London, 1960), and H. E. Norris, *Church Vestments: Their Origin and Development Illustrated* (London, 1941). A number of modern, colour, illustrations are included in R. Marks and P. Williamson (editors), *Gothic: Art for England 1400–1547* (London, 2003), which also includes a wealth of material relating to church furnishings more generally, and illustrations of some service books.

Chapter 3

The classic text relating to British music dating from before the Reformation is F. L. Harrison, *Music in Medieval Britain*, 2nd edn (London, 1963), which gives a readable summary of musical developments over the medieval centuries, as well as some detail relating to liturgical practices. A useful study of vocal performance practice is J. Morehen (editor), *English Choral Practice, 1400–1650* (Cambridge, 1995). The music cultivated in England's parish churches, particularly from the fifteenth century, has been the focus of several recent studies, including, F. Kisby (editor), *Music and Musicians in Renaissance Cities and Towns* (Cambridge, 2001).

The earliest substantial source of English choral polyphony to have survived from the Middle Ages is the Old Hall Manuscript. The most reliable of several editions is A. Hughes and M. Bent (editors), *The Old Hall Manuscript*, 3 vols, Corpus Mensurabilis Musicae 46 (Rome, 1969). The manuscript sources that concord with this collection are discussed in M. Bent, 'Sources of the Old Hall Manuscript', *Proceedings of the Royal Musical Association*, 94 (1968), pp. 19–35. Since Bent's article was published, several new sources have come to light, including one from York discussed in L. Colton, 'Music in pre-Reformation York: a new source and some thoughts on the York Masses', *Plainsong and Medieval Music*, 12 (2003), pp. 71–88. The music of the fifteenth and sixteenth centuries has been recorded by a number of choirs including the Hilliard Ensemble, The Orlando Consort, The Sixteen, Theatre of Voices and Gothic Voices, all of whose recordings are to be commended.

Chapters 4 and 5

There has recently been increased interest in the life of parish communities in the later middle ages. Notable studies include A. D. Brown, *Popular Piety in Late Medieval England: The Diocese of Salisbury, 1250–1550* (Oxford, 1995), and B. Kumin, *The Shaping of a Community: The Rise and Reformation of an English Parish c.1400–1560* (Aldershot, 1996). On the same theme are the contributions to K. L. French, G. G. Gibbs and B. A. Kumin (editors), *The Parish in English Life 1400–1600* (Manchester, 1997), and C. R. Burgess, 'London parishes: development in context', in R. Britnell (editor), *Daily Life in the Late Middle Ages* (Stroud, 1998), pp. 151–74. T. Cooper. *The Last Generation of English Catholic Clergy: Parish Priests in the Diocese of Coventry and Lichfield in the Early Sixteenth Century* (Woodbridge, 1999), has scrutinised recruits to the priesthood in one Midland diocese immediately before the Reformation. The importance placed by orthodox churchmen on physical monuments, in this case baptismal fonts, in the education of the laity, is demonstrated in A. E. Nichols, *Seeable Signs. The Iconography of the Seven Sacraments, 1350–1544* (Woodbridge, 1994). C. Richmond, 'Three Suffolk pieces', in S. Ditchfield (editor), *Christianity and Community in the West: Essays for John Bossy* (Aldershot, 2001), pp. 44–56, gives fascinating examples of mechanical images parishioners wanted to provide for their churches in the late middle ages.

Death, commemoration of the dead and care for departed souls in the late middle ages have also attracted recent attention. The best and most accessible account is C. Daniell, *Death and Burial in Medieval England, 1066–1550* (London and New York, 1997); P. Binski, *Medieval Death: Ritual and Representation* (London, 1996), places greater emphasis on physical forms of commemoration. The evidence contained in wills has been extensively explored in a series of papers by C. R. Burgess, including: '"For the increase of divine service": chantries in the parish in late medieval Bristol', *Journal of Ecclesiastical History*, 36 (1985), pp. 46–65; '"By quick and by dead": wills and pious provision in late medieval Bristol', *English Historical Review*, 102 (1987), pp. 837–58; 'A service for the dead: the form and function of the anniversary in late medieval Bristol', *Transactions of the Bristol and Gloucester Archaeological Society*, 105 (1987), pp. 183–211; '"A fond thing vainly invented": an essay on purgatory and pious motive in late medieval England', in S. J. Wright (editor), *Parish, Church and People: Local Studies in Lay Religion, 1350–1750* (London, 1988), pp. 56–84; 'Benefactions of mortality: the lay response in the late medieval urban parish', in D. M. Smith (editor), *Studies in Clergy and Ministry in Medieval England,* Borthwick Studies in History 1 (York, 1991), pp. 65–86. Most of Burgess's material is derived from Bristol. For York, see R. B. Dobson, 'The foundation of perpetual chantries by the citizens of York', in J. G. Cumming (editor), *The Province of York*, Studies in Church History 4 (Leiden, 1967), pp. 22–38; see also C. M. Barnett, 'Commemoration in the parish church: identity and social class in late medieval York', *Yorkshire Archaeological Journal*, 72 (2000), pp. 73–92. For a national synthesis of architectural evidence for chantry chapels, see G. H. Cook, *Medieval Chantries and Chantry Chapels*, revised edn (London, 1968).

There has been much recent interest in the use of churchwardens' accounts to reconstruct parish life in late medieval England. Such accounts have survived in much greater quantities in the South West than anywhere else in the country. K. L. French, *The People of the Parish: Community Life in a Late Medieval Diocese* (Philadelphia, 2001), has subjected churchwardens' accounts in the diocese of Bath and Wells to a detailed scholarly analysis. The value of such accounts for this kind of discussion is assessed in C. R. Burgess, 'Pre-Reformation churchwardens' accounts and parish government: lessons from London and Bristol', *English Historical Review*, 117 (2002), pp. 306–32. From a close examination of its sixteenth-century churchwardens' accounts, life in a remote Devon settlement has been brilliantly re-created in E. Duffy, *The Voices of Morebath: Reformation and Rebellion in an English Village* (New Haven and London, 2001). Pre-Reformation churchwardens' accounts are extremely rare for the north of England, and the only complete set is that for St Michael's, Spurriergate, York, which has recently been published in C. C. Webb (editor), *Churchwardens' Accounts of St Michael's, Spurriergate, York, 1518-1548*, Borthwick Texts and Calendars 20, 2 vols (York, 1997).

The church buildings of All Saints', North Street, and St Michael, Spurriergate, are described in Royal Commission on the Historical Monuments of England, *An Inventory of the Historical Monuments in York*, 5 vols (London, 1962–81), All Saints' in volume 3, South-West of the Ouse, St Michael in volume 5, The Central Area. All Saints' has been the subject of several other accounts, partly because of its fine collection of medieval glass, discussed in E. A. Gee, 'The painted glass of All Saints' Church, North Street, York', *Archaeologia*, 102 (1969), pp. 151–202. P. J. Shaw, *An Old York Church. All-Hallows in North Street: Its Medieval Stained Glass and Architecture* (York, 1908), contains a vast amount of information and includes translations of many of the surviving wills of medieval parishioners. There are many high-quality colour illustrations of the church in A. B. Barton, *A Guide to the Church of All Saints North Street, York* (York, 2003).

Chapter 6

The most evocative general account of the last years of medieval monasticism in England is still D. Knowles, *The Religious Orders in England, III. The Tudor Age* (Cambridge, 1959), while the suppression of chantries is effectively covered in A. Kreider, *English Chantries: The Road to Dissolution* (Cambridge, Mass, 1979). Much of his research into the early Reformation in Yorkshire was condensed in A. G. Dickens, *Lollards and Protestants in the Diocese of York 1509–1558* (London, 1958). D. M. Palliser, *The Reformation in York*, Borthwick Paper 40 (York, 1971), narrowed the focus to the religious changes within the city itself. The York chantry certificates have been printed in full in W. Page (editor), *The Certificates of the Commissioners Appointed to Survey the Chantries, Guilds, Hospitals, etc., in the County of York*, Part I, Surtees Society 91 (1894). All the surviving wills of York clergy for the greater part of the sixteenth century appear in C. Cross (editor), *York Clergy Wills 1520–1600: I Minster Clergy*, Borthwick Texts and Calendars 10 (York, 1984), and C. Cross (editor), *York Clergy Wills 1520–1600: II City Clergy*, Borthwick Texts and Calendars 15 (York, 1989). C. Cross and N. Vickers (editors), *Monks, Friars and Nuns in Sixteenth-Century Yorkshire*, Yorkshire Archaeological Society, Record Series 150 (Leeds, 1995), contains details of the later careers of some of the dispossessed York religious. J. C. H. Aveling, *Catholic Recusancy in the City of York, 1558–1791*, Catholic Record Society Monograph 2 (London, 1970), has included very detailed summaries of contemporary sources in addition to his account of the York recusant community. The positive (and negative) attractions of Protestantism, which some York citizens had come to appreciate by the middle of Elizabeth's reign, are portrayed in P. Marshall and A. Ryrie (editors), *The Beginnings of English Protestantism* (Cambridge, 2002), E. H. Shagan, *Popular Politics and the English Reformation* (Cambridge, 2002), and P. Collinson, *The Birthpangs of Protestant England: Religious and Cultural Change in the Sixteenth and Seventeenth Centuries* (London, 1988).

Chapter 7

A very useful introduction to the forms of service and the books in which they are contained is J. Harper, *The Forms and Orders of Western Liturgy from the Tenth to the Eighteenth Century. A Historical Introduction and Guide for Students and Musicians* (Oxford, 1991). Service books are discussed in C. Wordsworth and H. Littlehales, *The Old Service-Books of the English Church*, 2nd edn (London, 1910), and H. B. Swete, *Church Services and Service-Books Before the Reformation*, 2nd edn (London, 1905), both of which still contain useful material. More recent (and more technical) is A. Hughes, *Medieval Manuscripts for Mass and Office: A Guide to their Organisation and Terminology*, 2nd edn (Toronto, 1995).

The standard edition of the York Missal is W. G. Henderson (editor), *Missale ad Usum Insignis Ecclesiae Eboracensis*, 2 vols, Surtees Society 59–60 (1872), and there is a partial translation in T. F. Simmons (editor), *The Lay Folks Mass Book*, Early English Text Society, Original Series 71 (London, 1879). The other main York books are to be found in W. G. Henderson (editor), *Manuale et Processionale ad Usum Insignis Ecclesiae Eboracensis*, Surtees Society 63 (1875), which contains the Absolutions for the Dead, and S. W. Lawley (editor), *Breviarium ad Usum Insignis Ecclesiae Eboracensis*, 2 vols, Surtees Society 71, 75 (1880–3). The Gradual is in D. Hiley (editor), *Oxford, Bodleian Library, MS Lat. liturg. b.5*, Publications of Medieval Musical Manuscripts 20 (Ottawa, 1995).

The most accessible edition of the Sarum Missal is F. H. Dickinson (editor), *Missale ad Usum Insignis et Praeclarae Ecclesiae Sarum*, 2 vols (Burntisland, 1861–83). There are also a number of translations, including F. E. Warren, *The Sarum Missal in English*, 2 vols, Library of Liturgiology and Ecclesiology for English Readers 8–9 (London, 1911), and C. Walker, *The Liturgy of Sarum*, 2nd edn (London, c. 1870). The Sarum Manual, containing the Absolutions for the Dead, is available in A. J. Collins (editor), *Manuale ad Usum Percelebris Ecclesie Sarisburiensis*, Henry Bradshaw Society 91 (1960). The customs of Sarum are in W. H. Frere (editor), *The Use of Sarum*, 2 vols (Cambridge, 1898–1901).

Abbreviations

BIHR Borthwick Institute of Historical Research, York

       Abp. Reg.   Archbishops' Registers

       Prob. Reg.   Probate Registers

       Sede Vac. Reg.   Sede Vacante Registers

Chantry Certificates

       W. Page (editor), *The Certificates of the Commissioners Appointed to Survey the Chantries, Guilds, Hospitals, etc., in the County of York*, 2 vols, Surtees Society 91–2 (1894–5)

Churchwardens' Accounts

       C. C. Webb (editor), *Churchwardens' Accounts of St Michael's, Spurriergate, York, 1518–48*, 2 vols, Borthwick Texts and Calendars 20 (York, 1997)

RCHM Royal Commission on Historical Monuments

TE   J. Raine, J. Raine and W. Caley (editors), *Testamenta Eboracensia*, 6 vols, Surtees Society 4, 30, 45, 53, 79, 106 (1836–1902)

YCA   York City Archives

YMA   York Minster Archives

Notes & References

Chapter 1

1. E. Duffy, *The Stripping of the Altars: Traditional Religion in England, 1400–1580* (New Haven and London, 1992).

2. The fullest account is that of J. Le Goff, *The Birth of Purgatory* (Chicago, 1984).

3. J. Martos, *Doors to the Sacred: A Historical Introduction to Sacraments in the Christian Church* (London, 1981), pp. 181–2.

4. The most convenient assemblage of material is Duffy, *Stripping of the Altars*, esp. pp. 16, 23–31, 42–3 and 279–80; for Corpus Christi see M. Rubin, *Corpus Christi: The Eucharist in Late Medieval Culture* (Cambridge, 1991), esp., on York, pp. 255–7.

5. J. G. Davies, *The Secular Use of Church Buildings* (London, 1968), pp. 47–51.

6. B. Dobson, 'Later medieval York', in P. Nuttgens (editor), *The History of York from Earliest Times to the Year 2000* (Pickering, 2001), p. 116.

7. This section is dependent upon B. Dobson, 'The later middle ages, 1215–1500', in G. E. Aylmer and R. Cant (editors), *A History of York Minster* (Oxford, 1977), pp. 44–109.

8. P. H. Cullum, *Cremetts and Corrodies: Care of the Poor and Sick at St Leonard's Hospital, York, in the Middle Ages*, Borthwick Paper 79 (York, 1991); C. Rawcliffe, 'The eighth comfortable work: education and the medieval hospital', in C. M. Barron and J. Stratford (editors), *The Church and Learning in Later Medieval Society: Essays in Honour of R. B. Dobson* (Donington, 2002), pp. 384–5.

9. C. Cross and N. Vickers (editors), *Monks, Friars and Nuns in Sixteenth Century Yorkshire*, Yorkshire Archaeological Society, Record Series 150 (1995), pp. 67–95.

10. Cross and Vickers, *Monks, Friars and Nuns*, pp. 60–66.

11. Cross and Vickers, *Monks, Friars and Nuns*, pp. 407–11.

12. R. B. Dobson and S. Donaghey, *The History of Clementhorpe Nunnery*, The Archaeology of York, fascicule 2/1 (London, 1984).

13. A. F. Johnston, 'The York Cycle and the libraries of York', in Barron and Stratford, *Church and Learning*, pp. 355–70; Cross and Vickers, *Monks, Friars and Nuns*, p. 455; BIHR Prob. Reg. ix f. 129r, 293r, 355r–v.

14. F. Drake, *Eboracum* (London, 1736), appendix pp. xxix–xxx, xxxii; R. H. Skaife (editor), *The Register of the Guild of Corpus Christi in the City of York*, Surtees Society 57 (1872), pp. ix–xi.

15. D. M. Palliser, 'The union of parishes at York, 1547–86', *Yorkshire Archaeological Journal*, 46 (1974), pp. 87–102.

16. Palliser, 'Union of parishes', pp. 87–8; P. M. Tillott, 'The parish churches', in P. M. Tillot (editor), *The Victoria History of the Counties of England. A History of Yorkshire: The City of York* (London, 1961), pp. 396–402.

17. R. B. Dobson, 'The foundation of perpetual chantries by the citizens of medieval York', in J. G. Cumming (editor), *The Province of York*, Studies in Church History 4 (Leiden, 1967), pp. 22–38. Dobson, 'Late medieval York', p. 137.

18. C. Cross (editor), *York Clergy Wills 1520–1600: II City Clergy*, Borthwick Texts and Calendars 15 (York, 1989), pp. 7–8, 16–17; and see pp. 97-107 below.

19. D. E. O'Connor and J. Haselock, 'The stained and painted glass', in Aylmer and Cant, *History of York Minster*, pp. 364–7; Royal Commission on the Historical Monuments of England, *An Inventory of the Historical Monuments in the City of York*, 5 vols, (1962–81), vol. iii, pp. 7–8, vol. v, pp. 8, 28; O. Saunders, 'Minster and parish: the sixteenth century reconstruction of the church of St Michael-le-Belfrey in York', University of York, MA thesis in Medieval Studies (1996), pp. 47–57, 94–110.

20. BIHR Prob. Reg. ii ff. 451v–452v; iv ff. 263v–264r; ix ff. 58r, 355r–v; xi pt I f. 1v.

21. BIHR Prob. Reg. ix f. 108r–v; C. C. Webb (editor), *The Churchwardens' Accounts of St Michael, Spurriergate, York, 1518–1548*, Borthwick Texts and Calendars 20, 2 vols. (York, 1997), pp. 179, 194, 250, 262–3; J. A. Hoeppner Moran, *The Growth of English Schooling 1340–1548: Learning, Literacy and Laicization in Pre-Reformation York Diocese* (Princeton, 1985), pp. 232, 278–9.

22. Cross and Vickers, *Monks, Friars and Nuns*, pp. 62, 75, 409, 430, 454–5, 479, 496.

Chapter 2

1. E. Duffy, *The Stripping of the Altars: Traditional Religion in England 1400–1580* (New Haven and London, 1992).

2. Many medieval mensa slabs were used as paving after the Reformation and were rediscovered in the nineteenth century.

3. F. Bond, *The Chancel of English Churches* (Oxford, 1916), p. 16.

4. Bond, *Chancel*, p. 35.

5. H. King, *The Chancel and the Altar* (London, 1911), p. 89; J. Braun, *Der christliche Altar in seiner geschichtlichen Entwicklung*, 2 vols. (Munich, 1920), vol. i, p. 212, citing the York example, which is recorded in BIHR Prob. Reg. iii f. 439r.

6. The largest mensa know to survive, which is about 14 ft long, is the one at Tewkesbury Abbey. See Bond, *Chancel*, p. 7.

7. In certain circumstances the level of the chancel is raised higher than this, but only to incorporate some extra architectural feature under the altars, such as a vaulted processional way, crypt or ossuary. The high altar at St Peter Mancroft, Norwich, stands eight steps above the level of the choir pavement, and the high altar at Walpole St Peter, Norfolk, is approached up two flights of five steps. Both examples were constructed to create a processional way beneath the sanctuary.

8. The sedilia was used during the reading of the Epistle and the singing of the Gradual, Alleluia and Tract (see Chapter 7). For discussions of piscinae and sedilia, see Bond, *Chancel*, chapters 6 and 7.

9. Aumbries are discussed in Bond, *Chancel*, chapter 8, and Easter Sepulchres in chapter 9.

10. See C. E. Pocknee, *The Christian Altar in History and Today*, Alcuin Club Tract 33 (London, 1963), pp. 55–63 and various plates.

11. P. Dearmer, *Fifty Pictures of Gothic Altars*, Alcuin Club Collections 10 (London, 1910), plate xiii; Bond, *Chancel*, p. 19.

12. This is referred to in an early sixteenth-century manual to the Mass, G. van der Goude, *Dat Boexken vander Missen* (Antwerp, 1507), republished in English as *The Interpretacyon, and Sygnyfycacyon of the Masse* (London, 1532). In the thirteenth article the priest begins the Canon of the Mass 'hanging the curtains drawn: to the intent that he be not troubled'. There is a facsimile edition, P. Dearmer (editor), *Dat Boexken vander Missen. 'The Booklet of the Mass'. By Brother Gherit vander Goude. The Thirty-Four Plates Described, and the Explanatory Text of the Flemish Original Translated, with Illustrative Excerpts from Contemporary Missals and Tracts*, Alcuin Club Collections 5 (London, 1899).

13. Examples remain at Ludlow and Clun in Shropshire; the latter is illustrated in F. E. Howard and F. H. Crossley, *English Church Woodwork* (London, 1917), p. 142. See also Bond, *Chancel*, pp. 20–23.

14. The most detailed survey of the treatment of altar backdrops is in Bond, *Chancel*, chapter 2.

15. J. T. Micklethwaite, *The Ornaments of the Rubric*, Alcuin Club Tract 1 (London, 1901), p. 28.

16. See Bond, *Chancel*, pp. 26–8.

17. Micklethwaite, *Ornaments*, p. 28.

18. Dearmer, *Fifty Pictures*, p. 8.

19. J. Raine (editor), *A Description or Briefe Declaration of all the Ancient Monuments, Rites, and Customes Belonginge or Being Within the Monastical Church of Durham Before the Suppression. Written in 1593*, Surtees Society 15 (1844), p. 6 [subsequently *Durham Rites*].

20. Micklethwaite, *Ornaments*, p. 28.

21. See C. Norton, P. Binski and D. Park, *Dominican Painting in East Anglia: The Thornham Parva Retable and the Musée de Cluny Frontal* (Woodbridge, 1987).

22. Micklethwaite, *Ornaments*, p. 32.

23. A. H. Pearson (editor), *The Sarum Missal in English* (London, 1868), p. xliii.

24. Dearmer, *Fifty Pictures*, plate xx.

25. Micklethwaite, *Ornaments*, p. 32, n. 2 and p. 33 n. 1.

26. Micklethwaite, *Ornaments*, p. 33.

27. Dearmer, *Fifty Pictures*, p. 9.

28. R. C. Dudding (editor), *The First Churchwardens' Book of Louth* (Oxford, 1941), p. 151.

29. Micklethwaite, *Ornaments*, pp. 31–2.

30. Pearson, *Sarum Missal*, pp. xlii–xliii.

31. For example, when Thomas Cumberworth founded a chantry at Somerby in Lincolnshire in 1440, he provided for the chapel 'a box of copper and gilt for the blessed sacrament with a high foot thereto'. E. Peacock, *English Church Furniture, Ornaments and Decorations, At the Period of the Reformation, As Exhibited in a List of the Goods Destroyed in Certain Lincolnshire Churches, A.D. 1566* (London, 1866), p. 183.

32. J. C. Cox, *English Church Furniture* (London, 1907), p. 40.

33. *Rites of Durham*, p. 7.

34. The Hessett cover and the method of pyx suspension are illustrated in Cox, *English Church Furniture*, pp. 39–45. See also Micklethwaite, *Ornaments*, pp. 30–31.

35. *Rites of Durham*, p. 7.

36. *Rites of Durham*, p. 7.

37. For a full discussion of the origins and early developments of various vestments see C. E. Pocknee, *Liturgical Vesture — Its Origins and Development*, Alcuin Club Tract 30 (London, 1960), H. E. Norris *Church Vestments: Their Origin and Development Illustrated* (London, 1941), and P. Dearmer, *The*

Ornaments of the Ministers (London, 1908).

38. Pocknee, *Liturgical Vesture*, p. 18.

39. W. St John Hope and E.G.C.F. Atchley, *English Liturgical Colours* (London, 1918), p. 251 and passim.

40. Hope and Atchley, *English Liturgical Colours*, p. 15.

41. The general use of apparels on English albs is implied by the specific stipulation in the preface of the first Prayer Book of 1549, that the alb should be 'plain'.

42. The Latin word *casula* is a diminutive of the *casa*, a house. Pocknee, *Liturgical Vesture*, p. 28.

43. Two medieval conical chasubles survive on the continent; one, of the eleventh century, at Bayeaux, the other, of the twelfth century, at Sens. The former is said to have belonged to Thomas Becket. See Pocknee, *Liturgical Vesture*, p. 30.

44. In the translation of van der Goude, *Boexken*, article 18, 'lifting the chasuble upon his shoulders' is specifically mentioned as part of the priest's preparation for the consecration and Elevation of the Host. See also the panel painting, the *Mass of St Giles* by the Master of St Giles, now in the National Gallery, London, where St Giles has folded his black chasuble over his shoulders to reveal its crimson lining.

45. Pocknee, *Liturgical Vesture*, p. 37.

46. An English dalmatic of the early fifteenth century from Whalley Abbey, Lancashire, with a fringed skirt, is illustrated in R. Marks and P. Williamson (editors), *Gothic: Art for England 1400–1547* (London, 2003), p. 411.

47. Pocknee, *Liturgical Vesture*, p. 38.

48. For a fuller examination of medieval English vestment embroidery see A. Dryden, *Church Embroidery* (London, 1911), and D. King, *Opus Anglicanum: English Medieval Embroidery [an exhibition at] the Victoria and Albert Museum 26 September to 24 November 1963* (London, 1963). The Victoria and Albert Museum is perhaps the best place to study medieval English vestments first hand — see E. R. D. Maclagen, *Catalogue of English Ecclesiastical Embroideries of the XIII to XVI Centuries [in the Victoria and Albert Museum]*, 2nd edn (London, 1916).

49. For examples see Maclagen, *Catalogue of English Embroideries*, plates xxvi and xxvii, and Marks and Williamson, *Gothic*, pp. 169, 369.

50. The modern white, red, green, purple, black sequence is that of the Roman rite and only became standard in the Roman Catholic Church in the second quarter of the nineteenth century. Prior to that the local usage was employed throughout the western Church.

51. The earliest known sequence is in the statutes of 1240 drawn up by Bishop Pateshull for Lichfield; others are known for Wells, London, Canterbury and Exeter. See P. Dearmer, *The Parson's Handbook* 2nd edn

(London, 1907), pp. 120–26.

52. For a full commentary see Hope and Atchley, *English Liturgical Colours*, and J. W. Legg, *Notes on the History of Liturgical Colours* (London, 1881).

53. Dearmer, *Parson's Handbook*, pp. 511–13.

54. Hope and Atchley, *English Liturgical Colours*, pp. 113, 116.

55. *Rites of Durham*, p. 6.

Chapter 3

1. R. Bowers, 'To chorus from quartet: the performing resource for English church polyphony, *c.*1390–*c.*1559', in John Morehen (editor), *English Choral Practice, 1400–1650* (Cambridge, 1995), pp. 1–47.

2. J. Britton (editor), *The Natural History of Wiltshire by John Aubrey (Written between 1656 and 1691)* (London, 1847; repr. Trowbridge, 1969), p. 79.

3. Documents in the custody of the Borthwick Institute of Historical Research are reproduced and edited with permission. All editions are my own unless otherwise stated.

4. BIHR, MS Mus 2. See M. Bent, 'Sources of the Old Hall Manuscript', *Proceedings of the Royal Musical Association*, 94 (1968), pp. 19–35.

5. The Old Hall Manuscript is London, British Library, Additional Manuscript 57950. It is thought to have belonged to Thomas, Duke of Clarence, before passing to the royal chapel where more pieces were added to it. A recording of Bittering's *Nesciens mater* has been made by the Hilliard Ensemble, *The Old Hall Manuscript* (EMI Classics, 1991) CDC 7541112.

6. BIHR, MS Mus 9.

7. A full description and photographs of the binding strips can be found in L. Colton, 'Music in pre-Reformation York: a new source and some thoughts on the York Masses', *Plainsong and Medieval Music*, 12 (2003), pp. 71–88.

8. A. Hughes and M. Bent (editors), *The Old Hall Manuscript*, 3 volumes, Corpus Mensurabilis Musicae, 46 (Rome, 1969). In this edition the York squares concord with Gloria No.1 and Gloria No. 5. Margaret Bent identified the concordance with Gloria 1.

9. This identification was made by Peter Lefferts, following the publication of the description of the source in Colton, 'Music in pre-Reformation York'.

10. London, British Library, Cotton Titus D. XXIV, ff. 2–3v (preserved in the order 3v, 2, 3r) also found in Foligno, Biblioteca Communale, Frammenti Musicali, f. 1r–v, and Grottaferrata, Biblioteca dell'Abbazia, Collocazione Provisoria 197, ff. 1v–2. An edition of this piece can be found in F. Harrison, E. Sanders and P. Lefferts (editors), *Polyphonic Music of the Fourteenth Century*, 16 (Monaco, 1983), pp. 75–6.

11. The earliest source is the contract of Thomas Foderley, now Durham Cathedral, Reg. v, f. 34.

12. H. Baillie, 'Squares', *Acta Musicologica*, 32 (1960), pp. 178–93.

13. The opening of the Gloria from Mass II was recorded for the HMV *History of Music in Sound*.

14. M. Bent, *Dunstaple* (London, 1981), pp. 83–4.

15. For this identification see H. Baillie, 'Some biographical notes on English church musicians, chiefly working in London (1485–1569)', *Royal Musical Association Research Chronicle*, 2 (1962), p. 30.

16. *Venit dilectus meus* is the sixth antiphon at Matins on the Assumption of the Blessed Virgin Mary (15 August).

17. The fifteenth-century York Gradual is Oxford, Bodleian Library, MS Lat. liturg. b. 5; see W. H. Frere, 'The newly-found York Gradual', in J. H. Arnold and E. G. P. Wyatt (editors), *Walter Howard Frere: A Collection of His Papers on Liturgical and Hisorical Subjects*, Alcuin Club Collections 35 (Oxford, 1940), pp. 22–31.

18. A. Hughes, 'Fifteenth-century English polyphony discovered in Norwich and Arundel,' *Music and Letters*, 59 (1978), pp. 148–58.

19. London, British Library, Additional Manuscript 54324, f. 6v; see M. Bent, 'Dufay, Dunstable, Plummer – a new source', *Journal of the American Musicological Society*, 22 (1969), pp. 394–424. The second concordant source is Canterbury, Cathedral Library, Additional Manuscript 128/65; see N. Sandon, 'Fragments of medieval polyphony at Canterbury cathedral', *Musica Disciplina*, 30 (1976), p. 47.

20. R. Rastall, *The Heaven Singing: Music in Early English Religious Drama*, Volume 1 (Woodbridge, 1996), p. 134. The York Register, London, British Library, Additional Manuscript 35290, contains two-part music for three episodes in the Plays; the music is copied in score on ff. 250v, 251 and 253. A full discussion of the music used in the York Mystery Plays can be found in Rastall, *Heaven Singing*, pp. 121–37.

21. For more details relating to evidence for music performed in York, see Colton, 'Music in pre-Reformation York'.

Chapter 4

1. J. Bossy, 'The Mass as a social institution, 1200–1700', *Past and Present*, 100 (1983), p. 42. For full discussion of the development of the idea of Purgatory and its significance in the Middle Ages, see J. Le Goff, *The Birth of Purgatory* (London, 1984); see also E. Duffy, *The Stripping of the Altars: Traditional Religion in England 1400–1580* (New Haven and London, 1992), pp. 338–76, and C. R. Burgess, '"A fond thing vainly invented": an essay on purgatory and pious motive in late medieval England', in S. J. Wright (editor), *Parish, Church and People: Local Studies in Lay Religion, 1350–1750* (London, 1988), pp. 56–84.

2. P. Binski, *Medieval Death. Ritual and Representation* (London, 1996), pp. 71–2; C. R. Burgess, 'Benefactions of mortality: the lay response in the late medieval urban parish', in D. M. Smith (editor), *Studies in Clergy and Ministry in Medieval England*, Borthwick Studies in History 1 (York, 1991), pp. 67–9.

3. See, for example, Duffy, *Stripping of the Altars*, C. R. Burgess, '"For the increase of divine service": chantries in the parish in late medieval Bristol', *Journal of Ecclesiastical History*, 36 (1985), pp. 46–65, C. R. Burgess, '"By quick and by dead": wills and pious provision in late medieval Bristol', *English Historical Review*, 102 (1987), pp. 837-58, C. R. Burgess, 'A service for the dead: the form and function of the Anniversary in late medieval Bristol', *Transactions of the Bristol and Gloucestershire Archaeological Society*, 105 (1987), pp. 183–211, and Burgess, 'Benefactions of mortality', pp. 65–86: Burgess more than once notes dangers of generalising from Bristol. A. D. Brown, *Popular Piety in Late Medieval England: The Diocese of Salisbury, 1250–1550* (Oxford, 1995), draws some contrasts between parts of the diocese. See also B. Kumin, *The Shaping of a Community: The Rise and Reformation of the English Parish c.1400–1560* (Aldershot, 1996), and K. L. French, *The People of the Parish: Community Life in a Late Medieval Diocese* (Philadelphia, 2001).

4. By far the greater part of the wills are in BIHR Prob. Reg., and abbreviated translations of most are to be found in the appendix to P. J. Shaw, *An Old York Church. All-Hallows in North Street: Its Medieval Stained Glass and Architecture* (York, 1908). Wills are cited in their manuscript form, and a concordance of manuscripts, editions and translations consulted is provided in the Table at the end of this chapter.

5. The preponderance of tanners is clear from the 1381 Poll Tax, in which the occupations of 60 heads of household are recorded, 41 of whom were barkers — see J. N. Bartlett, 'The Lay Poll Tax returns for the City of York in 1381', *Transactions of the East Riding Antiquarian Society*, 30 (1953), pp. 72–6; this preponderance is so great that it is likely to reflect the reality of the time, even though the Tax appears to have been administered in such a way as to exclude the poor — see H. Swanson, *Medieval Artisans: An Urban Class in Late Medieval England* (Oxford, 1989), p. 151 and, on the North Street concentration of tanners, p. 160, cf. P. J. P. Goldberg, *Women, Work, and Life Cycle in a Medieval Economy: Women in York and Yorkshire, c.1300–1500* (Oxford, 1992), pp. 69–70.

6. Swanson, *Medieval Artisans*, pp. 42–3, 151–2, 157, 158.

7. E. Miller, 'Medieval York', in P. M. Tillot (editor), *The Victoria History of the Counties of England. A History of Yorkshire: City of York* (London, 1961), p. 71, cf. p. 79.

8. Swanson, *Medieval Artisans*, pp. 123–4, 168.

9. Figures based on J. Sheail, *The Regional Distribution of Wealth in England as*

Indicated in the 1524/5 Lay Subsidy Returns, 2 vols, List and Index Society 38–9 (London, 1998), vol. ii, pp. 433–4. In 1327, the parish ranked fourteenth out of nineteen York parishes assessed for a Subsidy — see J. W. R. Parker, 'Lay Subsidy Rolls, I Edward III. North Riding of Yorkshire and City of York', in *Miscellanea* 2, Yorkshire Archaeological Society, Record Series 71 (Leeds, 1929), pp. 160–71.

10. Miller, 'Medieval York', pp. 84–105; J. N. Bartlett, 'The expansion and decline of York in the later Middle Ages', *Economic History Review*, 2nd ser. 12 (1959–60), pp. 25–33.

11. J. Caley and J. Hunter (editors), *Valor Ecclesiasticus, temp. Henrici VIII, auctoritate regia instituta*, 6 vols. (London, 1810–34), vol. v, p. 24 (£4 19s. 9d.); cf. S. Ayscough and J. Caley (editors), *Taxatio Ecclesiastica Angliae et Walliae Auctoritate Papae Nicholae IV* (London, 1802), p. 298 (£5 6s. 8d.).

12. The proposals as a whole are discussed in D. M. Palliser, 'Unions of parishes at York, 1547–1586', *Yorkshire Archaeological Journal*, 46 (1974), pp. 87–102. For doubts as early as 1553 about including All Saints', see A. Raine (editor), *York Civic Records*, 9 vols, Yorkshire Archaeological Society, Record Series 98, 103, 106, 108, 110, 112, 115, 119, 138 (Leeds, 1939–76), vol. v, p. 90, cf. p. 5.

13. Swanson, *Medieval Artisans*, pp. 155–6; F. Pollock and F. W. Maitland, *The History of English Law*, rev. by S. F. C. Milsom, 2 vols. (Cambridge, 1968), vol. ii, p. 348.

14. Burgess, 'Benefactions of mortality', pp. 65–6.

15. The best short account is in C. Daniell, *Death and Burial in Medieval England, 1066–1550* (London and New York, 1997), pp. 44–54.

16. BIHR Prob. Reg. iii ff. 266v–268r; a hearse is also mentioned in Prob. Reg. ii ff. 168v–169r.

17. In the Vulgate, verse 9.

18. Dates from 1 January to 24 March are given in the form Old Style/New Style.

19. Respectively, BIHR Prob. Reg. iii f. 410r; ii f. 17r. The other reference to music is in the foundation document for Adam del Bank's chantry (YCA G.70 no. 27) — see below.

20. Duffy, *Stripping of the Altars*, pp. 361–2. Wax for lights to burn round the body is mentioned in BIHR Prob. Reg. i f. 10r; ii f. 8r; ii ff. 168v–169r; ii ff. 378r–380r; ii f. 506r (cf. YMA MS 2/6(e), f. 3v); iii f. 17r-v; iii ff. 66v–67r; iii ff. 266v–268r; iv f. 28r-v; iv f. 135r-v; v f. 44r; v f. 149r-v; v f. 271r; v f. 275r; v f. 310r; v f. 325v; v f. 331v; v ff. 391r–392v; vi ff. 23v–24r; vi f. 57r-v; YMA MS L2/4 ff. 157r–158v, and MS H2(1) ff. 2v–3v.

21. E.g., the will of Nicholas Blackburn, junior, BIHR Prob. Reg. ii ff. 168v–169r, which specifies that two torches were to be used at the altar of

the Blessed Virgin Mary, and one each at the altars of St James, St Nicholas and St Thomas of Canterbury. The siting of these altars is discussed below.

22. E.g., the will of Nicholas Blackburn, senior, BIHR Prob. Reg. ii ff. 605r–606v, which stipulated that two torches were to be used on Easter Day, for as many years as they lasted.

23. R. N. Swanson, *Religion and Devotion in Europe, c.1215–1515* (Cambridge, 1995), p. 100, 137–8, provides a good summary account. There is a wealth of detail in M. Rubin, *Corpus Christi: The Eucharist in Late-Medieval Culture* (Cambridge, 1991).

24. Blackburn was in fact buried at the Minster — see BIHR Prob. Reg. ii ff. 605r–606v; for similar instances, see Prob. Reg. i ff. 11v–12r; ii ff. 537v–538r.

25. Light of St Crux: BIHR Prob. Reg. ii ff. 154v–155r; ii f. 564v; ii ff. 622v–623r; iii ff. 266v–268v; light of the Holy Sepulchre: Prob. Reg. ii ff. 154v–155r; ii f. 564v; ii f. 662v; light before the image of the Virgin: Prob. Reg. ii f. 82r–v; ii ff. 154v–155r (specifying that the image was in the choir); iii ff. 266v–268v.

26. J. G. Davies, *The Secular Use of Church Buildings* (London, 1968), pp. 47–50.

27. BIHR Prob. Reg. v ff. 391r–392r.

28. BIHR Prob. Reg. vi ff. 19v–20r.

29. Swanson, *Religion and Devotion*, p. 214, comments on the contractual nature of many charitable bequests, while Burgess, 'A service for the dead', p. 189, indicates that this was often made explicit in Bristol wills. The All Saints' wills are not, however, unusual in York — see C. C. Webb, '"Toward the salary and fyndyng of Jhesu Mass:" the obit of Robert Dale, shipman and citizen of York', in D. M. Smith (editor), *The Church in Medieval York: Records Edited in Honour of Barrie Dobson*, Borthwick Texts and Calendars 35 (York, 1999), p. 127.

30. Respectively, BIHR Prob. Reg. iii f. 31r; iii ff. 107r–108v; ii ff. 114v–115r.

31. BIHR Prob. Reg. ii f. 174v.

32. E.g., William Vescy, who left £20 to the poor on the day of his burial, plus 60s. for pious works on the same day, and some £9 more to specific institutions or categories of indigent person — see BIHR Prob. Reg. iii ff. 266v–268v.

33. BIHR Prob. Reg. ii ff. 605r–606v; cf. ii ff. 378r–380r and iii ff. 266v–268v. For the importance of the feast of the Purification, and its ceremonial, see Duffy, *Stripping of the Altars*, p. 16.

34. BIHR Prob. Reg. ii ff. 378r–380r; ii ff. 605r–606v; iii ff. 266v–268v.

35. Duffy, *Stripping of the Altars*, pp. 367–8.

36. BIHR Prob. Reg. iii ff. 415v–417v.

37. The monetary bequests are too numerous to list. The reference to tiles is in BIHR Prob. Reg. ii ff. 154v–155r, and that to lead is in Prob. Reg. ii f. 174v.

38. E.g., William de Esyngwald left a quarter of a mark to the fabric of his native parish church, BIHR Prob.Reg. i f. 87r; William Vescy left money to York Minster, to a chapel near Whitby where he had formerly lived, Prob. Reg. iii ff. 266v–268v; while the far-flung connections of Robert Colynson are apparent from bequests to the fabric of the churches at Driffield and Penrith, to the Collegiate church at Ripon and to York Minster, Prob. Reg. ii ff. 378r–380r.

39. J. Myrc, *Instructions for Parish Priests*, J. Peacock (editor), Early English Text Society, Original Series 31, 2nd edn (London, 1902), pp. 10–11. More generally, see J. Martos, *Doors to the Sacred: A Historical Introduction to Sacraments in the Christian Church* (London, 1981), p. 260, and G. A. Mitchell, *Landmarks in Liturgy. The Primitive Rite - A Medieval Mass - The English Rite to 1662* (London, 1961), pp. 121–3, 278.

40. T. F. Simmons (editor), *The Lay Folks Mass Book*, Early English Text Society, Original Series 71 (London, 1879), p. 2.

41. T. Becon, The Displaying of the Popish Mass, in J. Ayre (editor), *Prayers and Other Pieces of Thomas Becon*, Publications of the Parker Society 17 (Cambridge, 1844), p. 286.

42. BIHR Prob. Reg. ii f. 506r, cf. YMA MS 2/6(e) f. 3v.

43. E.g., BIHR Prob. Reg. iv f. 28r–v.

44. For trentals on the day of burial, see BIHR Prob. Reg. i f. 122r; YMA MS L2/4 ff. 157r–158v; and for those within the octave, BIHR Prob. Reg. ii. f. 520r. The request for eight trentals is in Prob. Reg. v f. 275r.

45. BIHR Prob. Reg. iii ff. 266v–268v.

46. Evidence for the number and location of the altars is discussed below.

47. BIHR Prob. Reg. iii ff. 242v–243r; for another instance, seventy years later, see Prob. Reg. iv f. 135r–v.

48. BIHR Prob. Reg. ii f. 506r cf. YMA MS 2/6(e) f. 3v.

49. BIHR Prob. Reg. v f. 325v.

50. For discussion of annual obits, see G. H. Cook, *Medieval Chantries and Chantry Chapels* (London, 1947), p. 9; Burgess, 'A service for the dead', pp. 183, 190–91; Swanson, *Religion and Devotion*, p. 228.

51. BIHR Prob. Reg. iii f. 17r–v; iii ff. 266v -268r; M. Sellers and J. W. Percy (editors), *York Memorandum Book*, 3 vols, Surtees Society 120, 125, 186 (1912–69), vol. iii, pp. 43–4.

52. Burgess, 'A service for the dead', pp. 193–4.

53. The will is YMA MS H2(1) ff. 2v–3v; the chantry document (discussed

further below) is YCA G.70 no. 27.

54. BIHR Prob. Reg. iv f. 28r–v.

55. BIHR Prob. Reg. ii f. 82r–v; ii f. 153r–v; ii ff. 154v–155r; ii ff. 537v–538r; iii ff. 242v–243r; iii f. 510r; iv f. 28r–v; v f. 325v; v ff. 391r–392r.

56. Wills with specific requests attached to them include BIHR Prob. Reg. i f. 16v (where a feather bed, rather than money, is left); iii f. 17r–v; iii ff. 266v–268v; iii f. 510r; vi ff. 19v–20r; vi ff. 23v–24v.

57. BIHR Prob. Reg. iv f. 135r–v.

58. BIHR Prob. Reg. ii f. 506r cf. YMA MS 2/6(e) f. 3v; v f. 440r.

59. All the orders are left something in BIHR Prob. Reg. iii ff. 266v–268v, but specified services are only requested from the Carmelites; the Preaching Friars are singled out to provide particular services in BIHR Prob. Reg. v ff. 391r–392r and v f. 440r; and the Augustinians in BIHR Prob. Reg. ii f. 506r, cf. YMA MS 2/6(e) f. 3v.

60. BIHR Prob. Reg. ii f. 17r; ii ff. 378r–380r; iv f. 233r–v; v ff. 391r–392r (where the church is referred to as Holy Trinity 'in magno vico').

61. BIHR Prob. Reg. ii ff. 154v–155r; ii f. 183r; ii ff. 378r–380r; iii ff. 266v–268v; v ff. 391r–392r.

62. BIHR Prob. Reg. ii ff. 378r–380r; iii ff. 366v–368v; iii ff. 415v–417v, which states that there were three recluses in York; iii f. 510r (All Saints'); iv f. 233r–v.

63. BIHR Prob. Reg. ii ff. 378r–380r.

64. BIHR Prob. Reg. iii ff. 266v–268v.

65. BIHR Prob. Reg. ii f. 153r–v; ii ff. 154v–155r (8 marks); ii f. 174v; ii ff. 378r–380r; ii f. 510r; ii f. 520r; ii f. 610r–v; iv f. 135r–v; iii f. 277r–v; v f. 94v; v f. 250r; v f. 262r; v f. 271r.

66. BIHR Prob. Reg. v f. 325r.

67. BIHR Prob. Reg. iii f. 38r–v; cf. Prob. Reg. iii ff. 266v–268v, and YMA MS H2(1) ff. 2v–3v, both of which provide for multiple chaplains for the first year after death, though at slightly lower than the normal stipend, as part of complex packages of measures some of which were very long term.

68. BIHR Prob. Reg. i f. 29v.

69. BIHR Prob. Reg. i ff. 75r–76r.

70. BIHR Prob. Reg. ii ff. 154v–155r.

71. BIHR Prob. Reg. vi f. 57r–v (21 marks is left, which the will claims, erroneously, is 7 marks 4s per year).

72. 36 Edward III, i, cap. 8, in *Statutes of the Realm*, 11 vols. (London, 1810–28), vol. i, p. 373. The size of the stipend is perhaps reflected by the fact that in 1492 York priests who were so endowed were prohibited from taking second jobs as text writers or illuminators — see *York Civic Records*, vol. ii, pp. 79, 126. Many chantry priests in the north of England had considerably

lower incomes — see J. A. F. Thomson, *The Early Tudor Church and Society, 1485–1529* (London and New York, 1993), p. 179.

73. BIHR Prob. Reg. ii f. 572r–v.

74. BIHR Prob. Reg. i f. 63v.

75. BIHR Prob. Reg. ii ff. 378r–380r.

76. R. W. Pfaff, 'The English devotion of St Gregory's trental', *Speculum*, 49 (1974), pp. 75–90; Duffy, *Stripping of the Altars*, pp. 370–5.

77. M. A. Riley, 'The foundation of chantries in the counties of Nottingham and York', *Yorkshire Archaeological Journal*, 33 (1938), pp. 258–9.

78. R. B. Dobson, 'The foundation of perpetual chantries by the citizens of York', in J. G. Cumming (editor), *The Province of York*, Studies in Church History 4 (Leiden, 1967), p. 27.

79. Dobson, 'The foundation of perpetual chantries', pp. 32–3.

80. See R. B. Dobson (editor), *York City Chamberlain's Account Rolls, 1396–1500*, Surtees Society 192 (1978–9), p. xxxvi

81. A. G. Dickens, 'A municipal dissolution of chantries at York, 1536', in A. G. Dickens, *Reformation Studies* (London, 1982), pp. 47–56.

82. The Inquisition is The National Archives C143/166/3, and the licence is in *Calendar of Patent Rolls*, Edward II, vol. v (London, 1904), p. 31.

83. Royal Commission on the Historical Monuments of England, *An Inventory of the Historical Monuments in York*, 5 vols. (London, 1962–81), vol. iii, pp. 3–11; the account contains some inconsistencies, which can be only partially resolved by looking at the notes by Dr E. A. Gee held in the National Buildings Record file no. 61201 at the National Monuments Record, Swindon.

84. This interpretation, presented tentatively in the Royal Commission account, is the main problem with the evolution suggested there. The difficulty centres on the disposition of the piers of the north and south arcades. Had there been a crossing in the position postulated, the second bay from the east, the piers defining it should have been opposite each other, even allowing for later alterations: in fact, in what is already a very irregular pair of arcades, the alignment of those piers is the most eccentric (by nearly 3ft), making it difficult to propose a sequence of development including a crossing at that point.

85. C. Kerry, 'History and antiquities of All Saints' Church, North Street, York', *Associated Architectural Societies, Reports and Papers*, 9 part I (1967), p. 62.

86. See notes in National Buildings Record File, pp. xxi with revision on p. xxii. See also E. A. Gee, 'The roofs of All Saints, North Street, York,' *York Historian*, 3 (1980), p. 3. If the suggestion made here is correct, it accounts for the significant oddity in the original design of the roof over the north chancel aisle for, while there has clearly always been a gable to the east end,

implying a roof running east–west, the top of the east window in the north wall is truncated by the eaves, indicating that there was formerly also a gable facing north. Had the entire chancel aisle been constructed at one time, it is likely that it would simply have been roofed east–west, rather than with a structurally complex and leak-prone intersection between ridges at right-angles to each other. If, however, there was a pre-existing transeptal chapel, which would already have been roofed north–south, the aesthetic advantage of covering it with north and east gables might have outweighed the structural disadvantages.

87. YCA G.70, nos 19–21.

88. The will is BIHR Prob. Reg. iii ff. 266v–268r, the Inquisition is The National Archives C143/441/20, and the licence to alienate in mortmain is in *Calendar of Patent Rolls,* Henry IV, vol. iv (London, 1909), p. 162.

89. The first north nave aisle was of thirteenth-century date, as indicated by the third pier from the east wall.

90. Listed in the inventory associated with YMA MS L2/4 ff. 154v–155r.

91. The will is YMA MS H2(1) ff. 2v–3v; the document relating to the foundation of the chantry is YCA G.70 no. 27.

92. William Savage's burial is recorded in the will of his son, Robert, who died in 1398/9: BIHR Prob. Reg. iii f. 17r–v. For the date of the glass, see RCHM, *Inventory*, vol. iii, pp. 8–9.

93. A. H. Thomson, *The English Clergy and their Organization in the Later Middle Ages* (Oxford, 1947), pp. 134, 144. Burgess, '"For the increase of divine service"', pp. 52–3.

94. Payments to chaplains of both chantries are recorded in *York City Chamberlain's Account Rolls*, pp. 14, 24, 43, 62, 74, 93, 109, 125, 136, 151, 169, 185 and 202, referring to years ranging form the 1430s to 1500. For the dissolution, see Dickens, 'Municipal dissolution', p. 172, citing the record printed in *York Civic Records*, vol. iv, p. 144. *The Valor Ecclesiasticus*, vol. v, p. 27, records that the Bank chantry still had an annual income of £5 6s. 8d. in 1535.

95. Dobson, 'Foundation of perpetual chantries', p. 29.

96. YCA York House Book, ix f. 49r–v; reference is made to the inventory in *York Civic Records*, vol. iii, pp. 28–30, though it is not printed there. Bolton's will, BIHR Prob. Reg. ii f. 107v, does not mention the chantry. See C. M. Barnett, 'Commemoration in the parish church: identity and social class in late medieval York', *Yorkshire Archaeological Journal*, 72 (2000), p. 84. It has also been suggested (Kerry, 'History and antiquities of All Saints' Church'; Shaw, *An Old York Church*, p. 9; *Victoria History of the Counties of England, City of York*, p. 369), that there was a chantry founded by Allan Hamerton. The basis for that suggestion seems to be one of the documents

relating to the City's dissolution of chantries in the 1530s, which associates him with a chantry. The document (printed in *York Civic Records*, vol. iv, p. 144) is, however, clear, that it was not a separate foundation: 'Item one chantry within the church of All Hallows in North Street founded by Allan Hamerton, somtime of the said City, merchant, William Skelton, late citizen of York, John Catton of the said City and Emote his wife by year £4'. Hamerton did have an independent chantry in the chapel of St William on Ouse Bridge.

97. Dobson, 'Foundation of perpetual chantries', p. 24.

98. Such is the likely implication of the will of James Bagule, rector (BIHR Prob. Reg. ii f. 17r), in which a book of motets was left to the chaplain Thomas Astell. See A. Wathey, 'Lost books of polyphony in England: a list to 1500', *Royal Musical Association Research Chronicle*, 21 (1988), item 1438. I am grateful to Lisa Colton for advice concerning this.

99. Several of the wills which include provision for the re-use of funeral lights at the altars contain formulae for their distribution which yield a total of five altars: BIHR Prob. Reg. ii ff. 168v–169r; ii f. 572r–v; iii ff. 66v–67r; iii ff. 266v–268v; YMA MS H2(1) ff. 2v–3v.

100. BIHR Prob. Reg. vi f. 57r–v. See E. A Gee, 'The painted glass of All Saints' Church, North Street, York', *Archaeologia*, 102 (1969), pp. 164–5.

101. BIHR Prob. Reg. ii f. 572r–v.

102. RCHM, *Inventory*, vol. iii, p. 9; Gee, 'The painted glass of All Saints' Church', p. 174.

103. YMA MS H2(1) ff. 2v–3v; cf. BIHR Prob. Reg. vii f. 21r, of 1507/8.

104. BIHR Prob. Reg. iii ff. 66v–67r, which refers to the making of six torches, two for the high altar and one for every remaining altar.

105. BIHR Prob. Reg. iii ff. 250v–251r.

106. BIHR Prob. Reg. ii ff. 371v–372r.

107. For comments on the phenomenon more generally, see Binski, *Medieval Death*, p. 27.

108. See n. 19 above for the references to this practice in the wills. On the importance of Elevation lights, see Rubin, *Corpus Christi*, p. 60.

109. Duffy, *Stripping of the Altars*, p. 96.

110. The legacy is in BIHR Prob. Reg. v f. 44r; on sacring bells in general, see Myrc, *Instructions for Parish Priests*, p. 9, *Lay Folks Mass Book*, pp. 36–40, and Duffy, *Stripping of the Altars*, pp. 97–8.

111. BIHR Prob. Reg. ii ff. 52v–53r. For houseling cloths, see Duffy, *Stripping of the Altars*, p. 128. For other measures to avoid loss of the Host, see Myrc, *Instructions for Parish Priests*, pp. 58–9 and, for similar provisions regarding the wine, pp. 56–7. See also Mitchell, *Landmarks in Liturgy*, pp. 178–80.

112. BIHR Prob. Reg. iii ff. 266v–268r.

113. BIHR Prob. Reg. ii ff. 371v–372r; for the association with the chantry, see *York City Chamberlain's Account Rolls*, pp. 62, 74, 93.

114. BIHR Prob. Reg. ii f. 17r; ii ff. 335v–336; ii f. 682r; iii f. 510r; iv f. 233r–v, the last being the will of Howren; Dobley's own will is BIHR Prob. Reg. v f. 94v, while payments to him as chaplain are recorded in *York City Chamberlain's Account Rolls*, pp. 109, 125, 136, 151 and 169.

115. BIHR Prob. Reg. iii f. 63r–v.

116. John Cliffe's will is BIHR Prob. Reg. ii ff. 333v–334r; his association with the St Mary's altar is noted there, and with the Catton chantry is apparent from *York City Chamberlain's Account Rolls*, pp. 23, 32 62, 74, 93. Nicholas Clyff's will is BIHR Prob. Reg. ii ff. 335v–336r; it records a gift of vestments to an altar in St William's Chapel on Ouse Bridge.

117. BIHR Prob. Reg. iii ff. 266v–268v.

118. BIHR Prob. Reg. iii f. 38r–v;

119. *York Memorandum Book*, vol. iii, pp. 43–4.

120. YCA York House Book, ix f. 49r–v.

121. Rubin, *Corpus Christi*, p. 74, Duffy, *Stripping of the Altars*, pp. 124–6.

122. BIHR Prob. Reg. ii f. 572r–v.

123. The first window from the east in the south aisle, for example, commemorates, the parish priest, James Bagule († 1440/1) and several parishioners, while the fourth window (originally the second) commemorates Richard Killyngholme († 1451) and his wives Joan († 1436) and Margaret: see Gee, 'The painted glass of All Saints' Church', pp. 187–8.

124. RCHM, *Inventory*, vol. iii, pp. 6–7, but see also pp. xxi and xxii of Dr Gee's notes.

125. Drawings of most are to be found in Shaw, *An Old York Church*. I am grateful to Philip Lankester, Sally Badham and Brian and Moira Gittos for advice concerning the dates of those illustrated in Fig. 5.13.

126. BIHR Prob. Reg. ii f. 153r–v; iii ff. 266v–268v; see also v f. 149r–v, relating, interestingly, to a tanner.

127. St Mary: BIHR Prob. Reg. i f 29v; i ff. 75r–76r; ii f. 82r–v; ii ff. 168v–169r; v f. 57r–v; v f. 235v; St Nicholas and/or St Katherine: BIHR Prob. Reg. ii ff. 371v–372r; ii f. 682r; iii f. 17r–v; iii f. 38r–v; iii ff. 250v–251r; iii f. 510r; v f. 44r; v f. 94v; *York Memorandum Book*, iii pp. 42–3; St Thomas: BIHR Prob. Reg. vi ff. 19v–20r. For the hierarchy of spaces in which burial might be sought, see Daniell, *Death in the Middle Ages*, pp. 95–9.

128. BIHR Prob. Reg. iv f. 233r–v; v f. 94v.

129. BIHR Prob. Reg. v ff. 391r–392r.

130. YMA MS H2(1) ff. 2v–3v, where his wife and his kinsman John Bawtre later joined him — see YMA MS L2/4 ff. 157r–158r. A similar request was made by a less prominent parishioner, the tanner Adam Atkinson, who, in

1502, wished to be buried in the church 'in medio le aley': BIHR Prob. Reg. vi ff. 23v–24r.

131. See Binski, *Medieval Death*, pp. 91–2.

132. Binski, *Medieval Death*, pp. 71–2.

Chapter 5

1. C. Burgess, 'The benefactions of mortality: the lay response in the late medieval urban parish', in D. M. Smith (editor), *Studies in Clergy and Ministry in Medieval England*, Borthwick Studies in History 1 (York, 1991), pp. 65–86; C. Burgess, 'Pre-Reformation churchwardens' accounts and parish government: lessons from London and Bristol', *English Historical Review*, 117 (2002), pp. 306–32; R. Hutton, *The Rise and Fall of Merry England: The Ritual Year 1400–1700* (Oxford, 1994), p. 292; B. Kumin, *The Shaping of a Community: The Rise and Reformation of the English Parish c.1400–1560* (Aldershot, 1996); K. L. French, G. G. Gibbs and B. A. Kumin (editors), *The Parish in English Life 1400–1600* (Manchester, 1997); K. L. French, *The People of the Parish: Community Life in a Late Medieval Diocese* (Philadelphia, 2001); E. Duffy, *The Voices of Morebath: Reformation and Rebellion in an English Village* (New Haven and London, 2001); J. R. Boyle, *The Early History of the Town and Port of Hedon in the East Riding of the County of York* (Hull, York and London, 1895), pp. ciii–cxxxviii, clxii–clxxxvii; P. Hoskin (editor), 'Some late fourteenth-century gild accounts and fabric wardens' accounts from the church of St Margaret's, Walmgate, York', in D. M. Smith (editor), *The Church in Medieval York: Records edited in Honour of Professor Barrie Dobson*, Borthwick Texts and Calendars 24 (York, 1999), pp. 75–86; C. C. Webb (editor), *Churchwardens' Accounts of St Michael's, Spurriergate, York, 1518–1548*, 2 vols, Borthwick Texts and Calendars 20 (York, 1997) [subsequently *Churchwardens' Accounts*]. The Ecclesfield churchwardens' accounts contain some receipts for the 1520s and rather more for the 1530s but are now too incomplete and damaged to yield much material on religion in the parish: A. S. Gatty (editor), *The First Book of the Marriage, Baptismal and Burial Registers of Ecclesfield Parish Church, Yorkshire, from 1558 to 1619 and also the Churchwardens' Accounts from 1520–1546* (London, 1878), pp. 148–62. The Sheriff Hutton churchwardens' accounts, of great value for charting the religious changes of the reigns of Henry VIII, Edward VI, Mary and Elizabeth in Yorkshire, have not been classed as pre-Reformation churchwardens' accounts in the context of this chapter since, apart from an inventory of church ornaments of 1524, they begin only in 1537: BIHR PR SH/13; J. S. Purvis, 'The churchwarden's book of Sheriff Hutton, A.D. 1524–1568', *Yorkshire Archaeological Journal*, 36 (1947), pp. 178–89.

2. W. Page (editor), *The Certificates of the Commissioners Appointed to Survey the*

Chantries, Guilds, Hospitals etc. in the County of York. Part II [subsequently *Chantry Certificates, Part II*], Surtees Society 92 (1895), p. 460; Duffy, *Morebath*, p. 5.

3. *Churchwardens' Accounts*, pp. 154, 221, 249–50.

4. A. Raine, *Medieval York: A Topographical Survey based on Original Sources* (London, 1955), pp. 157–62.

5. *Churchwardens' Accounts*, pp. 108, 163, 186, 190, 193, 262, 325, 326; BIHR Prob. Reg. vii f. 121r; ix f. 107r–v.

6. *Churchwardens' Accounts*, pp. 74, 123, 154–5, 187, 194, 195, 221, 248–9, 250, 262–3; BIHR Prob. Reg. ix f. 5r; C. Burgess and A. Wathey, 'Mapping the soundscape: church music in English towns, 1450–1550', *Early Music History*, 19 (2000), pp. 1–46.

7. E. Duffy, *The Stripping of the Altars: Traditional Religion in England 1400–1580* (New Haven and London, 1992), pp. 91–130; BIHR Prob. Reg. v ff. 473v, 510v–511v; vi f. 223r; A. G. Dickens, 'A municipal dissolution of chantries at York, 1536', in A. G. Dickens, *Reformation Studies* (London, 1982), pp. 47–56; *Chantry Certificates, Part II*, p. 460.

8. BIHR Prob. Reg. vii ff. 52r–53v; ix ff. 5r, 58r, 368v; xi pt I f. 1v; PRY/MS F86.

9. BIHR Prob. Reg. ix ff. 87v, 92v, 253r, 293r; xi pt I f. 9r.

10. G. Lawton, *Collectio Rerum Ecclesiasticarum de Diocesi Eboracensi*, 2 vols. (London,1840), vol. i, pp. 7–37; J. and J. A. Venn, *Alumni Cantabrigienses*, Part I, vol. iii (Cambridge, 1924), p. 147; BIHR *Sede Vac.* Reg. v A f. 529v; Abp. Reg. xxv ff. 116r, 117v, 118v; xxvii f. 68v; xxviii f. 2v; Prob. Reg. vii ff. 52r–53v.

11. BIHR Prob. Reg. vi f. 187r; ix ff. 57r, 74r, 87v, 92v, 368v, 416v; C. Cross (editor), *York Clergy Wills 1520–1600: II City Clergy*, Borthwick Texts and Calendars 15 (York, 1989), pp. 25–6, 85–6; *Churchwardens' Accounts*, pp. 9, 87–8, 93–4, 101, 108, 116, 123, 128–9, 134–5, 139–40, 147, 153–4; C. Cross (editor), *York Clergy Wills 1520–1600: I Minster Clergy*, Borthwick Texts and Calendars 10 (York, 1984), pp. 34–5.

12. In local documents his name variously appears as Werell, Wirall, or Wyrall; Worrall seems to be the form most frequently used in his latter years; *Chantry Certificates, Part II*, p. 460; *Churchwardens' Accounts*, p. 331; BIHR Abp. Reg. xxvi ff. 118v, 121v; Prob. Reg. ix f. 74r; D & C Original Wills 1550; T. Cooper, *The Last Generation of English Clergy: Parish Priests in the Diocese of Coventry and Lichfield in the Early Sixteenth Century* (Woodbridge, 1999) pp. 8–10.

13. R. H. Skaife (editor), *The Register of the Corpus Christi Guild in the City of York*, Surtees Society 57 (1872), pp. v–vi, 184, 186; BIHR Prob. Reg. ix f. 74r.

14. *Churchwardens' Accounts*, p. 91.

15. *Churchwardens' Accounts*, pp. 11, 276, 304; Hutton, *Rise and Fall of Merry*

England, pp. 5–48; Duffy, *Stripping of the Altars*, p. 334.

16. *Churchwardens' Accounts*, pp. 194, 304, 316 n. 7; C. Richmond, 'Three Suffolk pieces', in S. Ditchfield (editor), *Christianity and Community in the West: Essays for John Bossy* (Aldershot; 2001), p. 55.

17. BIHR Prob. Reg. viii f. 121r; ix f.107r–v; *Churchwardens' Accounts*, p. 221.

18. *Churchwardens' Accounts*, pp. 153, 250–52.

19. BIHR Prob. Reg. v f. 473v; vii ff. 52r–53v; ix ff. 257v–258r, 368v; xi pt I ff. 1v, 15v, 290v; xi pt II ff. 403r–v, 760v–761r.

20. BIHR Prob. Reg. ix ff. 74r, 92v, 107r–v, 355r–v; xi pt I f. 1v.

21. BIHR Prob. Reg. xi pt I ff.147v–148r.

22. BIHR Abp. Reg. xxvii f. 95r; xxviii f. 5v.

23. BIHR PRY/MS F89; *Churchwardens' Accounts*, pp. 1–2, 191–2.

24. *Churchwardens' Accounts*, pp. 2–3, 191, 192, 204, 299.

25. *Churchwardens' Accounts*, pp. 250, 262–3, 272–3, 281.

26. Duffy, *Morebath*, pp. 115–17; K. French, 'Parochial fund-raising in late medieval Somerset', in French, Gibbs and Kumin, *Parish in English Life*, pp. 115–32; *Churchwardens' Accounts,* pp. 94, 115–16, 179, 250, 262–3.

27. BIHR Prob. Reg. ix ff. 107r–v, 368v; xi pt I f. 9r; xi pt II ff. 403r–v, 760v–761r.

28. *Churchwardens' Accounts*, p. 194.

29. *Chantry Certificates*, Part II, p. 460.

30. *Chantry Certificates*, Part II, p. 460; BIHR D & C Original Wills 1550 (inventory of Worrall's goods).

31. BIHR D & C Original Wills 1550.

Chapter 6

1. A. G. Dickens, *The German Nation and Martin Luther* (London, 1974), p. 89; A. Kreider, *English Chantries. The Road to Dissolution* (Cambridge, Mass., 1979), p. 96.

2. C. Cross (editor), *York Clergy Wills 1520–1600: I Minster Clergy*, Borthwick Texts and Calendars 10 (York, 1984), pp. 9–25.

3. A. G. Dickens, *Lollards and Protestants in the Diocese of York 1509–1558* (London, 1959), pp. 17–19.

4. C. Cross and N. Vickers (editors), *Monks, Friars and Nuns in Sixteenth Century Yorkshire*, Yorkshire Archaeological Society, Record Series 150 (1995), pp. 134–5; C. C. Webb (editor), *The Churchwardens' Accounts of St Michael's, Spurriergate, York, 1518–1548*, 2 vols, Borthwick Texts and Calendars 20 (York, 1997) p. 172 [subsequently *Churchwardens' Accounts*].

5. Cross and Vickers, *Monks, Friars and Nuns*, pp. 61–6, 552–3.

6. A. G. Dickens, 'A municipal dissolution of chantries, 1536', in A. G. Dickens, *Reformation Studies* (London, 1982), pp. 47–56.

7. D. M. Palliser, *The Reformation in York*, Borthwick Paper 40 (York, 1971), pp. 7–9; Cross and Vickers, *Monks, Friars and Nuns*, pp. 431, 496.

8. Palliser, *Reformation* in York, pp. 7–9; Cross and Vickers, *Monks, Friars and Nuns*, pp. 431, 496–7.

9. *Churchwardens' Accounts*, p. 195.

10. Cross and Vickers, *Monks, Friars and Nuns*, pp. 408–9, 439, 454–5, 479, 496.

11. Cross and Vickers, *Monks, Friars and Nuns*, pp. 75, 511–12.

12. Cross and Vickers, *Monks, Friars and Nuns*, pp. 62, 64–5, 78, 85, 87, 92, 410, 515, 516.

13. Cross and Vickers, *Monks, Friars and Nuns*, pp. 66, 80, 433, 434, 455–6, 457–8, 459, 460, 483, 497, 498, 499, 515, 552–3.

14. Kreider, *English Chantries*, pp. 93–124; C. Cross, 'From the Reformation to the Restoration', in G. E. Aylmer and R. Cant (editors), *A History of York Minster* (Oxford, 1977), p. 198; *Churchwardens' Accounts*, p. 208.

15. A. Raine (editor), *York Civic Records*, 9 vols, Yorkshire Archaeological Society, Record Series 98, 101, 106, 108, 110, 112, 115, 119, 138 (1939–76), vol. iv, pp. 68–70; Cross, 'Reformation to Restoration', pp. 196–7, 198.

16. *Churchwardens' Accounts*, p. 304; W. Page (editor), *The Certificates of the Commissioners Appointed to Survey the Chantries, Guilds, Hospitals etc., in the County of York, Part I*, Surtees Society 91 (1894), pp. 5–83 [subsequently *Chantry Certificates*, Part I].

17. Kreider, *English Chantries*, pp. 190–91; *Chantry Certificates*, Part I, p. xii; Cross, 'Reformation to Restoration', p. 200.

18. Cross, 'Reformation to Restoration', pp. 199–200.

19. J. Raine (editor), *The Fabric Rolls of York Minster*, Surtees Society 35 (1859), pp. 306–14.

20. *Churchwardens' Accounts*, pp. 328–32; W. Page (editor), *Inventories of Church Goods for the Counties of York, Durham and Northumberland*, Surtees Society 97 (1897), pp. 85–92.

21. C. Cross (editor), *York Clergy Wills 1520–1600: II City Clergy*, Borthwick Texts and Calendars 15 (York, 1989), p. 46.

22. A. G. Dickens, 'Robert Parkyn's narrative of the Reformation', in Dickens, *Reformation Studies*, pp. 298–9.

23. V. Staley (editor), *The First Prayer Book of Edward VI*, Library of Liturgiology and Ecclesiology for English Readers 2 (London, 1903), p. 4; Dickens, 'Robert Parkyn's narrative', p. 301.

24. Dickens, 'Robert Parkyn's narrative', p. 304.

25. Cross, 'Reformation to Restoration', pp. 200–202; P. Aston, 'Music since the Reformation', in Aylmer and Cant, *History of York Minster*, p. 402.

26. Cross, 'Reformation to Restoration', pp. 202–3.

27. Dickens, 'Robert Parkyn's narrative', p. 309.

28. A. G. Dickens, 'Robert Holgate Archbishop of York and President of the King's Council in the North', in Dickens, *Reformation Studies*, p. 349; A. G. Dickens, 'Archbishop Holgate's Apology', in Dickens, *Reformation Studies*, pp. 353–62; Cross, 'Reformation to Restoration', pp. 201–3.

29. Cross, 'Reformation to Restoration', p. 202.

30. Cross, *York Clergy Wills: II City Clergy*, pp. 70–71; 72–3, 76–8, 78–80, 82.

31. J. C. H. Aveling, *Catholic Recusancy in the City of York, 1558–1791*, Catholic Record Society Monograph 2 (London, 1970), pp. 17–19.

32. Cross, 'Reformation to Restoration', p. 203.

33. W. Bright (editor), *The Prayer Book of Queen Elizabeth 1559*, Ancient and Modern Library of Theological Literature 34 (London, 1890), pp. 9–14, 16.

34. The National Archives SP 12/10 pp. 29–40; Cross, 'Reformation to Restoration', pp. 203–5.

35. Cross, 'Reformation to Restoration', pp. 205, 207–8; I. Green, *Print and Protestantism in Early Modern England* (Oxford, 2000), p. 506; I. Green, '"All People that on Earth do dwell. Sing to the Lord with cheerful Voice": Protestantism and music in early modern England', in S. Ditchfield (editor), *Christianity and Community in the West: Essays for John Bossy* (Aldershot, 2001), pp. 148–64; T. Mace, *Musick's Monument* (London, 1676), pp. 18–20.

36. Aveling, *Catholic Recusancy*, pp. 170–71; Cross, *York Clergy Wills: II City Clergy*, pp. 91–4; Cross and Vicars, *Monks, Friars and Nuns*, p. 399.

37. Aveling, *Catholic Recusancy*, p. 29.

38. A. F. Johnston and M. Rogerson (editors), *Records of Early English Drama, York I* (Toronto, 1979), pp. 353, 354, 355, 361, 365, 366–7; *York Civic Records*, vol. vii, p. 13.

39. Aveling, *Catholic Recusancy*, p. 168; BIHR PRY/J1 ff. 27v, 29r; C. Cross, 'The genesis of a godly community: two York parishes 1590–1640', in W. J. Sheils and D. Wood (editors), *Voluntary Religion*, Studies in Church History 23 (Oxford, 1986), pp. 209–22.

40. BIHR Prob. Reg. xix pt. I ff. 296v–297r; xxii pt. II f. 607v; xxiv pt. I ff. 262v–263r.

41. YCA Housebook xxix f.124v.

Chapter 7

1. The best introduction to the complexities of medieval liturgy, and to the books in which that liturgy was contained, is J. Harper, *The Forms and Orders of Western Liturgy from the Tenth to the Eighteenth Century. A Historical Introduction and Guide for Students and Musicians* (Oxford, 1991).

2. For detailed discussion of the origins and evolution of the Elevation, see T. W. Drury, *Elevation in the Eucharist. Its History and Rationale* (Cambridge, 1907).

3. T. F. Simmons (editor), *The Lay Folks Mass Book*, Early English Text Society, Original Series 71 (London, 1897). For discussion of this and other evidence, see J. Bossy, 'The Mass as a Social Institution, 1200–1700', *Past and Present*, 100 (1983), pp. 29–61, and E. Duffy, *The Stripping of the Altars: Traditional Religion in England 1400–1580* (New Haven and London, 1992), esp. pp. 118, 124–6.

4. There are several editions of the Sarum Missal. See, for example, F. H. Dickinson (editor), *Missale ad Usum Insignis et Praeclarae Ecclesiae Sarum*, 2 vols (Burntisland, 1861–83). For English translations, see F. E. Warren, *The Sarum Missal in English*, 2 vols, Library of Liturgiology and Ecclesiology for English Readers 8–9 (London, 1911); C. Walker, *The Liturgy of Sarum*, 2nd edn (London, c. 1870) contains very full rubrics and other information on ceremonial.

5. For a full discussion of service books, see A. Hughes, *Medieval Manuscripts for Mass and Office: A Guide to Their Organisation and Terminology*, 2nd edn (Toronto, 1995). Still useful amongst older literature are C. Wordsworth and H. Littlehales, *The Old Service-Books of the English Church*, 2nd edn (London, 1910), and H. B. Swete, *Church Services and Service-Books Before the Reformation* (London, 1905).

6. Book of Common Prayer, 'Concerning the Service of the Church'.

7. Manuscripts containing books of the York Use are discussed in W. H. Frere, 'York Service Books', in J. H. Arnold and E. G. P. Wyatt (editors), *Walter Howard Frere: A Collection of His Papers on Liturgical and Historical Subjects*, Alcuin Club Collections 35 (London, 1940), pp. 158–68. The principal editions are: the Missal — W. G. Henderson (editor), *Missale ad Usum Insignis Ecclesiae Eboracensis*, 2 vols, Surtees Society 59–60 (1872); the Manual and Processional — W. G. Henderson (editor), *Manuale et Processionale ad Usum Insignis Ecclesiae Eboracensis*, Surtees Society 63 (1875); the Breviary — S. W. Lawley (editor), *Breviarium ad Usum Insignis Ecclesie Eboracensis*, 2 vols, Surtees Society 71, 75 (1880–3); the Gradual — D. Hiley (editor), *Oxford, Bodleian Library, MS Lat. liturg. b.5*, Publications of Mediaeval Musical Manuscripts 20 (Ottawa, 1995). There is a basic Mass text with a 'liturgical' translation in the *Lay Folks Mass Book*, pp. 90–117. A Book of Hours, or Primer, for the laity to read during the Mass, is edited in C. Wordsworth (editor), *The Prymer or Hours of the Blessed Virgin Mary, According to the Use of the Illustrious Church of York*, Surtees Society 132 (1920).

Chapter 8

1. Daniel Rock, *The Church of Our Fathers as seen in St Osmund's Rite for the Cathedral of Salisbury* (3 vols in 4, London, 1849–53; 2nd edn, revised by G. W. Hart and W. H. Frere, 4 vols, London, 1905).

2. Percy Dearmer, *The Parson's Handbook* (London, 1899; revised and

illustrated edition, 1907; many subsequent editions).

3. P. J. Shaw, *An Old York Church. All-Hallows in North Street: Its Medieval Stained Glass and Architecture* (York, 1908).

Glossary

Absolutions of the Dead	Service which followed the Requiem Mass, said before the body was taken away from the church.
Acolyte	The second of the two minor orders, the other being the subdeacon, responsible for directing the ceremonial of the Mass.
Advent	The penitential season lasting for a month before Christmas.
Advowson	The right to appoint a cleric to an ecclesiastical living.
Agnus Dei	Formula beginning 'O Lamb of God' sung in the Mass shortly before the communion.
Aisle	A compartment extending along the side of a nave or chancel.
Alb	A white linen garment reaching from the neck to the knees and tied at the waist by a girdle.
Almuce	see Tippet.
Altar	The table on which the sacrifice of the Mass was offered.
Altarpiece	Decorated panel behind an altar.
Amice	A rectangular piece of linen worn round the neck over the cassock to prevent the outer vestments from soiling.
Antiphon	a) Sentences from the Scriptures sung during the Mass which vary with the season or feast.
	b) Sentences from the Scriptures said alternately by the priest and choir or by two separate parts of the choir.
Antiphonal	Book containing the antiphons.
Apparel	A coloured panel of embroidery used to decorate both the alb and the amice.
Appropriation	Assumption of an ecclesiastical benefice to a monastic house.
Apse	The semicircular eastern end of a chancel.

Ascension Day	A feast commemorating Christ's ascent into heaven after the Resurrection; kept on the sixth Thursday (that is, the fortieth day) after Easter.
Asperges me	'Sprinkle me', a chant sung during the sprinkling of holy water upon the altar and the people during the principal Mass on Sundays.
Aumbry	A cupboard in the wall of a church in which the sacred Mass vessels were stored.
Baldric	Leather from which the clapper of a bell was suspended.
Basilica	An early form of building used for Christian worship after the conversion of Constantine.
Beads	A rosary.
Bede Roll	List of deceased parishioners publicly prayed for at High Mass each Sunday.
Benedictus	'Blessed is he', the hymn of thanksgiving, originally spoken by Zacharias at the birth of John the Baptist, sung after the offertory during the Mass.
Benefice	An ecclesiastical living such as a rectory or vicarage which an incumbent enjoyed for life.
Book of Common Prayer	The Prayer Book (in English) adopted by the Church of England at the Reformation.
Book of Hours	see Primer.
Boss	Projection at the intersecting point of a vault rib, often decorated.
Breviary	Liturgical book containing antiphons, lessons, psalms, and sometimes hymns, for the daily offices; sometimes divided into the separate books of the antiphonal, legend, psalter and hymnal.
Candlemas	see Purification of the Blessed Virgin Mary.
Canon	a) A musical piece with close imitation between the parts in the manner of a 'round'. b) Clergy belonging to a cathedral or collegiate church.
Canon of the Mass	Otherwise known as the 'Still Mass', the most sacred part of the Mass when the priest consecrates the bread and wine.
Canonical Hours	Matins and Lauds, Prime, Terce, Sext, None, Vespers and Compline, the seven daily services set out in the Breviary.
Cappa Nigra	A version of the cope worn out of doors.
Cassock	A long sleeved, skirted gown, buttoned at the shoulders and waist.
Censer	Vessel in which incense is burnt, otherwise known as a 'thurible'.
Cere	Waxed cloth placed immediately over the top of an altar.
Chalice	The cup for the wine consecrated at the Eucharist.
Chancel	The part of the church nearest to the altar east of the nave and transepts; also known as the 'choir'.
Chantry	An office established for a priest in a special chapel or at a designated altar within a church to offer Masses in perpetuity for the soul of the founder and his or her nominees.
Chasuble	A full circular cloak of costly material with a hole at the centre for the head, worn by the celebrant at Mass, sometimes known simply as 'the vestment'.

Chrisom	Robe put on a child after baptism.
Christmas	The feast commemorating Christ's birth.
Church Ale	A parish festivity, which usually involved a special brewing of ale, to raise money for the upkeep of the parish church.
Ciborium	A canopy resting on four pillars erected over an altar.
Clavichord	A stringed instrument with a keyboard, a predecessor of the piano.
Clearstorey	Set of windows high in the nave or chancel walls of a church, above the aisle roofs.
Cod	Pillow or cushion.
Collect	A short prayer which may be fixed or may vary to accord with a specific feast.
Communion	The eating of the consecrated bread and the drinking of the consecrated wine at the Mass.
Consuetudinary	Book containing directions for the ceremonial of various services.
Cope	A hooded cloak formed from a semi-circular piece of fabric secured at the breast by a morse or clasp, worn in processions, choir offices and other occasional services.
Corbel	A support or bracket projecting from a wall.
Corporal	Cloth upon which the consecrated bread and wine are placed during celebration of the Mass, and with which their remains are afterwards covered.
Corporal Acts of Mercy	The seven good works: feeding the hungry, giving drink to the thirsty, clothing the naked, sheltering the stranger, visiting the sick, relieving prisoners and burying the dead. The first six are prescribed in Matthew xxv. 35.
Corpus Christi	The feast celebrating the institution of the Eucharist held on the Thursday after Trinity Sunday.
Coucher	A book so large that it needed to rest on a desk; synonym for breviary.
Credence	A shelf to hold the sacred vessels during Mass.
Creed	see Nicene Creed.
Crucifer	Cross bearer.
Crucifix	Cross bearing the figure of Christ.
Cruets	Vessels in which the wine and water for the Eucharist are brought to the altar.
Customary	see Consuetudinary.
Dalmatic	A woollen tunic decorated with orphreys and apparels worn by a deacon, and therefore sometimes known as a 'deacon coat'.
Damask	Twilled linen.
Deacon	Minister in major orders immediately below the priest, able to baptise but not celebrate the Eucharist.
Deo Gracias	'Thanks be to God', a formula sung frequently during the Mass.

Dirge	see Dirige
Dirige	'Direct [my way]', the opening words of the second part of the Office of the Dead, performed on the morning of burial.
Dorsal	A cloth hung behind an altar in place of a reredos, sometimes know as an upper frontal.
Easter	The period commemorating Christ's crucifixion and resurrection.
Easter Sepulchre	A place, often on top of a tomb, beside the altar in which the Host was symbolically buried from Good Friday until Easter Day.
Epistle	A reading from one of the letters in the New Testament.
Epistoller	The subdeacon who reads or sings the Epistle at the Mass.
Eschatology	The doctrine of the four last things: Death, Judgement, Heaven and Hell.
Eucharist	see Mass.
Evensong	The service of Evening Prayer in the Book of Common Prayer.
Extreme Unction	see Unction.
Fanon	see Maniple.
Ferial Day	A day on which no special feast or fast has been appointed.
Fiddleback Chasuble	An etiolated form of chasuble which left a priest's arms entirely free, sometimes known as a 'Roman chasuble'.
Frieze	In this context, coarse woollen cloth.
Frontal	Covering for the front of an altar.
Frontal, Upper	see Dorsal.
Frontlet	A short cloth which covered the frontal, sometimes called the 'super-frontal'.
Fustian	Thick twilled cotton cloth.
Gloria (in excelsis)	'Glory be to God on High', the hymn in praise of God sung during the Ordinary of the Mass.
Gloria Patri	'Glory be to the Father...', an ascription of praise to God the Father, God the Son and God the Holy Spirit.
Gospel	A reading from one of the first four books, Matthew, Mark, Luke and John, in the New Testament.
Gospeller	The deacon who reads or sings the Gospel at the Mass.
Gradual	a) Set of antiphons, usually taken from the Psalms, sung after the first reading from the Scriptures.
	b) A book containing such antiphons.
Gradual Psalms	Psalms 120-34.
Gregorian chant	see Plainchant.
Hearse	Frame of timber or iron, which held candles and was placed over the coffin at funerals.
High Mass	The main Mass on Sundays and holy days at which the priest was assisted by the deacon and subdeacon and other ministers.
Holy Sacrament	see Host.
Holy Week	The week before Easter.

Host	The bread, usually a round wafer, consecrated at the Eucharist.
Hours, Book of	see Primer.
Hours of the Blessed Virgin Mary	A brief office or form of prayer in honour of the Blessed Virgin Mary divided into the traditional seven hours with lessons, psalms and prayers.
Houseling cloth	Cloth held below the chins of kneeling communicants to catch any crumbs which might fall from the Host.
Impropriation	Assignation of an ecclesiastical benefice to a lay proprietor or corporation.
Incle	Ribbon or string.
Indulgence	Remission of a period of punishment in Purgatory.
Indent	Indentation left on the floor of a church after the removal of a memorial brass.
Jamb	Stone side of a door or window.
Kyrie Eleison	Transliteration of the Greek 'Lord, have mercy', a brief prayer for divine compassion during the Mass.
Lady Chapel	Chapel dedicated to the Blessed Virgin Mary.
Latten	Brass, or a mixed metal resembling brass.
Lectureship	A post voluntarily established by town corporations and occasionally by individual laymen after the Reformation to provide additional preaching.
Legend	Book containing extracts from the Scriptures appointed to be read at the Mass.
Lent	The fast of forty days before Easter.
Lent Cloth	A great cloth or veil hung across the sanctuary during Lent.
Litany	A form of general supplication.
Litany of the Saints	Intercessions for mercy and deliverance addressed to the Holy Trinity, the Blessed Virgin Mary and a list of angels and saints.
Louvre	A protected opening on the roof of a hall to let smoke out and air in. Also used of openings in towers through which the sound of bells can penetrate.
Low Mass	The simplified form of daily Mass, usually celebrated by one priest without any other ministers apart from a server.
Maniple	A strip of material worn over a priest's left wrist.
Manual	Book containing the forms of occasional services.
Mark	13s. 4d., two-thirds of a pound sterling.
Martinmas	The feast of St Martin celebrated on 11 November.
Mass	Otherwise called the Eucharist, the re-enactment of the Last Supper, the central act of Christian worship.
Matins	In origin the first canonical office of the day, said at or around midnight. Also used more generally for the public service preceding the first Mass of Sunday.
Maundy Thursday	The Thursday before Easter, commemorating Christ's washing of his disciples' feet.

Metrical Psalms	The Psalms translated into English metre. First issued in a complete edition by Thomas Sternhold and John Hopkins in 1562.
Michaelmas	The feast of St Michael, kept on 29 September.
Misericord	The underside of an uphinged choir-stall on which standing members of the choir could lean during long services.
Missal	The liturgical book containing everything necessary for the celebration of the Mass.
Mitre	Liturgical head-dress which is part of the insignia of a bishop.
Morrow Mass priest	A priest appointed to say or sing a Mass celebrated very early in the morning.
Morse	A clasp.
Mortmain	Lands, which could not be alienated, held by an ecclesiastical or other corporation.
Mosterdeviles	A kind of mixed grey woollen cloth.
Motet	One of the most important forms of polyphonal chant popular from the late fourteenth century onwards.
Nave	The western part of a church assigned to the laity, usually separated from the chancel by a screen.
Nicene Creed	The statement of belief issued by the Council of Nicaea in 325.
Noble	3s. 4d., one sixth of a pound sterling.
Obit	A repetition of the Office of the Dead, including the Requiem Mass, on the anniversary of the death of the deceased.
Octave	The eighth day after a feast day or funeral.
Offertory	The offering of the bread and wine for consecration during the Mass.
Opus Anglicanum	'English Work', embroidered fabric for which England was famous in the late Middle Ages.
Ordinal	A handbook of instructions for the variations in services throughout the ecclesiastical year.
Ordinary of the Mass	That part of the Mass which precedes the Canon and contains the confession and absolution of sins, the Gloria, readings from the Epistles and Gospels and the Nicene Creed.
Orphrey	A strip of embroidered fabric.
Pall	A cloth draped over the coffin at funerals.
Palm Sunday	The Sunday before Easter which celebrates Christ's triumphal entry into Jerusalem.
Pastedown	A leaf stitched into the binding of a book to protect the first or last page of the text.
Paten	Shallow dish or plate on which the Host is placed at the Mass.
Pax	A small metal or wooden plate, usually with a depiction of the crucifixion, used at Mass for conveying the Kiss of Peace, being kissed first by the priest and then by members of the congregation. Sometimes called the 'Paxbred'.

Pentecost	The feast, popularly known as Whitsun, commemorating the descent of the Holy Spirit upon the Apostles, celebrated seven weeks after Easter.
Pica	see Pie.
Pie	Book of directions for observing the correct services throughout the year, also known as a 'pica'.
Piscina	A basin for washing the sacred Mass vessels, often built into the wall of the church.
Placebo	'I shall please', the usual name for the Vespers of the Dead, the first part of the Office of the Dead.
Plainchant	Gregorian chant, the ancient, unaccompanied chant of the Roman church sung to a single melodic line, sometimes known as plainsong; sometimes known as 'pricksong'.
Polyphony	Music in two or more parts.
Portus	Portiforium, or portable breviary.
Postcommunion	Prayer or prayers said after the communion.
Prebend	A part of the endowment of a secular, that is a non-monastic cathedral, which supported a canon.
Prebendary	A canon of a secular cathedral maintained by a prebend.
Predella	The platform on which the priest stood when celebrating Mass.
Preface	A prayer or prayers, said or chanted by the priest as he prepares for the Canon of the Mass. Prefaces vary according to the day of the celebration.
Presbytery	see Sanctuary.
Pricksong	see Polyphony.
Primer	In this context, a Latin book of devotions popular among the educated laity which contained the Hours, or Little Office, of the Blessed Virgin Mary, the fifteen Gradual Psalms, the Litany of the Saints and the Office of the Dead. Sometimes known as a 'Book of Hours'.
Processional	Book containing instructions for religious processions.
Proper	A passage from scripture appropriate for the particular occasion on which a Mass is being performed.
Psalter	Book containing the Psalms, one of the books of the Bible.
Pulpit	Raised enclosed platform in a church from which a cleric delivers a sermon.
Purgatory	Place of purification where those who have died in the Grace of God undergo penance for their unforgiven sins before they can be received into heaven.
Purification of the Blessed Virgin Mary	Otherwise known as 'Candlemas'. The commemoration on 2 February of the purification of the Blessed Virgin Mary in the Temple.
Pyx	Receptacle for the reserved Host suspended above an altar.
Ratchet	see Rochet.

Recluse	A man or woman who has taken vows to live apart from the world for the sake of religion.
Regular priest	A priest belonging to a monastic order.
Requiem Mass	A Mass offered specifically for the welfare of the soul of the departed.
Reredos	A decorated panel above or behind an altar.
Responsory	a) An anthem said or chanted antiphonally. b) The reply to a versicle (see below).
Retable	A decorative panel placed at the back of an altar.
Riddel	Altar curtain.
Rochet	A short, ungirded form of the alb worn over the cassock.
Rogationtide	Days of prayer and fasting kept on the Monday, Tuesday and Wednesday before Ascension Day.
Roman Chasuble	see Fiddleback chasuble.
Rood	Large crucifix, which hung above the rood screen, or stood on a beam above it.
Rood Light	Candle which burnt before the rood.
Rood Screen	A screen which separated the chancel from the nave on which stood a crucifix with the figures of the Virgin and St John on either side.
Root of Jesse	A depiction of the descent of Jesus from Old Testament kings which usually took the form of a tree springing from the recumbent form of Jesse, the father of David.
Rosary	A form of prayer involving the recitation of fifteen decades of 'Hail Mary', each decade being preceded by the Lord's Prayer, and followed by the Gloria Patri; a string of 165 beads for counting out the prayer.
Rubric	Directions for the conduct of part of a service.
Sacrament house	Secure receptacle for the reserved Host.
Sacring bell	Bell rung immediately before the elevation of the Host.
St Gregory's Trental	Series of thirty Masses celebrated by a priest while undertaking a severe regime of fasting and self mortification.
Sanctuary	The part of the church containing the altar.
Sanctus	The hymn of adoration following the offertory during the Mass, beginning 'Holy, Holy, Holy'.
Say	Fine cloth resembling serge.
Scala Celi	'Staircase to Heaven', an altar at which certain indulgences could be obtained.
Secular priest	A priest not a member of a monastic order.
Sedilia	Two or three seats near the altar used by the ministers during the Mass.
Sentences	see Gradual and Tract.
Serge	In this context, a twisted torch, otherwise a kind of woollen fabric.
Sindon	A cloth to cover a pyx, also known as a 'pyx-cloth'.
Still Mass	see Canon of the Mass.
Stipend	Income from an ecclesiastical living.
Stipendiary priest	An unbeneficed priest hired for the performance of specified religious services.

Stole	A narrow strip of material placed over a priest's shoulders and secured by the girdle of the alb.
Square	A polyphonic composition in which the lowest, tenor, part contained an old melody and rhythm but the upper parts were new.
Square Chasuble	A chasuble which left a priest's arms entirely free.
Subdeacon	A major order above the acolyte but below the deacon.
Superaltar	see Reredos.
Surplice	A full white vestment.
Tabernacle	a) A secure receptacle for the reserved Host.
	b) A niche to house an image.
Table	see Retable.
Taper	Thin wax candle.
Taperer	A candle bearer.
Tester	Canopy without posts suspended above an altar.
Thurible	see Censer.
Thurifer	Bearer of the thurible.
Tippet	A fur scarf, otherwise called an 'almuce'.
Tithe	Tax of one tenth paid on the proceeds of land and personal industry for the upkeep of the clergy.
Title	In this context, financial guarantee, usually provided by a monastic house, which a candidate required before ordination.
Tracery	Ornamental open-work at the head of a window.
Tract	A chant sung at Mass on certain penitential days.
Transept	The side arm of a cruciform church (that is, one with the plan of a cross).
Transubstantiation	The belief that at the Mass the bread and wine at the consecration was transformed into the body and blood of Christ.
Trental	A set of 30 Masses offered for the departed on the day of, or on successive days after, the burial.
Trinity Sunday	The feast in honour of the Holy Trinity celebrated on the first Sunday after Pentecost or Whitsun.
Troper	Book of sequences, or hymns, sung at the Mass.
Tunicle	A woollen tunic decorated with apparels and orphreys worn by a subdeacon.
Twill	A fabric woven to produce diagonal lines.
Tympanum	The space at the head of an arch.
Unction, Extreme	The anointing with holy oils of the sick on the point of death.
Use	A local modification of the standard Roman religious observance or rite.
Valor Ecclesiasticus	Valuation of all ecclesiastical corporations, including monasteries, and all parochial livings produced for the government of Henry VIII in 1535.
Veni Creator	'Come, Creator', hymn to the Holy Spirit sung particularly at Whitsuntide.
Versicle	A short sentence, often from a psalm, said as a prayer by the celebrant, or a short series of such sentences, said or chanted antiphonally.

Vespers	The last of the daily offices (religious services).
Vestments	The distinctive dress of the clergy which originated in the secular costume of ancient Rome.
Vicar Choral	The clerical deputy of a prebendary responsible for singing cathedral services.
Vigil	Nocturnal service of prayer; the eve of a festival, usually kept as a fast.
Votive Mass	Mass said for a particular purpose or intention.
Whitsun	see Pentecost.

Notes on Authors and Editors

P. S. Barnwell obtained his Ph.D. at the University of Leeds, and is now Head of Medieval and Later Rural Research at English Heritage and an Honorary Visiting Fellow at the University of York. He has published on many medieval topics including the construction of Beverley Minster and the churches of Northamptonshire.

Allan B. Barton studied at the University of York, where he was awarded his D.Phil. for a thesis on the stained glass of Derbyshire and Nottinghamshire, 1400-1550. He is president of the Guild of Clerks, a society which reconstructs early liturgies and studies the ceremonies and vestments of the Church of England.

Lisa Colton obtained her D.Phil. at the University of York, where her dissertation was on Music and Sanctity in England, c.1260-1400. She is now Lecturer in Music at the University of Huddersfield. Her research interests include medieval music, popular music and the relationship between music and gender.

Claire Cross, a graduate of Girton College, Cambridge, taught history at the University of York, from which she retired as a professor in 2000. She has published books and articles on late-medieval and early-modern English religious and political history, and has edited the wills of sixteenth-century York clergy.

John Hawes is Head Server at the church of St Mary the Virgin, Primrose Hill, and secretary of the Guild of Clerks. He has published a booklet, *Ritual and Riot*, on Anglo-Catholicism in Brighton. He works at HM Prison Wandsworth.

Ann Rycraft graduated from Oxford and was for a time an archivist at the Borthwick Institute, University of York. She then taught palaeography at the Centre for Medieval Studies in York University, where she is now a Teaching Fellow. She is tutor to the Latin project, which is currently working on all the surviving documents relating to the Blackburn family.

Index

222